I'M A ROCK.
I ROCK OUT.

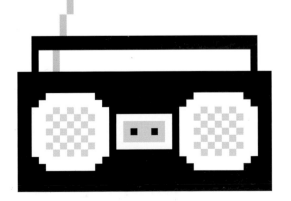

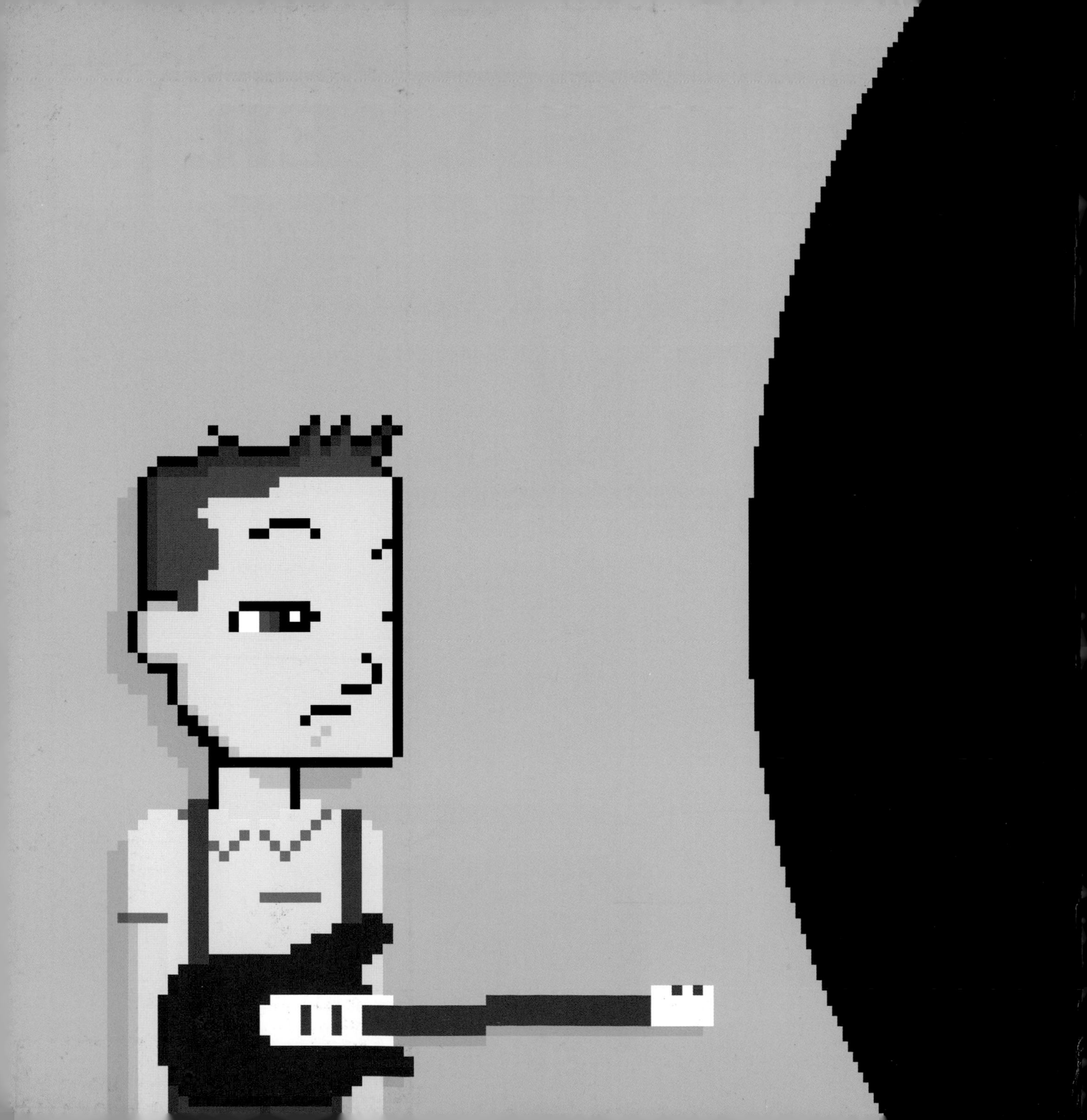

I'M A ROCKER.
I ROCK OUT.

WRITTEN, ILLUSTRATED,
AND DESIGNED BY
R STEVENS

EDITED BY
JILL BEATON

Oni Press, Inc.
publisher, Joe Nozemack
editor in chief, James Lucas Jones
art director, Keith Wood
director of sales & marketing, Tom Shimmin
editor, Jill Beaton
editor, Charlie Chu
graphic designer, Jason Storey
digital prepress lead, Troy Look
administrative assistant, Robin Herrera

Oni Press, Inc.
1305 SE Martin Luther King Jr. Blvd.
Suite A
Portland, OR 97214

onipress.com
facebook.com/onipress
twitter.com/onipress
onipress.tumblr.com

dieselsweeties.com
twitter.com/rstevens
rstevens@mac.com

First Edition: July 2013

ISBN: 978-1-62010-090-5

Diesel Sweeties: I'm a Rocker. I Rock Out. July 2013.
Published by Oni Press, Inc. 1305 SE Martin Luther King Jr. Blvd., Suite A, Portland, OR 97214.

10 9 8 7 6 5 4 3 2 1

Library of Congress Control Number: 2013937906

Printed in China.

WARM-UP ACT

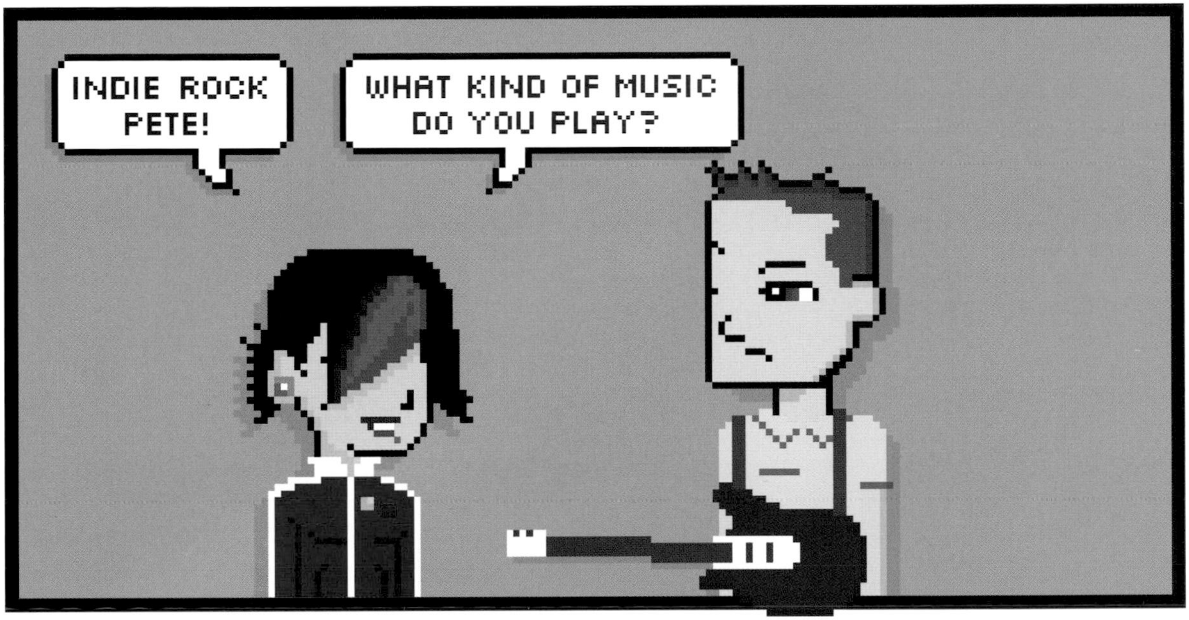

INDIE ROCK PETE!
WHAT KIND OF MUSIC DO YOU PLAY?

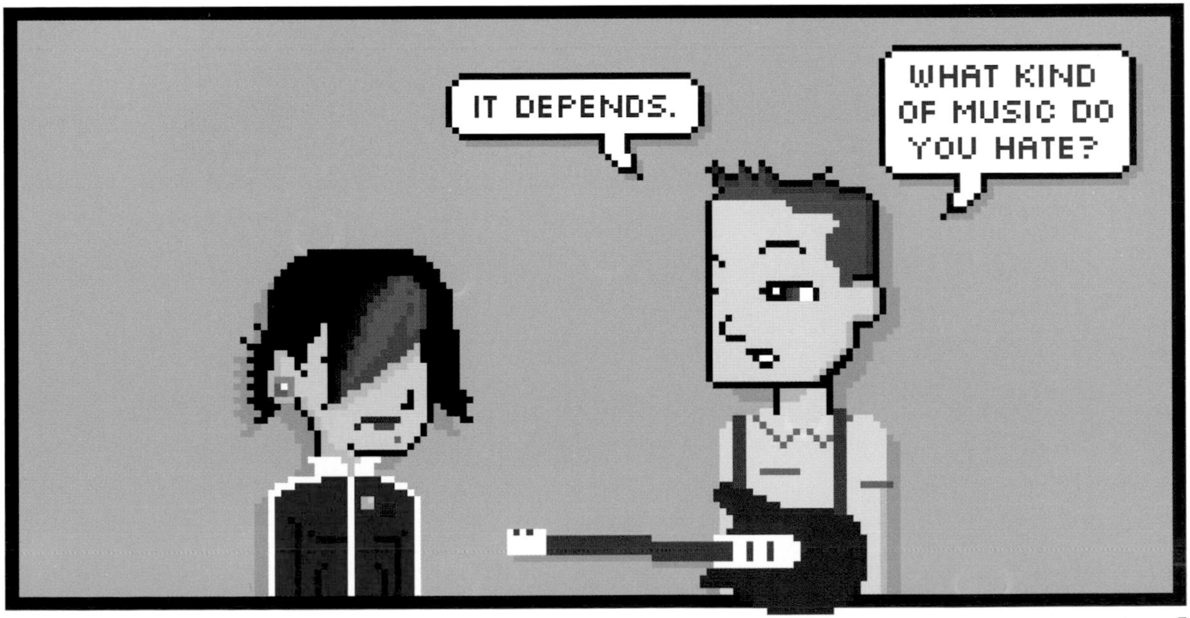

IT DEPENDS.
WHAT KIND OF MUSIC DO YOU HATE?

THE CORNER OF SWINGER AND VINE

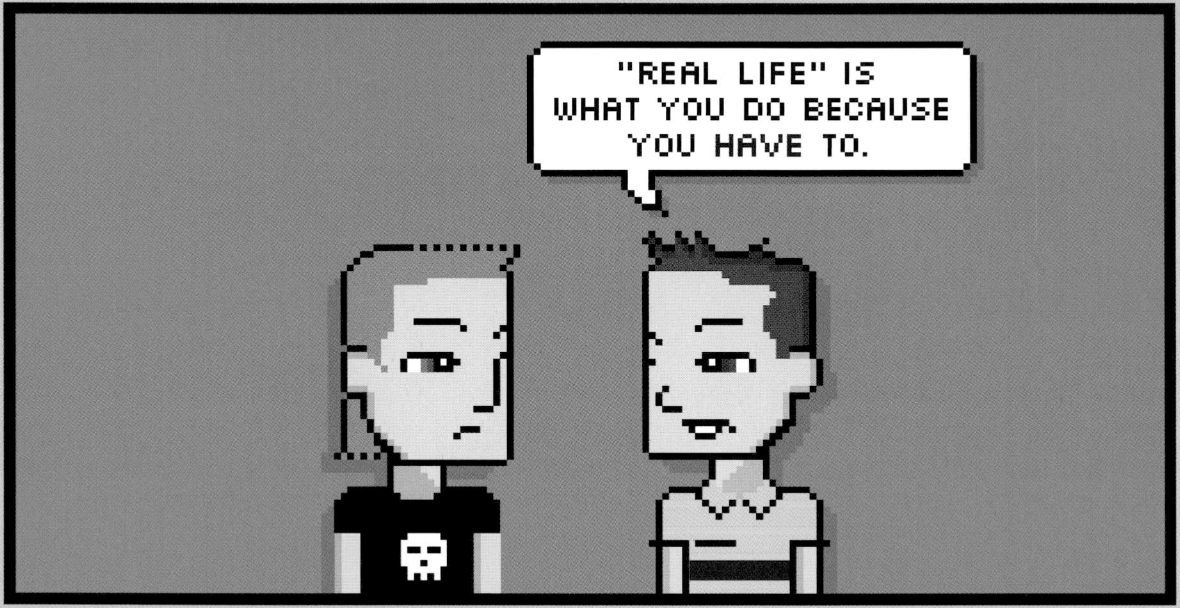
"REAL LIFE" IS WHAT YOU DO BECAUSE YOU HAVE TO.

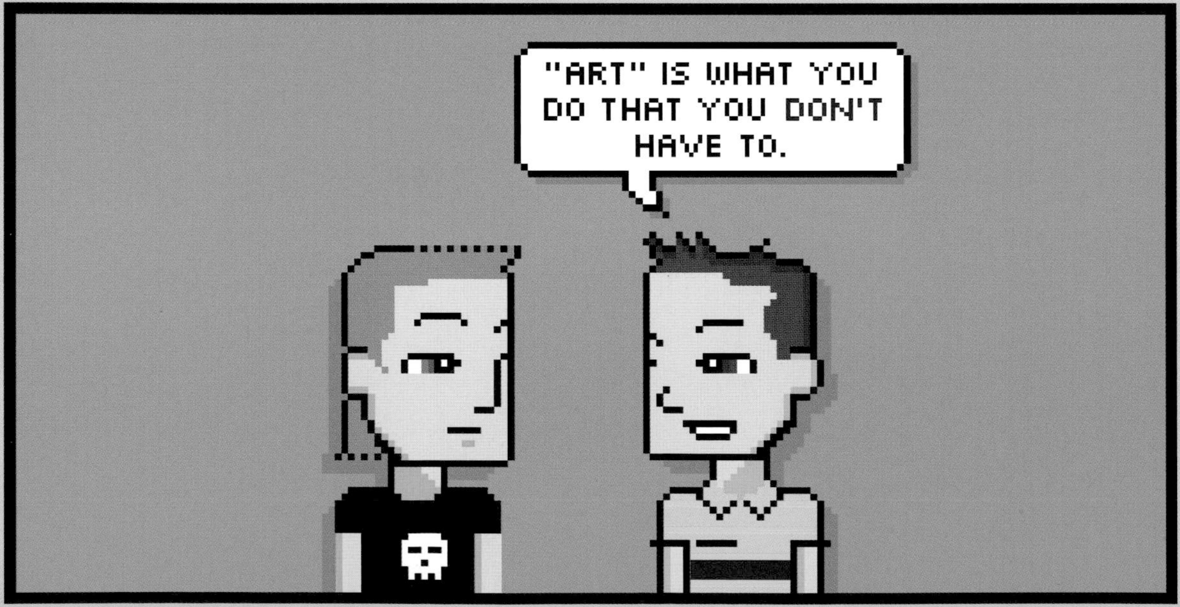
"ART" IS WHAT YOU DO THAT YOU DON'T HAVE TO.

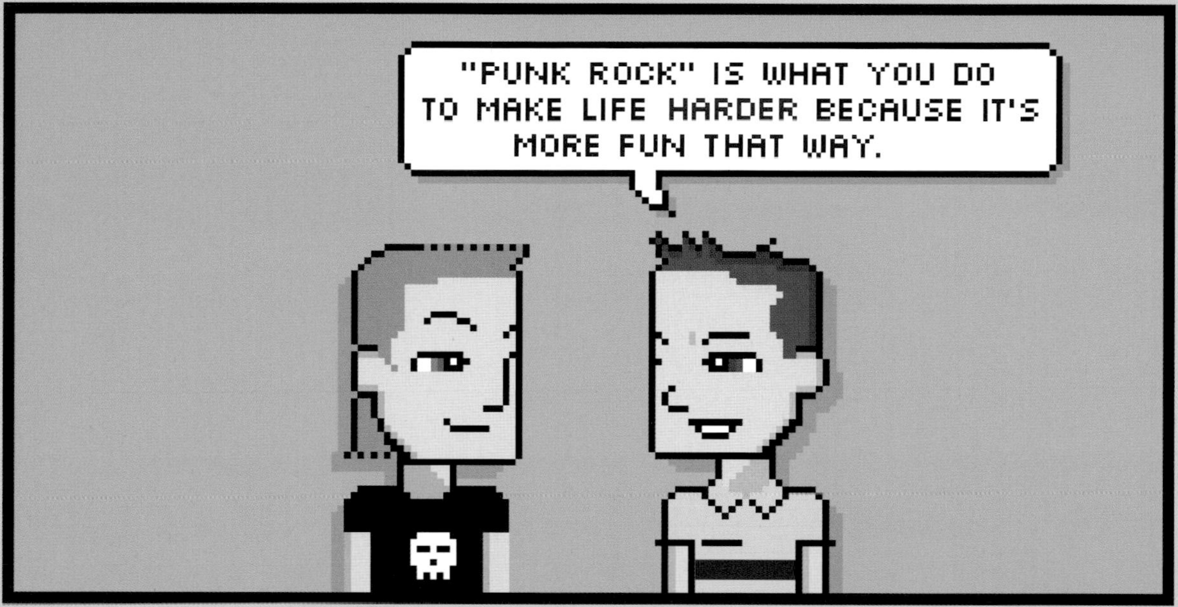
"PUNK ROCK" IS WHAT YOU DO TO MAKE LIFE HARDER BECAUSE IT'S MORE FUN THAT WAY.

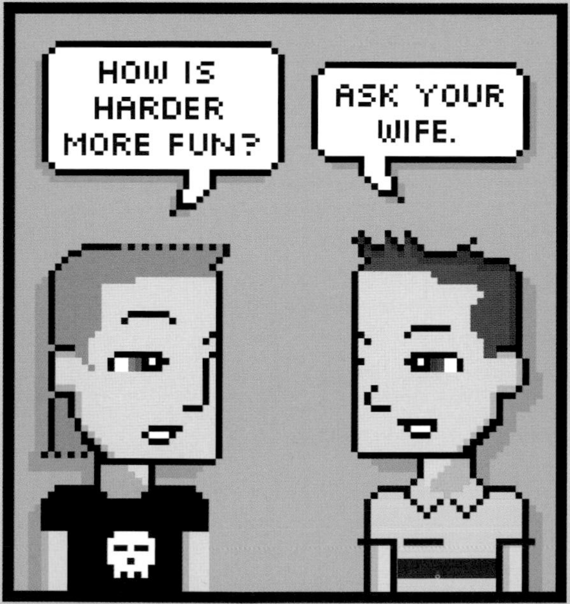
HOW IS HARDER MORE FUN?
ASK YOUR WIFE.

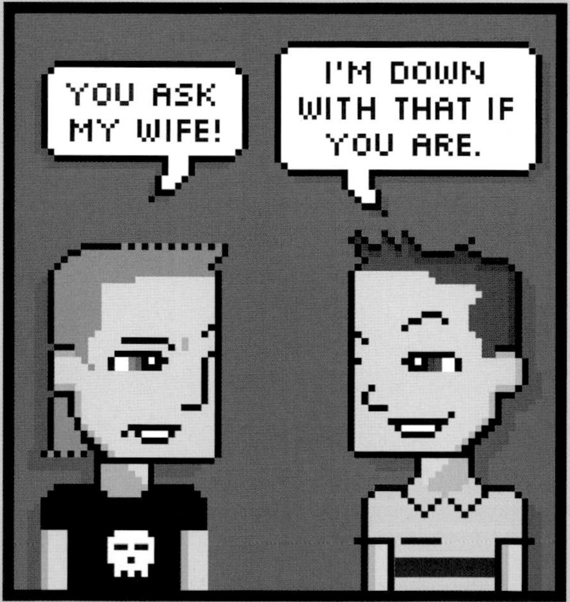
YOU ASK MY WIFE!
I'M DOWN WITH THAT IF YOU ARE.

THE CALL BOX OF PUBLIC OPINION

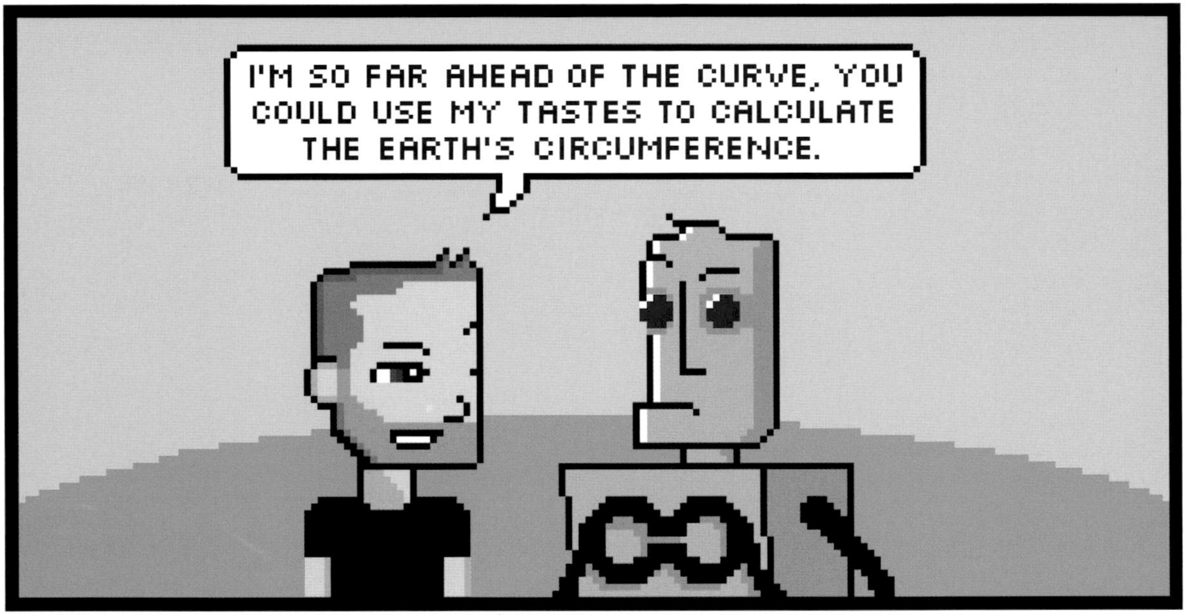
I'M SO FAR AHEAD OF THE CURVE, YOU COULD USE MY TASTES TO CALCULATE THE EARTH'S CIRCUMFERENCE.

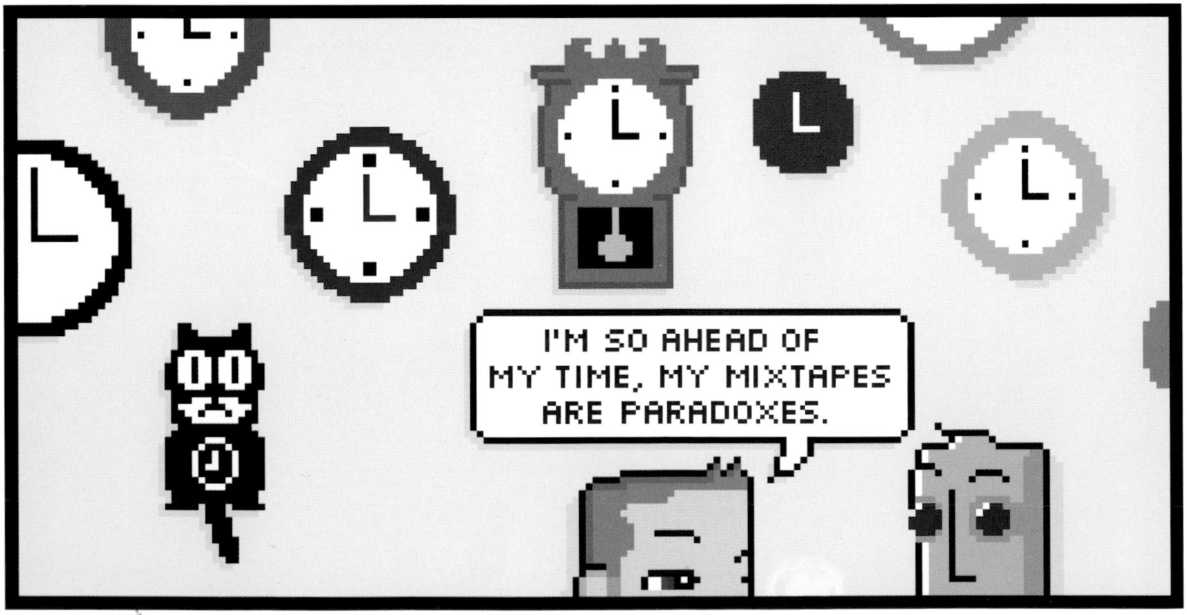
I'M SO AHEAD OF MY TIME, MY MIXTAPES ARE PARADOXES.

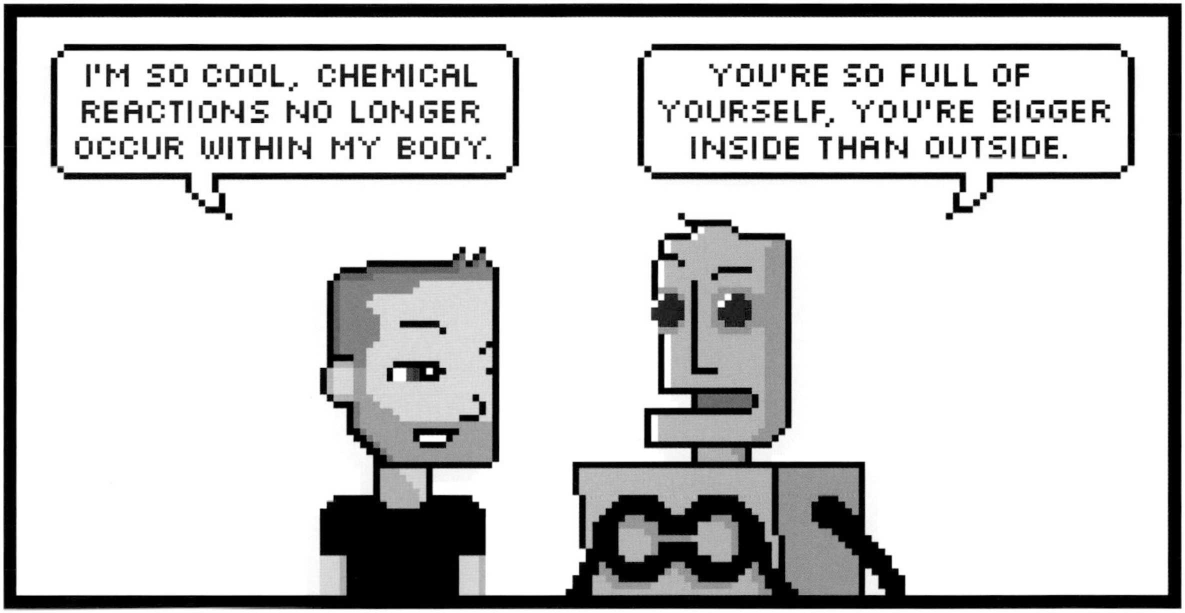
I'M SO COOL, CHEMICAL REACTIONS NO LONGER OCCUR WITHIN MY BODY.
YOU'RE SO FULL OF YOURSELF, YOU'RE BIGGER INSIDE THAN OUTSIDE.

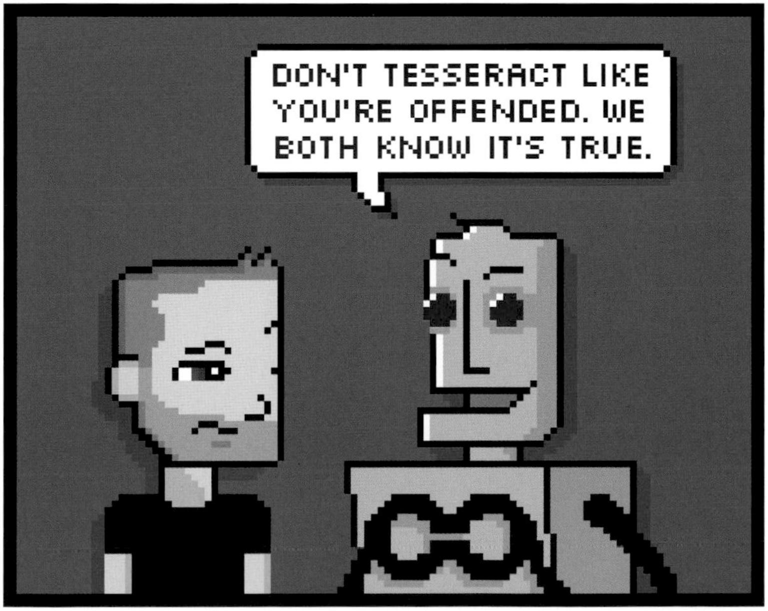
DON'T TESSERACT LIKE YOU'RE OFFENDED. WE BOTH KNOW IT'S TRUE.

DIAGRAM OF DISAGREEMENT

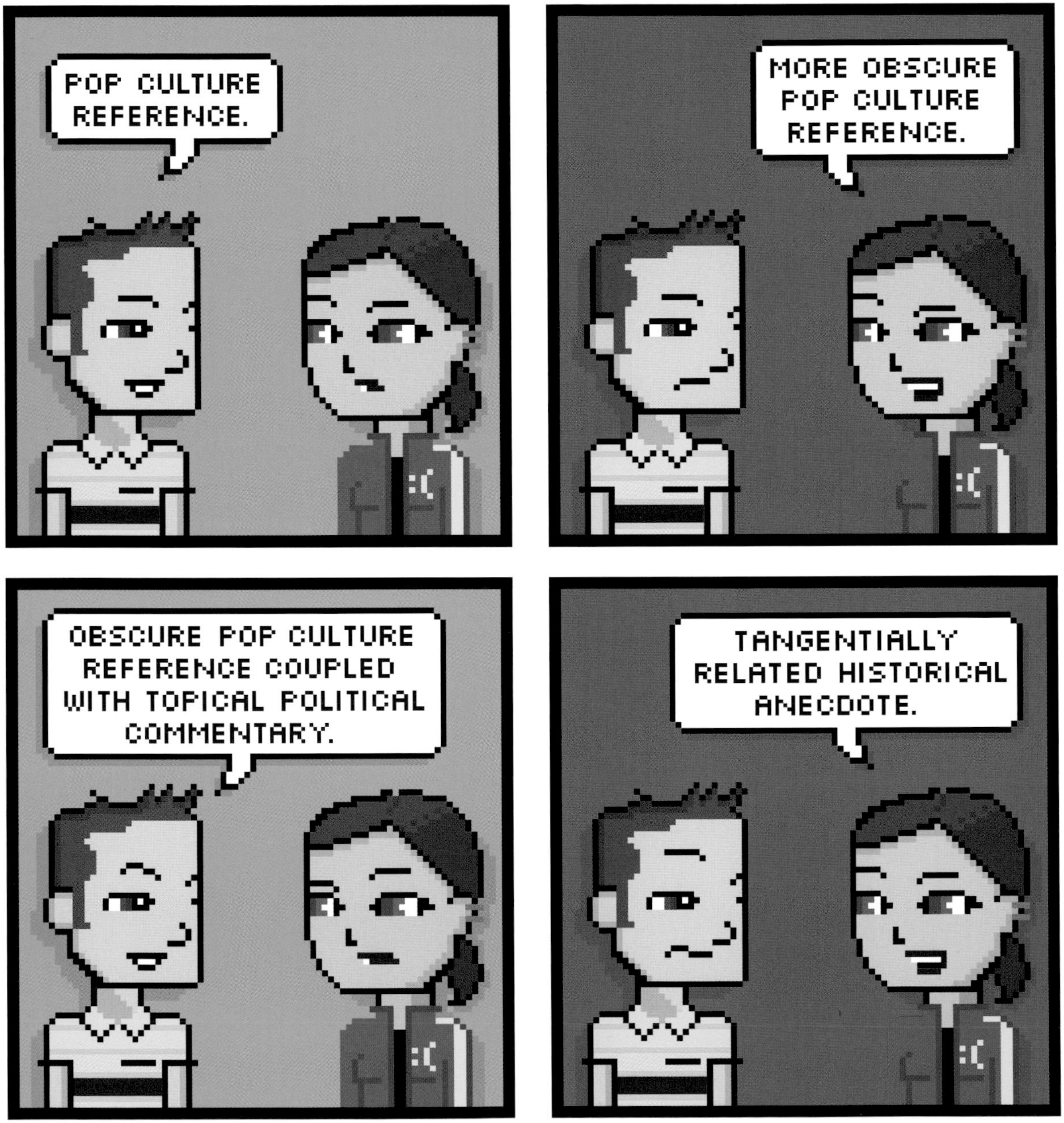
POP CULTURE REFERENCE.
MORE OBSCURE POP CULTURE REFERENCE.
OBSCURE POP CULTURE REFERENCE COUPLED WITH TOPICAL POLITICAL COMMENTARY.
TANGENTIALLY RELATED HISTORICAL ANECDOTE.

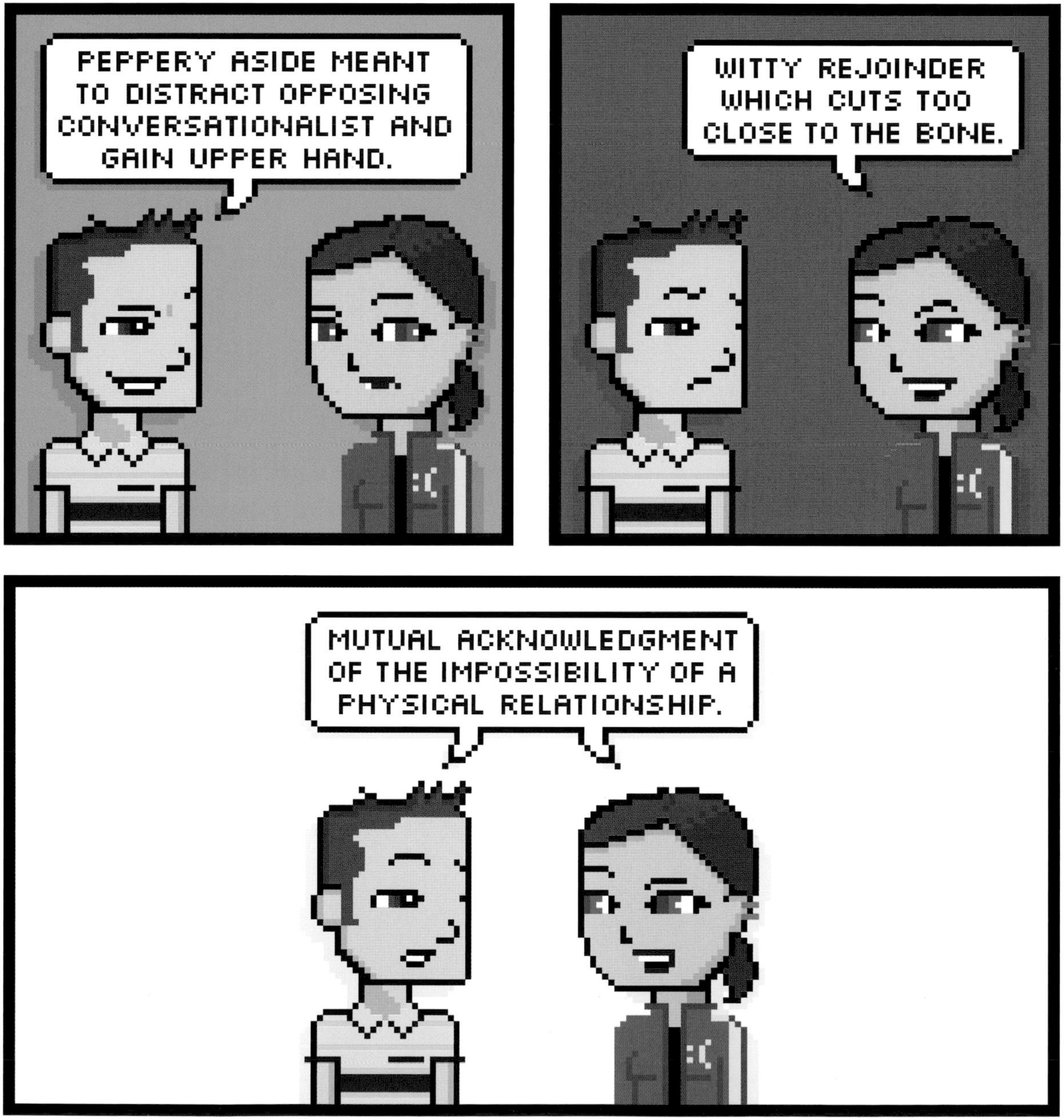
PEPPERY ASIDE MEANT TO DISTRACT OPPOSING CONVERSATIONALIST AND GAIN UPPER HAND.
WITTY REJOINDER WHICH CUTS TOO CLOSE TO THE BONE.
MUTUAL ACKNOWLEDGMENT OF THE IMPOSSIBILITY OF A PHYSICAL RELATIONSHIP.

REACH FOR THE STARS

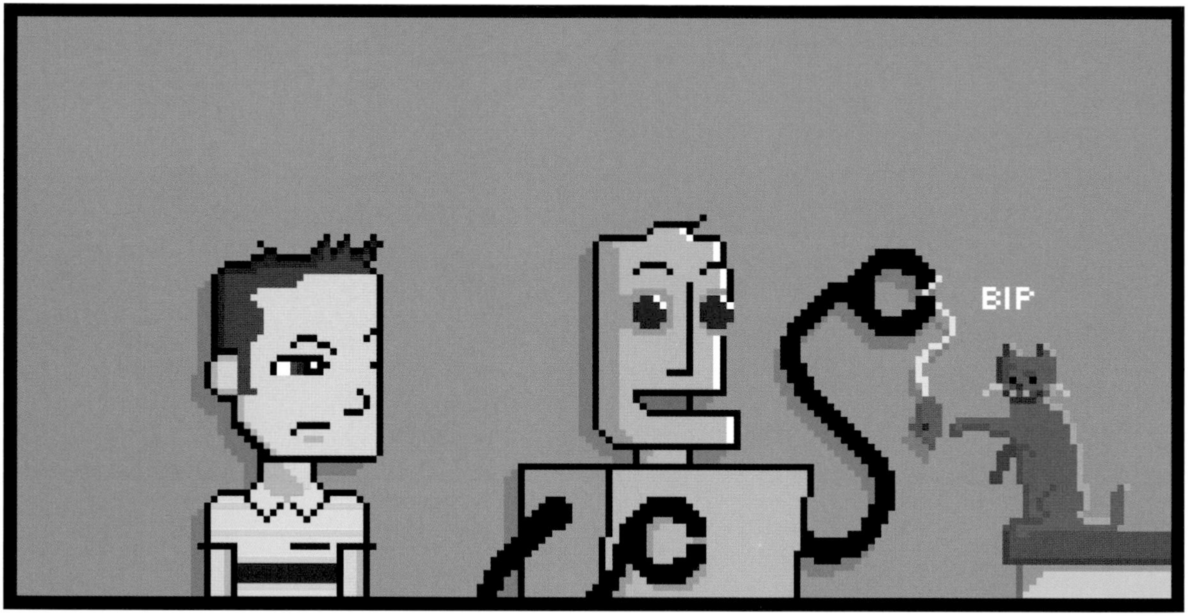
BIP

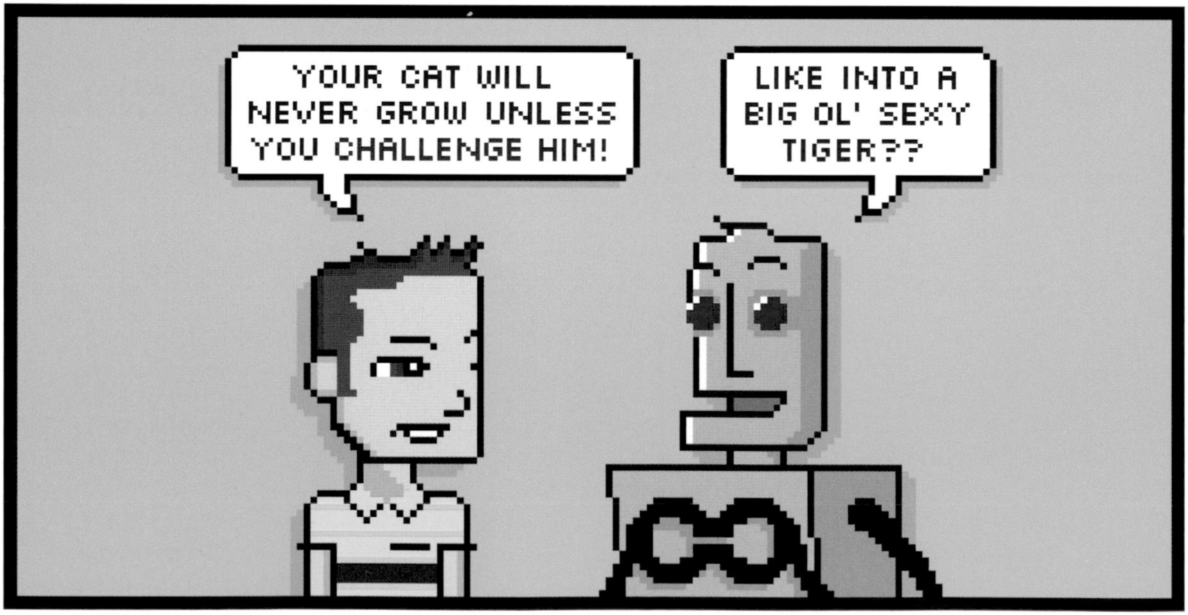
YOUR CAT WILL NEVER GROW UNLESS YOU CHALLENGE HIM!
LIKE INTO A BIG OL' SEXY TIGER??

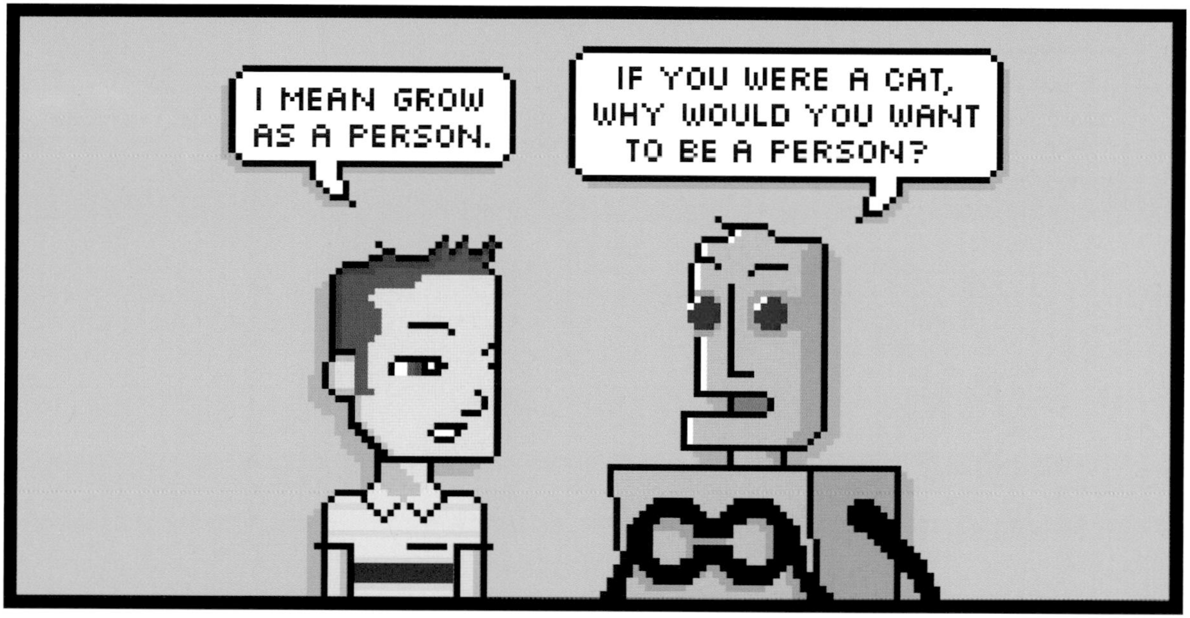
I MEAN GROW AS A PERSON.
IF YOU WERE A CAT, WHY WOULD YOU WANT TO BE A PERSON?

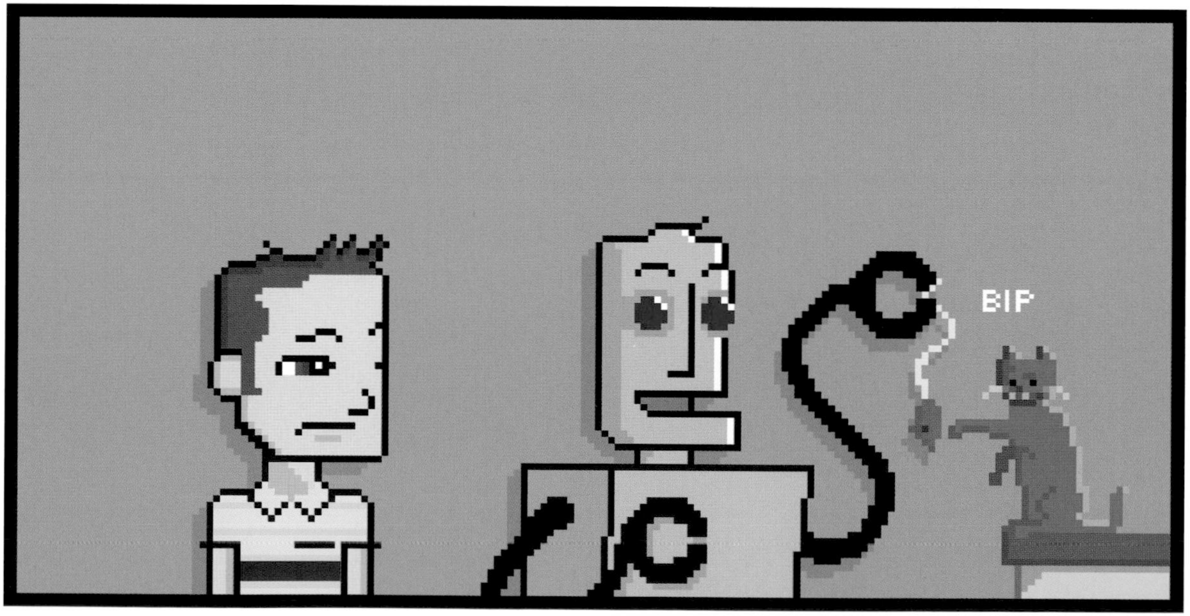
BIP

R.I.P. IRONY?

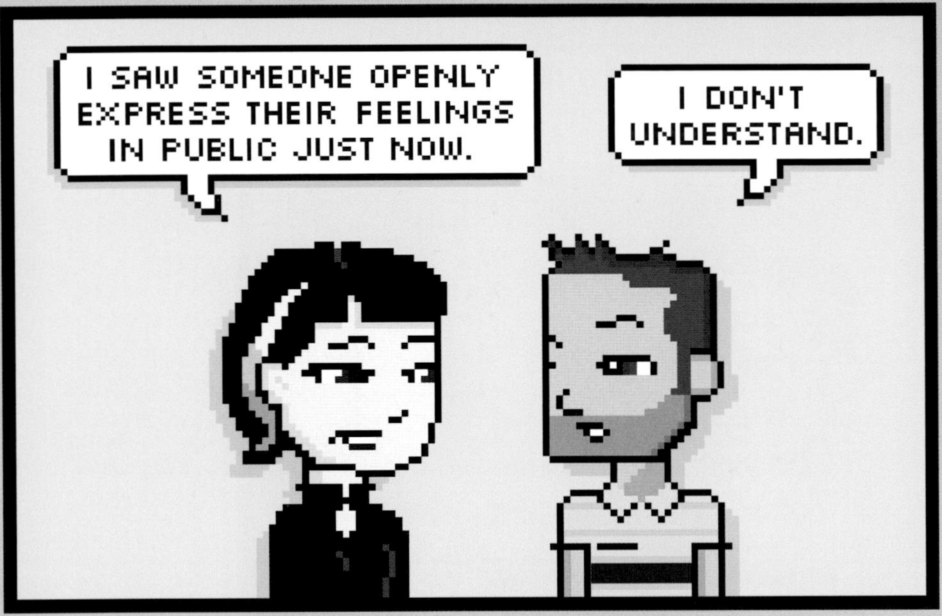
I SAW SOMEONE OPENLY EXPRESS THEIR FEELINGS IN PUBLIC JUST NOW.
I DON'T UNDERSTAND.

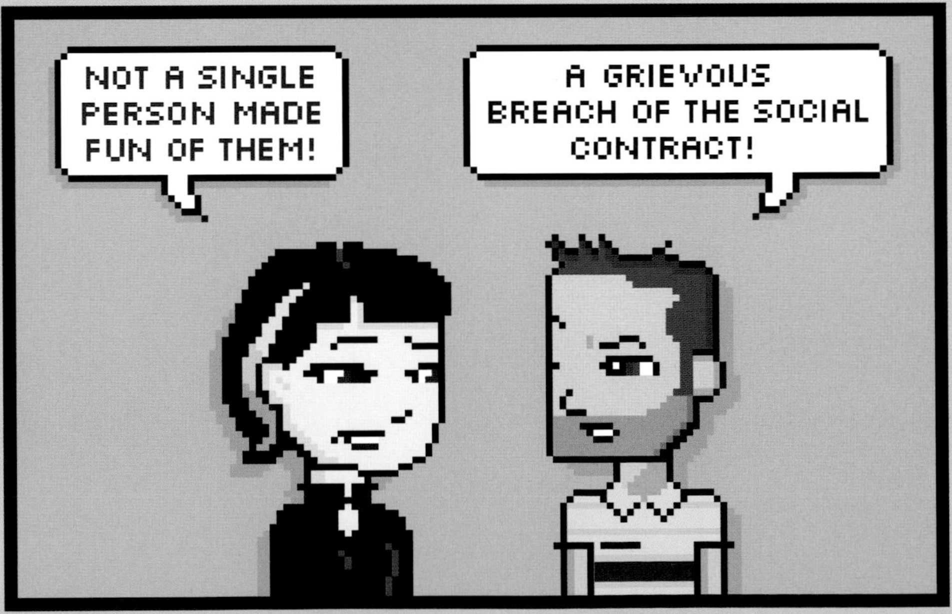
NOT A SINGLE PERSON MADE FUN OF THEM!
A GRIEVOUS BREACH OF THE SOCIAL CONTRACT!

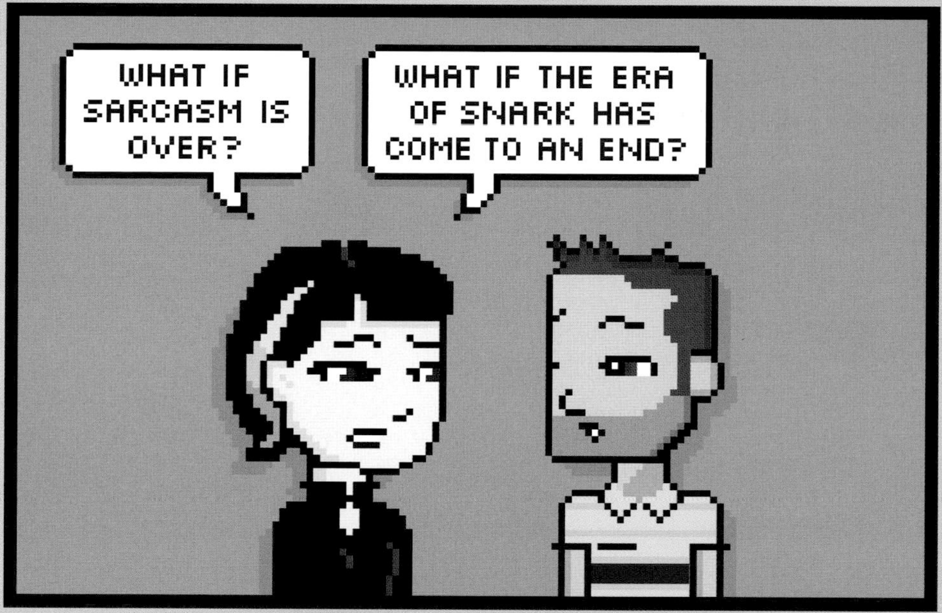
WHAT IF SARCASM IS OVER?
WHAT IF THE ERA OF SNARK HAS COME TO AN END?

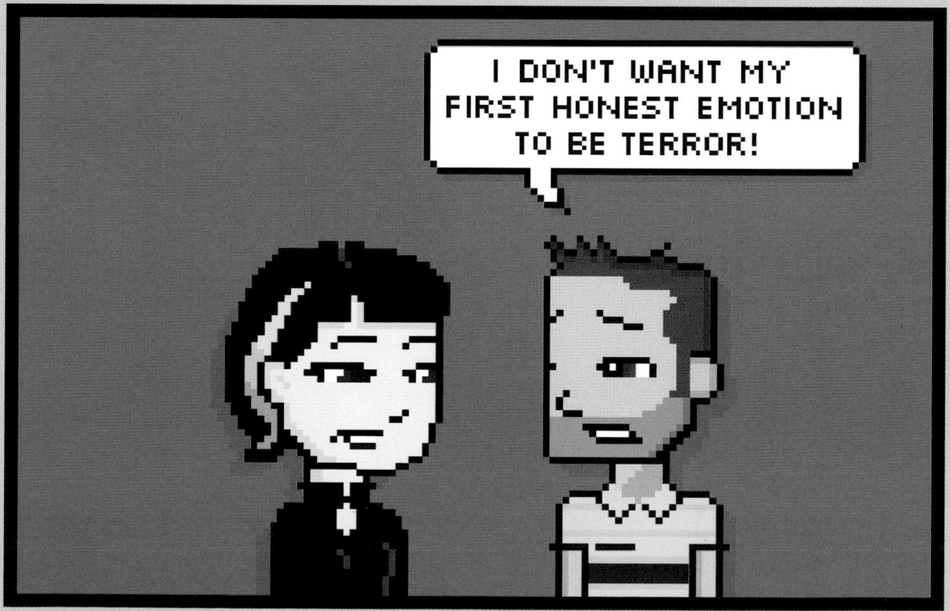
I DON'T WANT MY FIRST HONEST EMOTION TO BE TERROR!

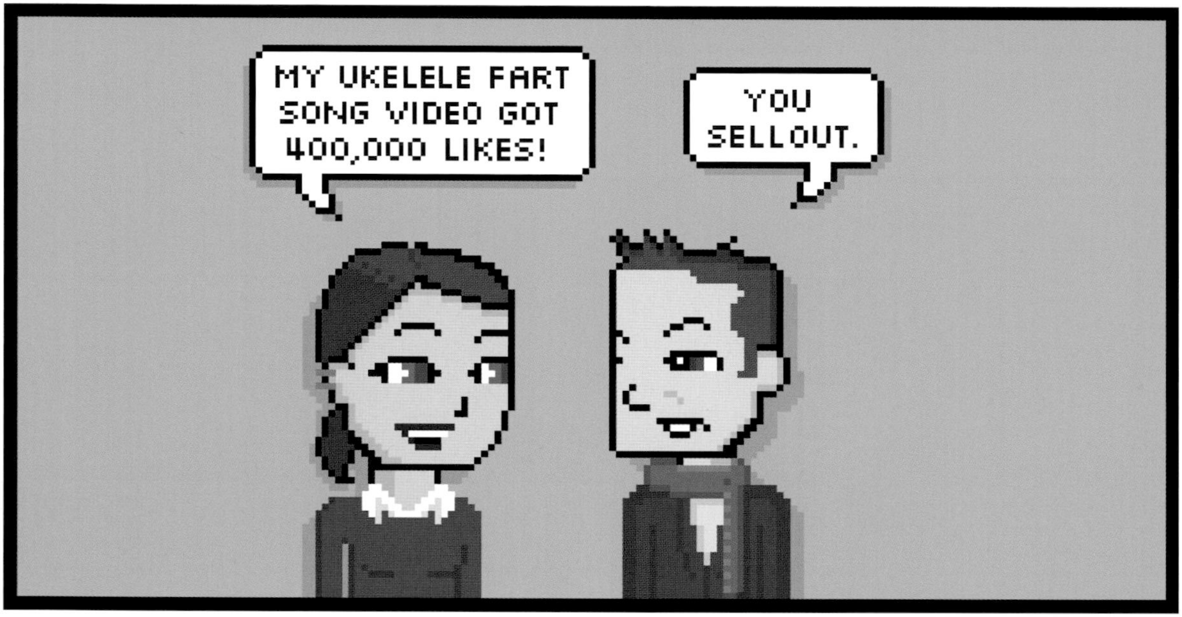
MY UKELELE FART SONG VIDEO GOT 400,000 LIKES!
YOU SELLOUT.

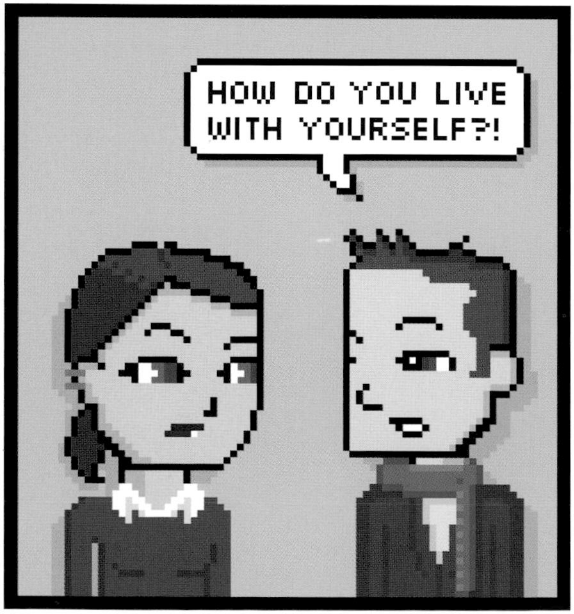
HOW DO YOU LIVE WITH YOURSELF?!

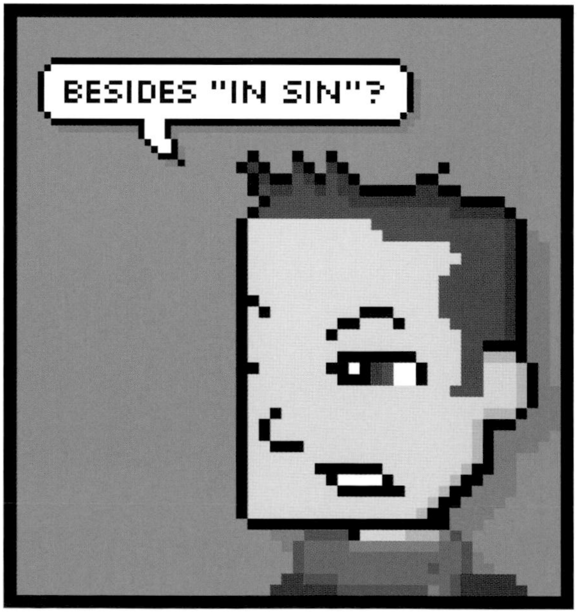
BESIDES "IN SIN"?

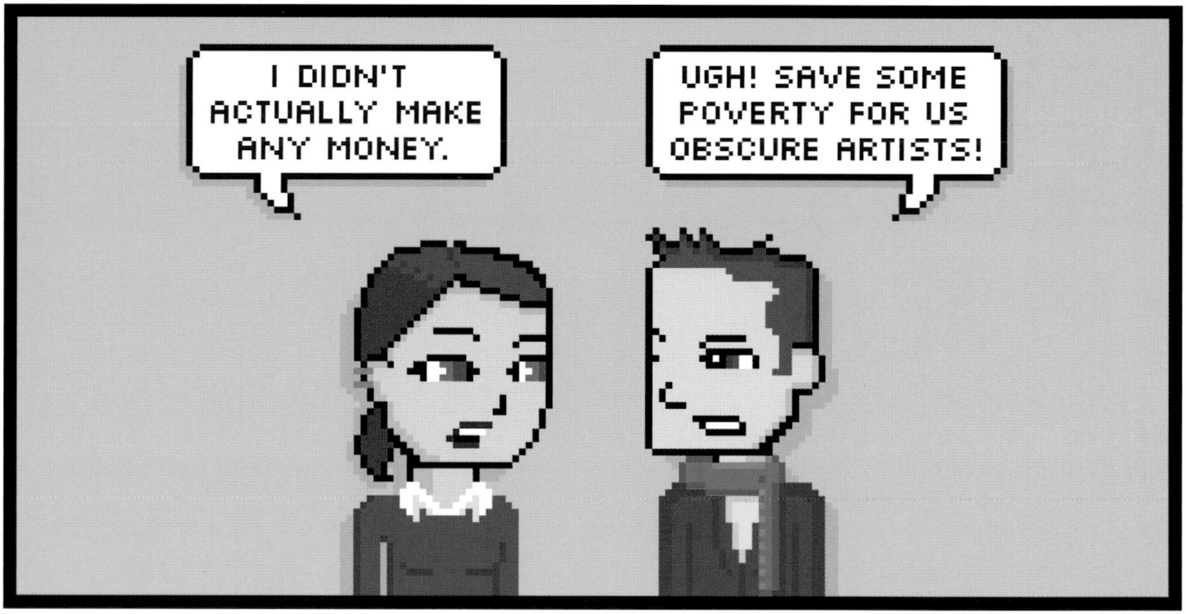
I DIDN'T ACTUALLY MAKE ANY MONEY.
UGH! SAVE SOME POVERTY FOR US OBSCURE ARTISTS!

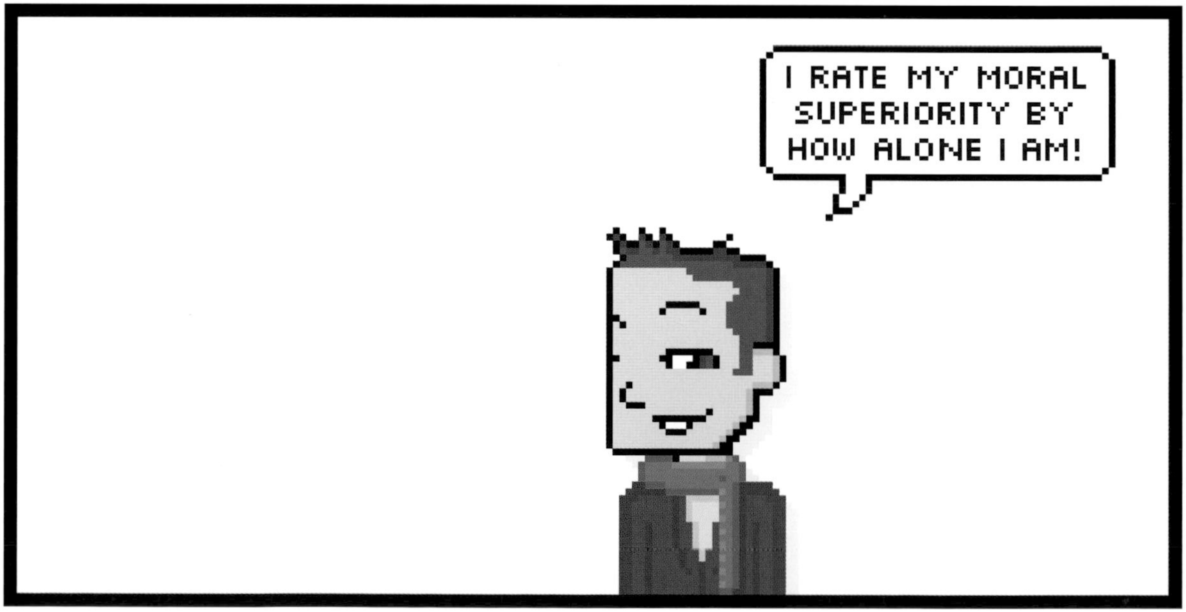
I RATE MY MORAL SUPERIORITY BY HOW ALONE I AM!

SEND PICS, PREFERABLY DAGUERREOTYPES

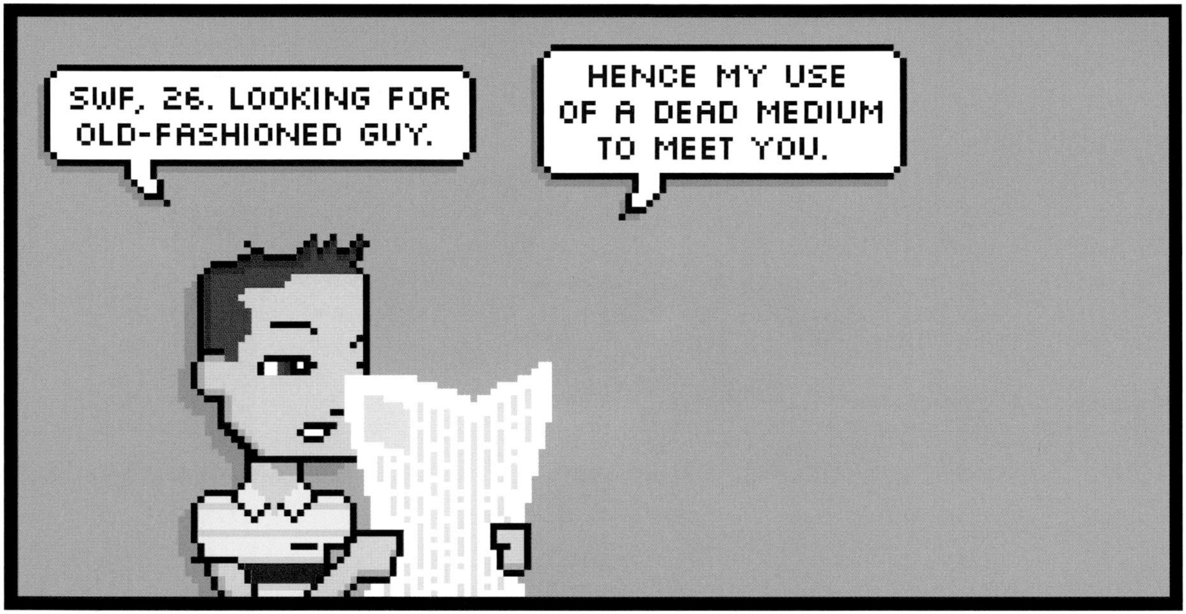
SWF, 26. LOOKING FOR OLD-FASHIONED GUY.
HENCE MY USE OF A DEAD MEDIUM TO MEET YOU.

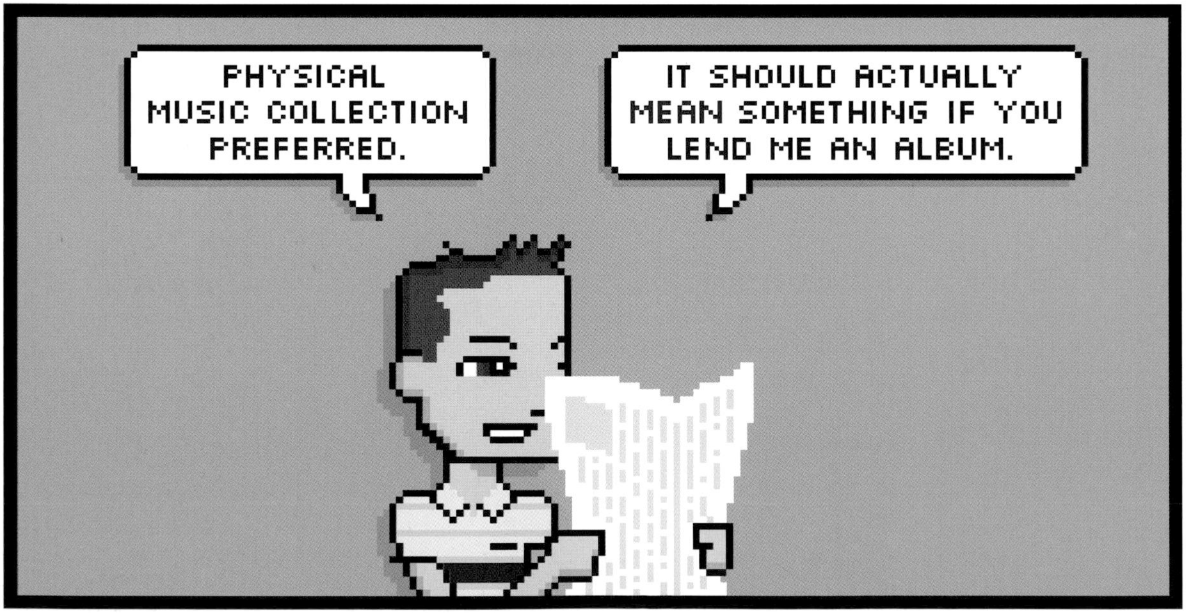
PHYSICAL MUSIC COLLECTION PREFERRED.
IT SHOULD ACTUALLY MEAN SOMETHING IF YOU LEND ME AN ALBUM.

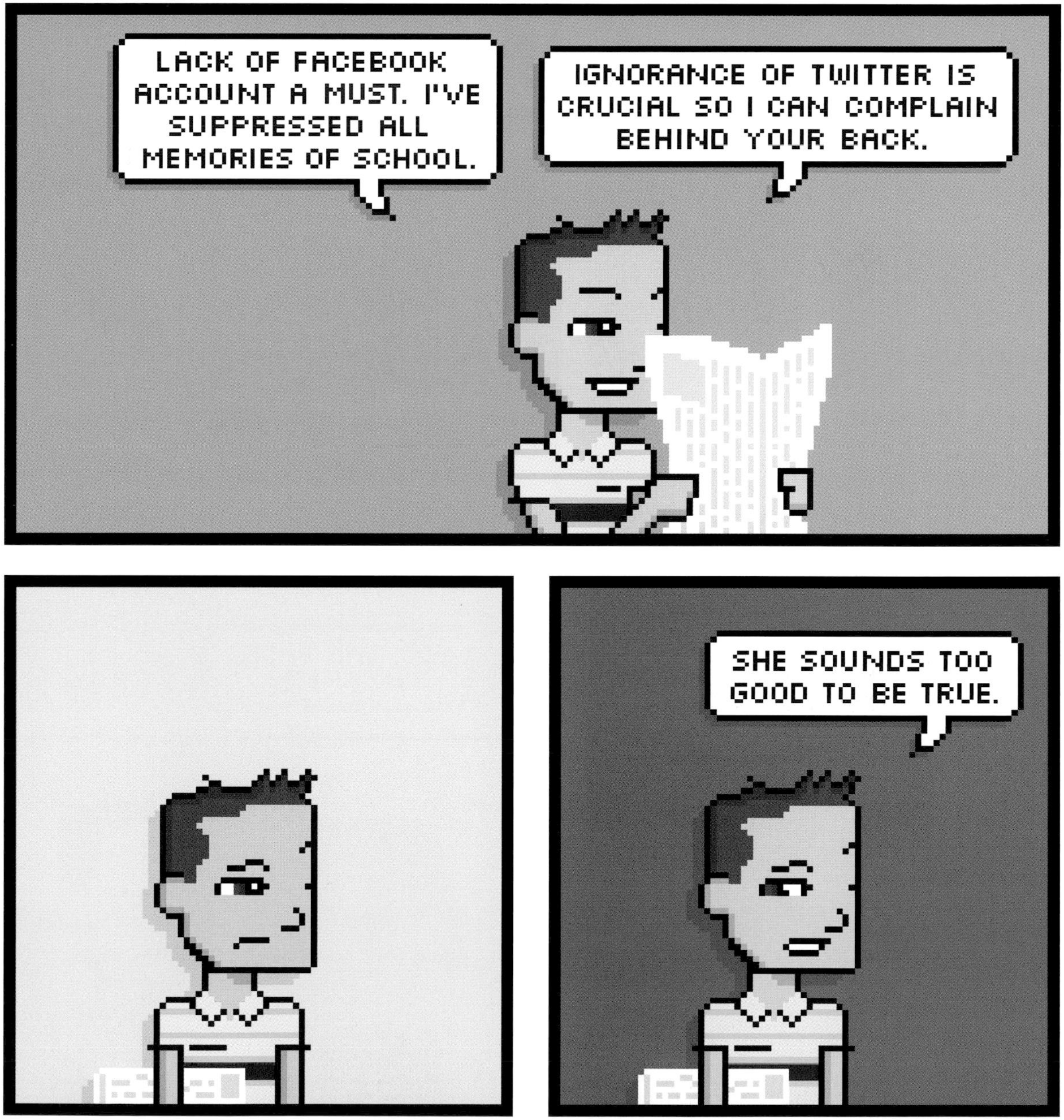
LACK OF FACEBOOK ACCOUNT A MUST. I'VE SUPPRESSED ALL MEMORIES OF SCHOOL.
IGNORANCE OF TWITTER IS CRUCIAL SO I CAN COMPLAIN BEHIND YOUR BACK.
SHE SOUNDS TOO GOOD TO BE TRUE.

YOUR OLD SEX WAS BETTER

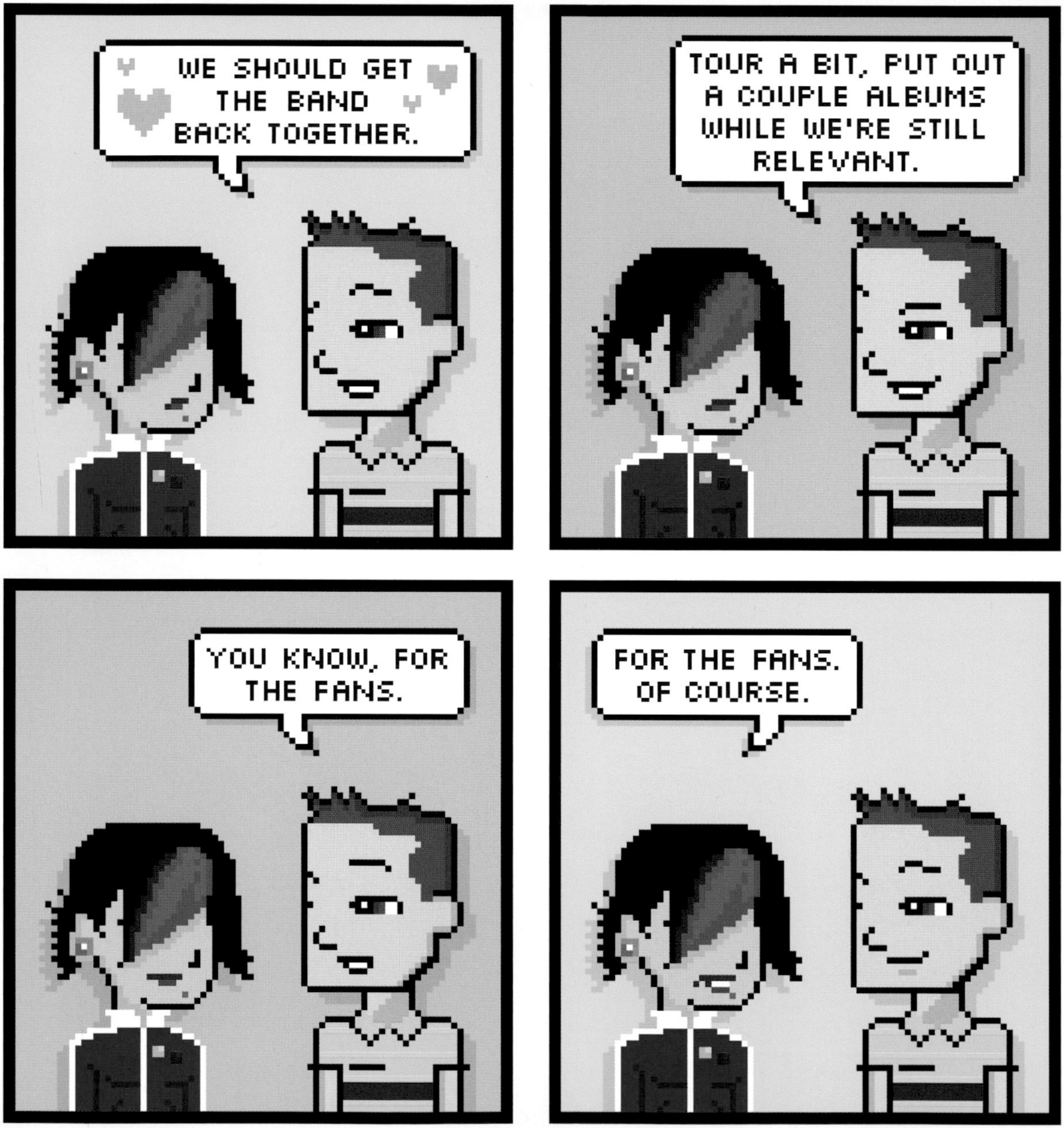

WE SHOULD GET THE BAND BACK TOGETHER.
TOUR A BIT, PUT OUT A COUPLE ALBUMS WHILE WE'RE STILL RELEVANT.
YOU KNOW, FOR THE FANS.
FOR THE FANS. OF COURSE.

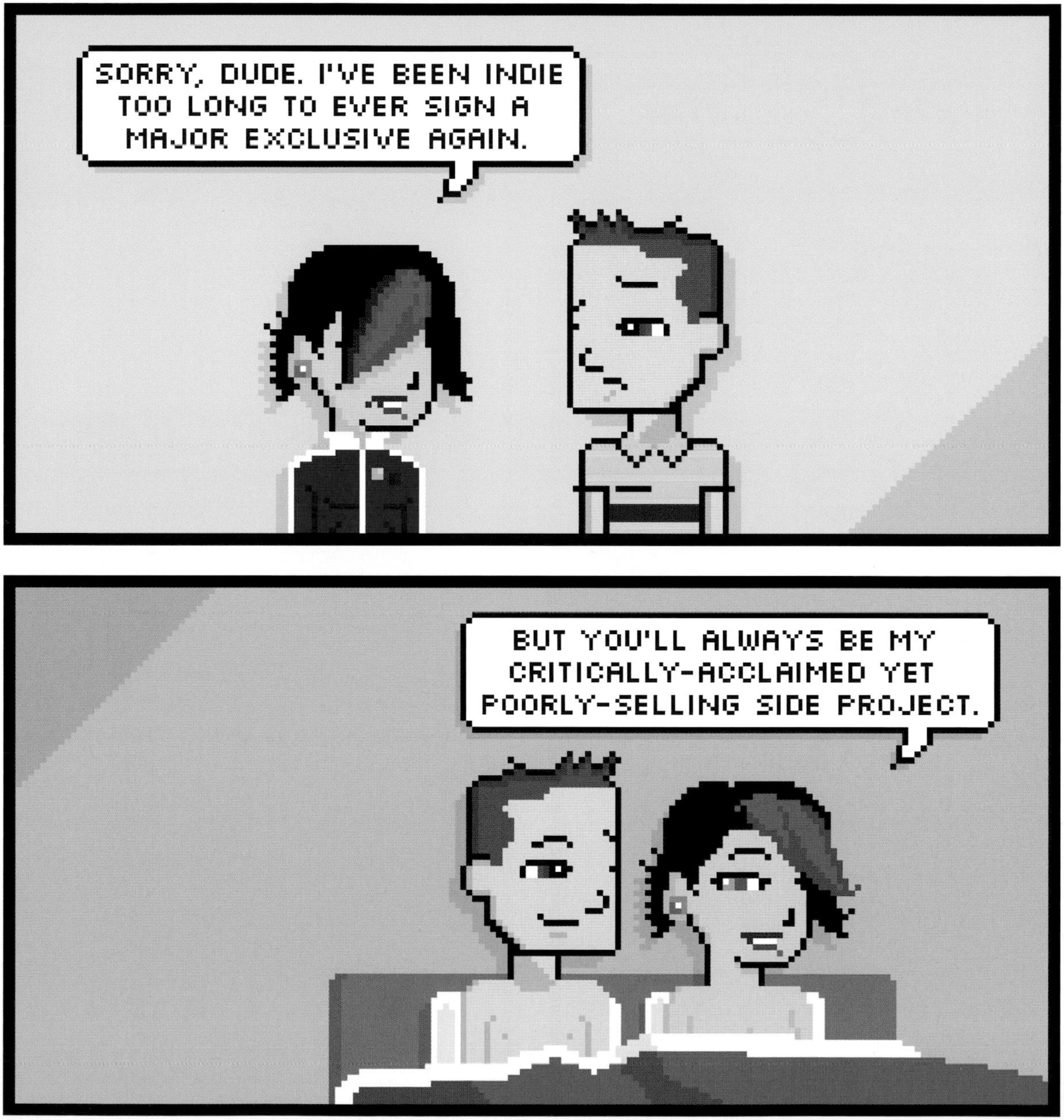
SORRY, DUDE. I'VE BEEN INDIE TOO LONG TO EVER SIGN A MAJOR EXCLUSIVE AGAIN.
BUT YOU'LL ALWAYS BE MY CRITICALLY-ACCLAIMED YET POORLY-SELLING SIDE PROJECT.

SIMPLE TRANSLATIONS FOR CRAPPY THINGS MUSIC FANS SAY

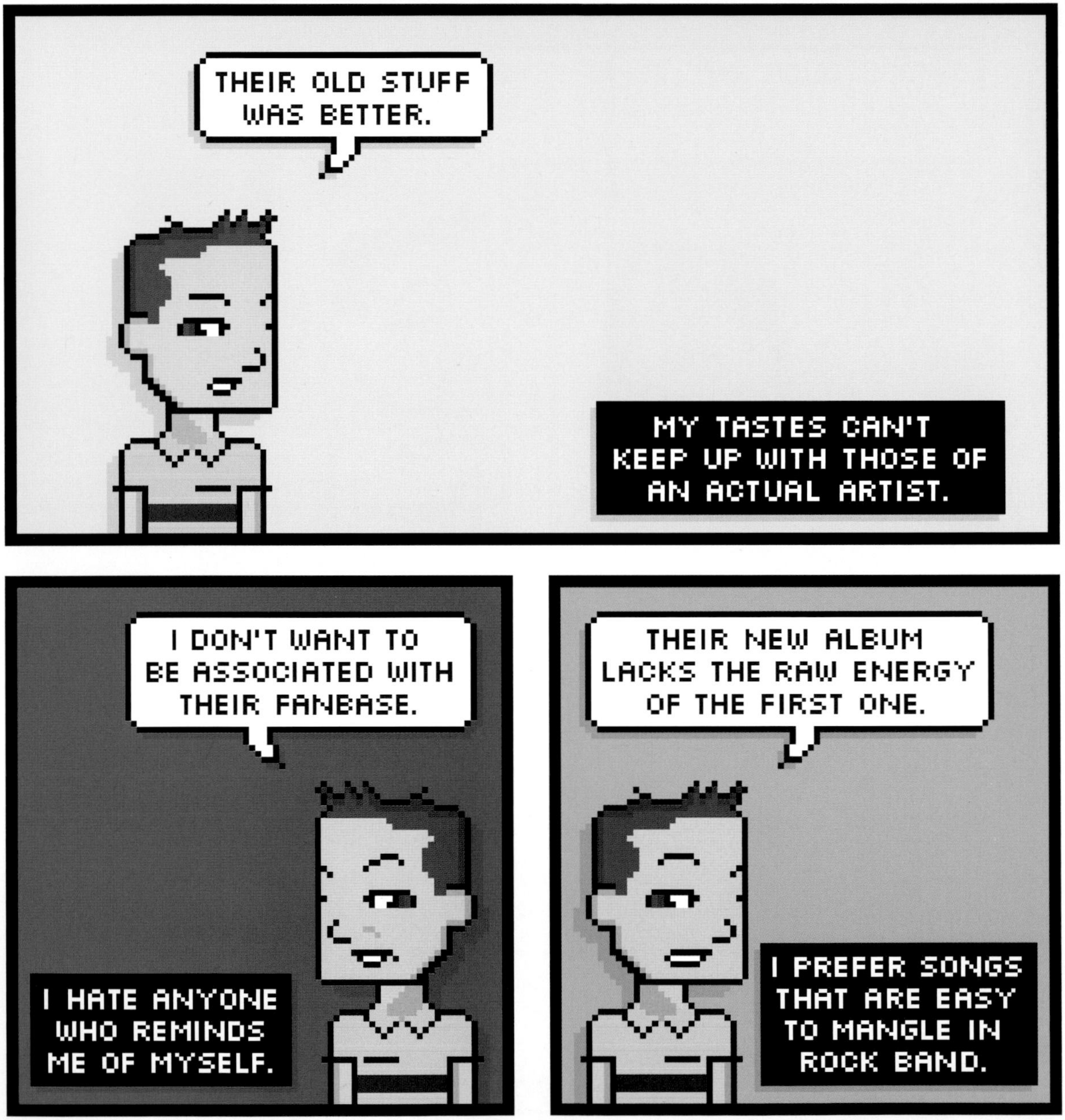

THEIR OLD STUFF WAS BETTER.
MY TASTES CAN'T KEEP UP WITH THOSE OF AN ACTUAL ARTIST.
I DON'T WANT TO BE ASSOCIATED WITH THEIR FANBASE.
I HATE ANYONE WHO REMINDS ME OF MYSELF.
THEIR NEW ALBUM LACKS THE RAW ENERGY OF THE FIRST ONE.
I PREFER SONGS THAT ARE EASY TO MANGLE IN ROCK BAND.

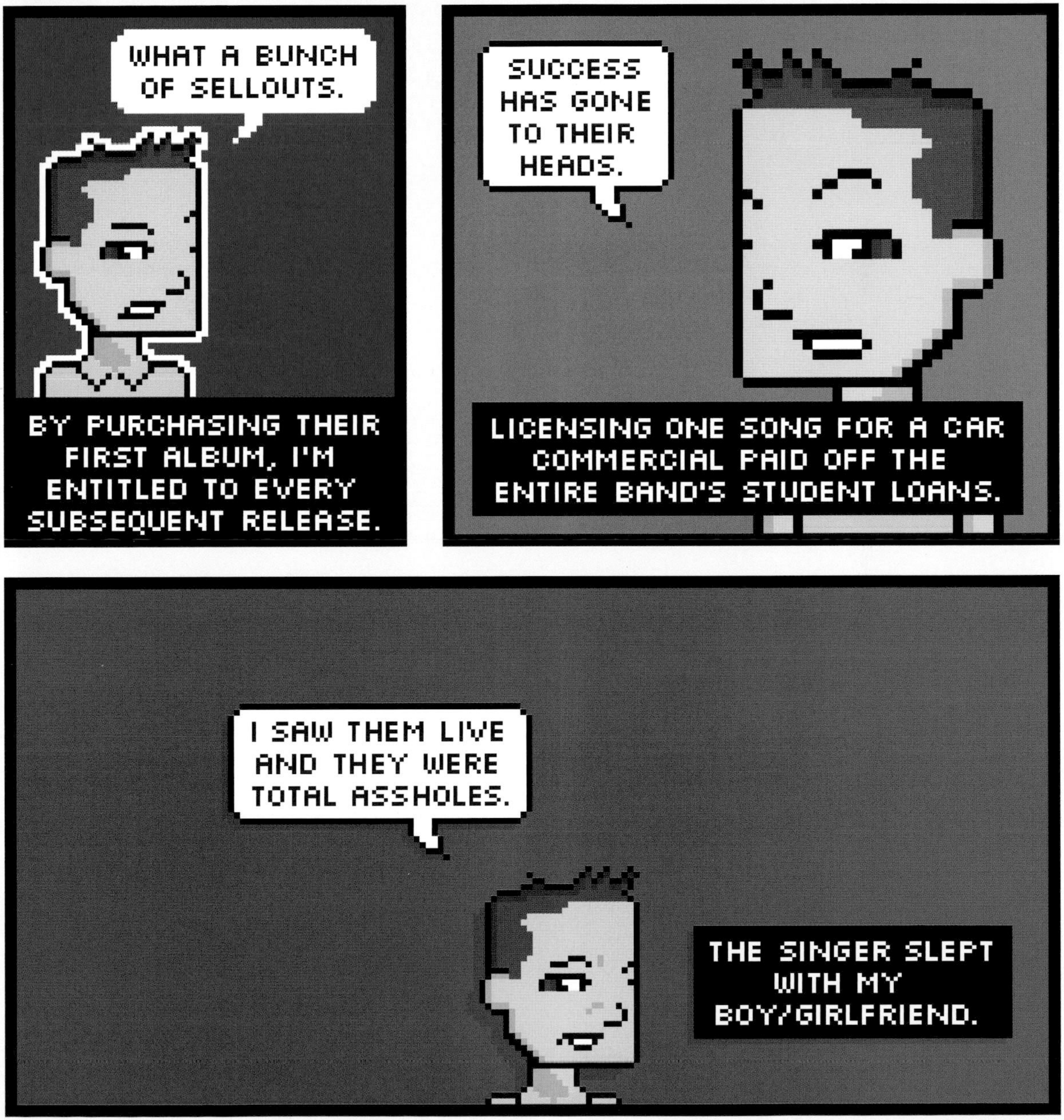
WHAT A BUNCH OF SELLOUTS.
BY PURCHASING THEIR FIRST ALBUM, I'M ENTITLED TO EVERY SUBSEQUENT RELEASE.
SUCCESS HAS GONE TO THEIR HEADS.
LICENSING ONE SONG FOR A CAR COMMERCIAL PAID OFF THE ENTIRE BAND'S STUDENT LOANS.
I SAW THEM LIVE AND THEY WERE TOTAL ASSHOLES.
THE SINGER SLEPT WITH MY BOY/GIRLFRIEND.

A HERO OF OUR TIME

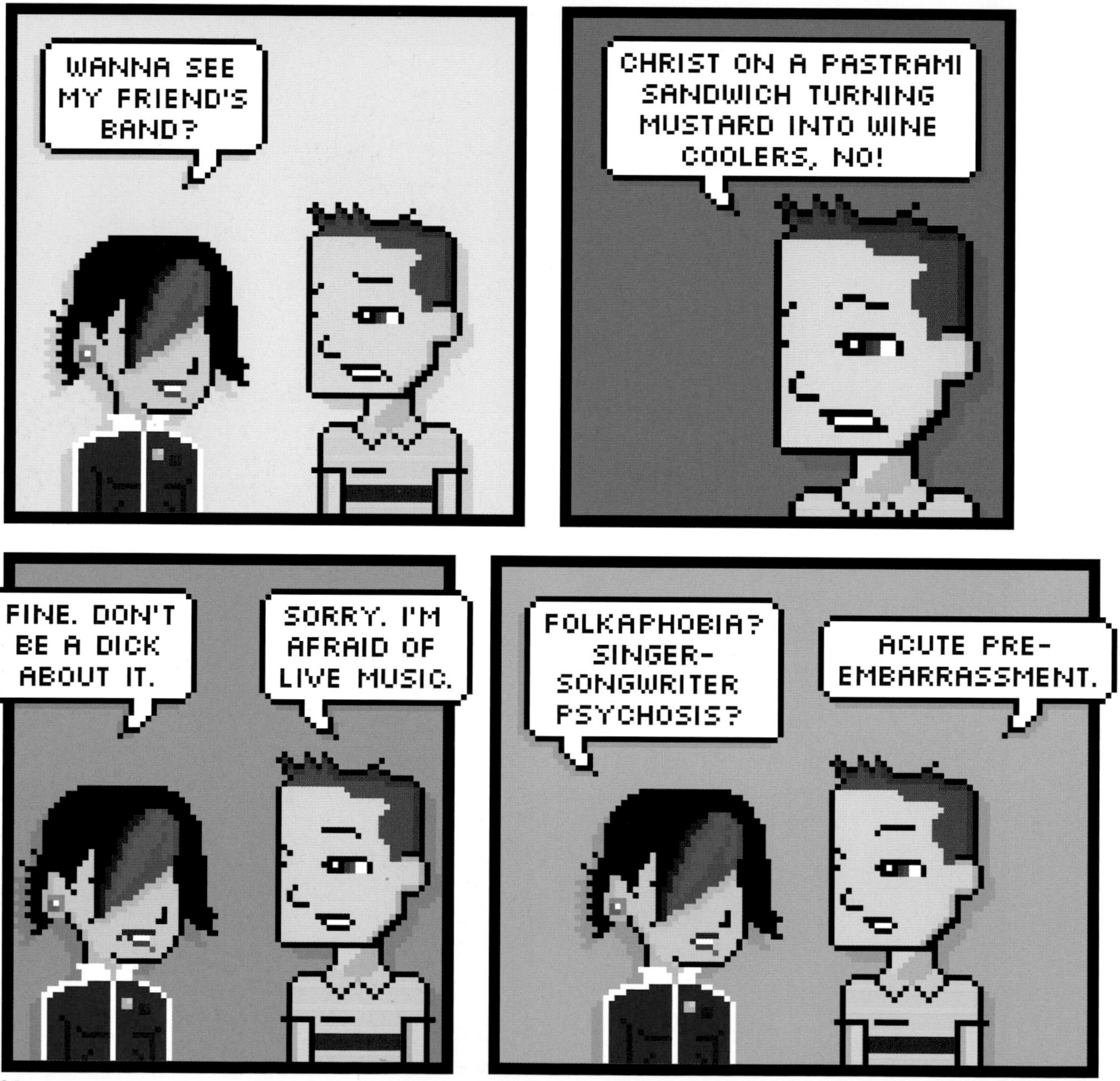
WANNA SEE MY FRIEND'S BAND?
CHRIST ON A PASTRAMI SANDWICH TURNING MUSTARD INTO WINE COOLERS, NO!
FINE. DON'T BE A DICK ABOUT IT.
SORRY. I'M AFRAID OF LIVE MUSIC.
FOLKAPHOBIA? SINGER-SONGWRITER PSYCHOSIS?
ACUTE PRE-EMBARRASSMENT.

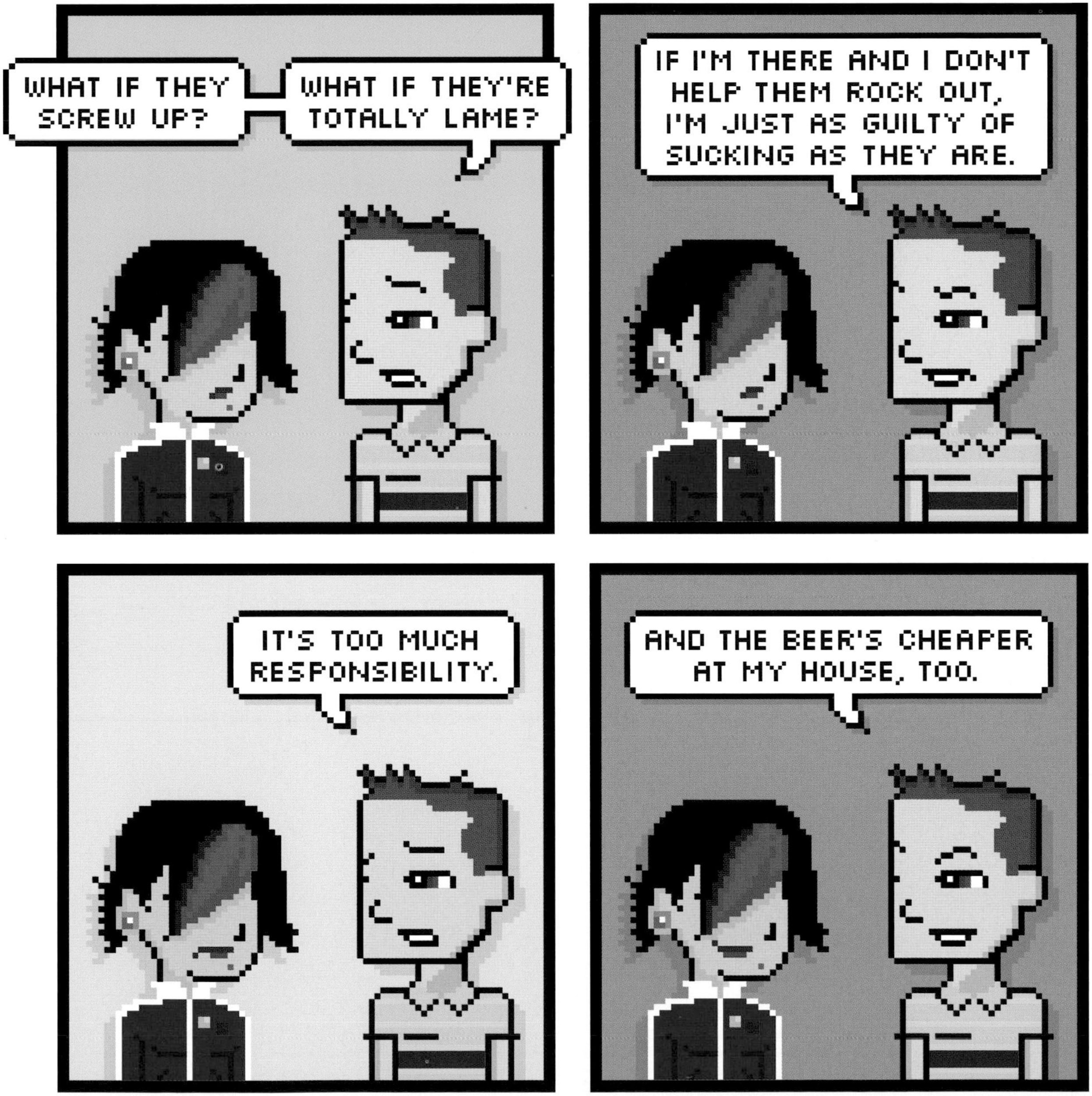
WHAT IF THEY SCREW UP?
WHAT IF THEY'RE TOTALLY LAME?
IF I'M THERE AND I DON'T HELP THEM ROCK OUT, I'M JUST AS GUILTY OF SUCKING AS THEY ARE.
IT'S TOO MUCH RESPONSIBILITY.
AND THE BEER'S CHEAPER AT MY HOUSE, TOO.

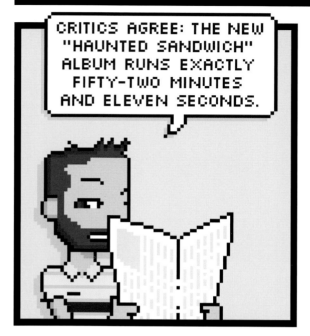

CRITICS AGREE: THE NEW "HAUNTED SANDWICH" ALBUM RUNS EXACTLY FIFTY-TWO MINUTES AND ELEVEN SECONDS.

AND IS AVAILABLE IN VINYL, CD, AND MP3 FORMATS.

IT CARRIES A SUGGESTED RETAIL PRICE OF $15.99.

HOWEVER, ITS VALUE IS THE SUBJECT OF GREAT DEBATE.

MY SO-CALLED STRIFE

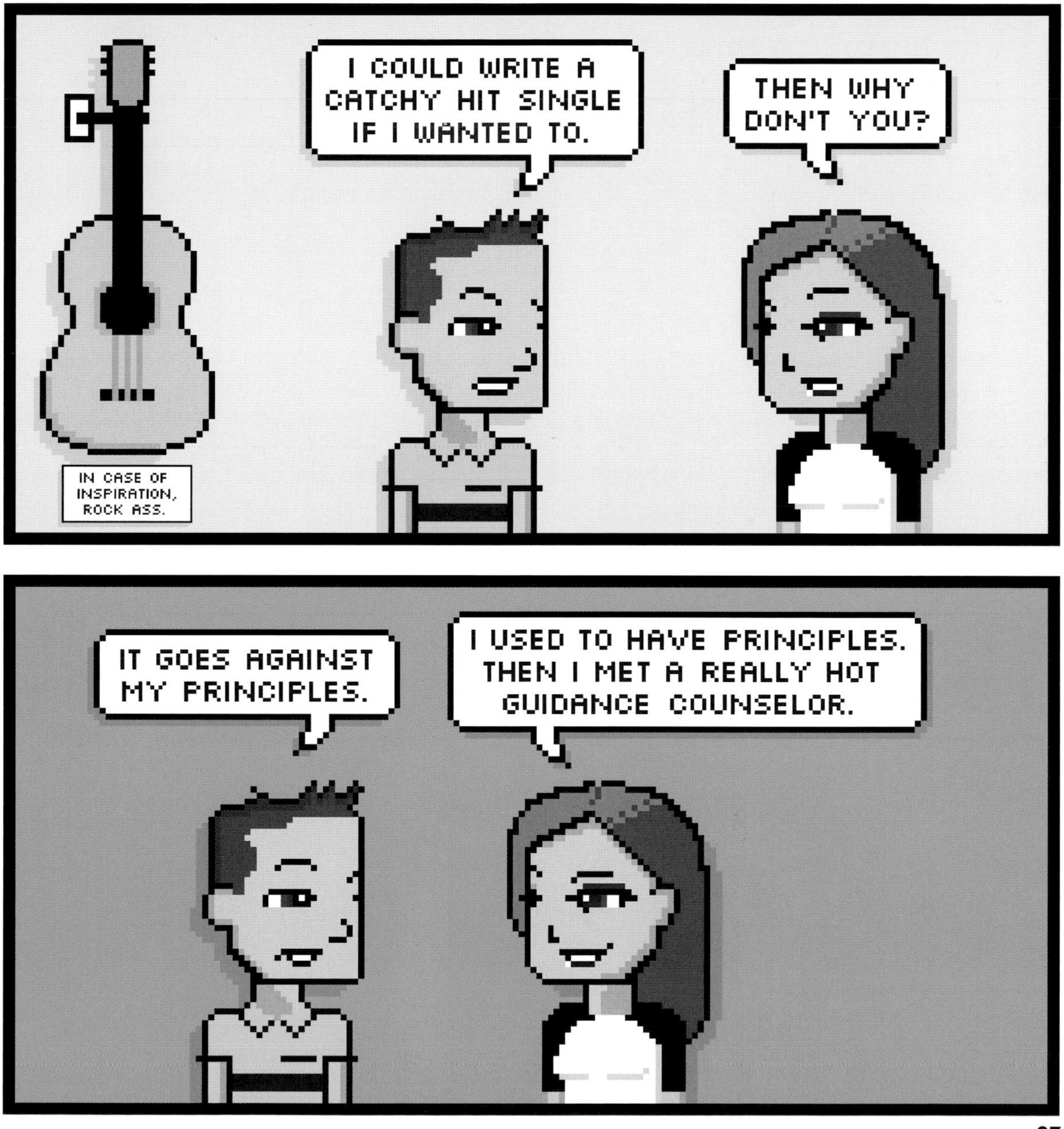
IN CASE OF INSPIRATION, ROCK ASS.
I COULD WRITE A CATCHY HIT SINGLE IF I WANTED TO.
THEN WHY DON'T YOU?
IT GOES AGAINST MY PRINCIPLES.
I USED TO HAVE PRINCIPLES. THEN I MET A REALLY HOT GUIDANCE COUNSELOR.

NOCTURNAL AMBITIONS

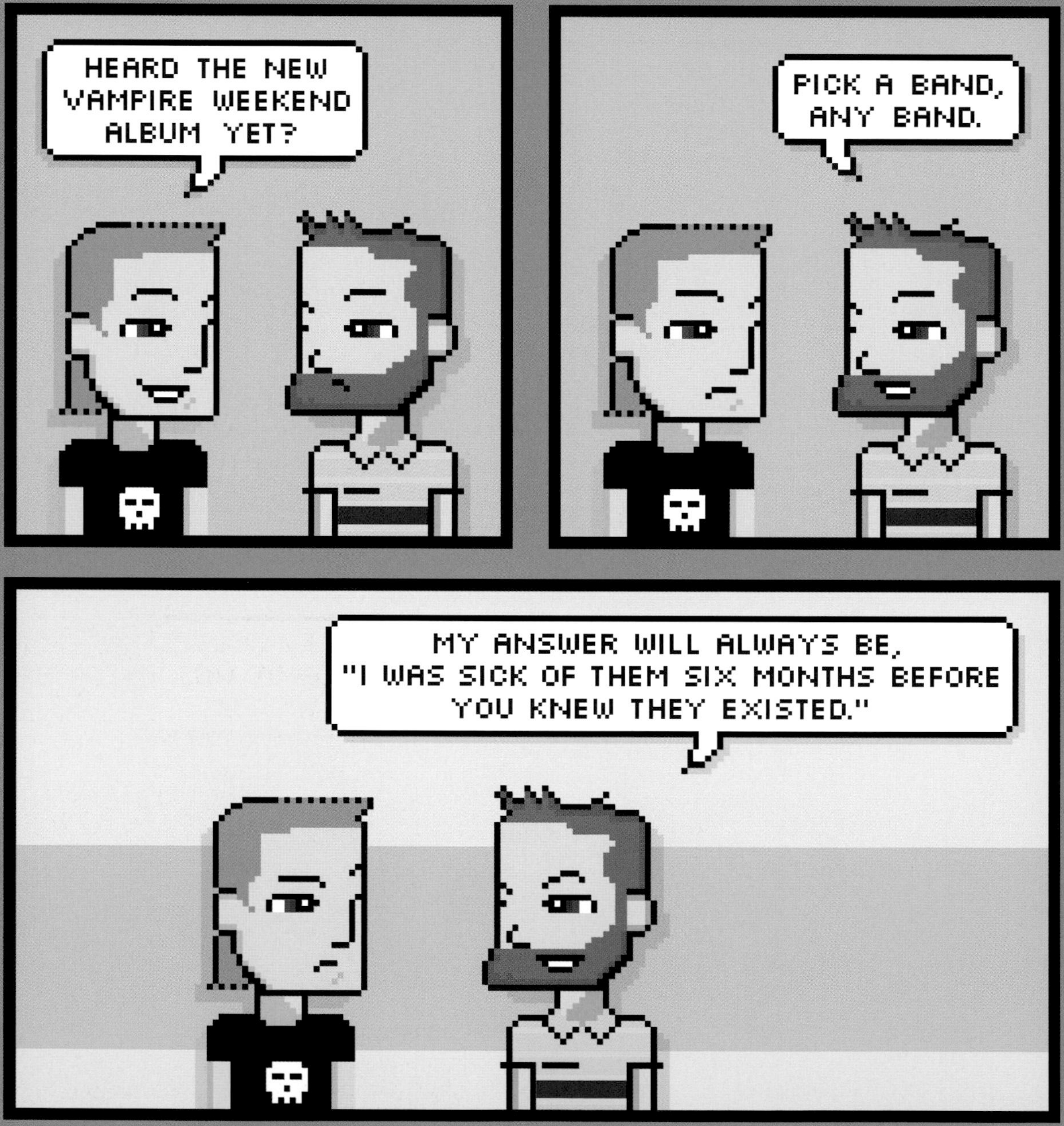
HEARD THE NEW VAMPIRE WEEKEND ALBUM YET?
PICK A BAND, ANY BAND.
MY ANSWER WILL ALWAYS BE, "I WAS SICK OF THEM SIX MONTHS BEFORE YOU KNEW THEY EXISTED."

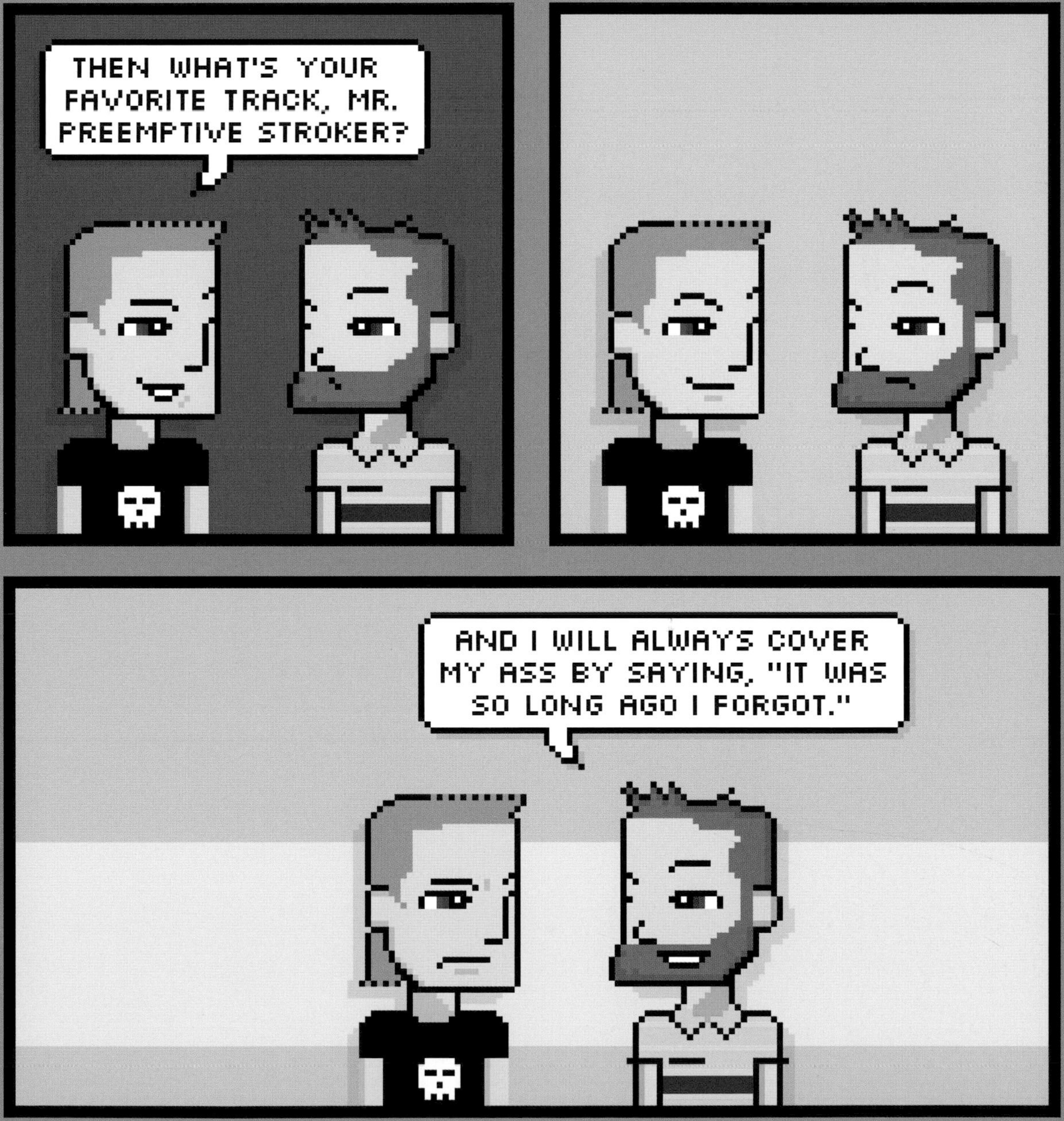
THEN WHAT'S YOUR FAVORITE TRACK, MR. PREEMPTIVE STROKER?
AND I WILL ALWAYS COVER MY ASS BY SAYING, "IT WAS SO LONG AGO I FORGOT."

AUDIOPHILES DO IT ON BOTH SIDES

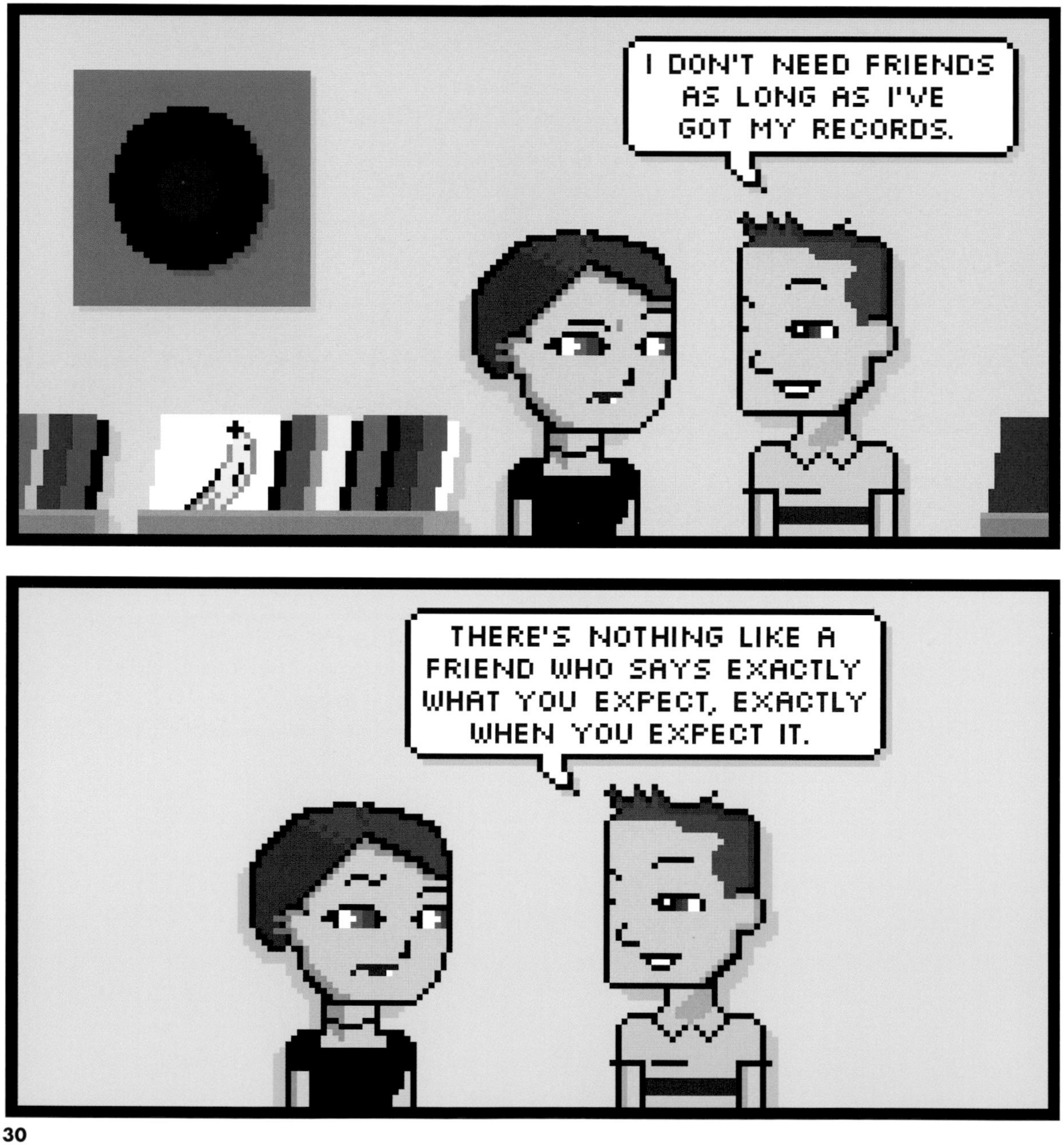
I DON'T NEED FRIENDS AS LONG AS I'VE GOT MY RECORDS.
THERE'S NOTHING LIKE A FRIEND WHO SAYS EXACTLY WHAT YOU EXPECT, EXACTLY WHEN YOU EXPECT IT.

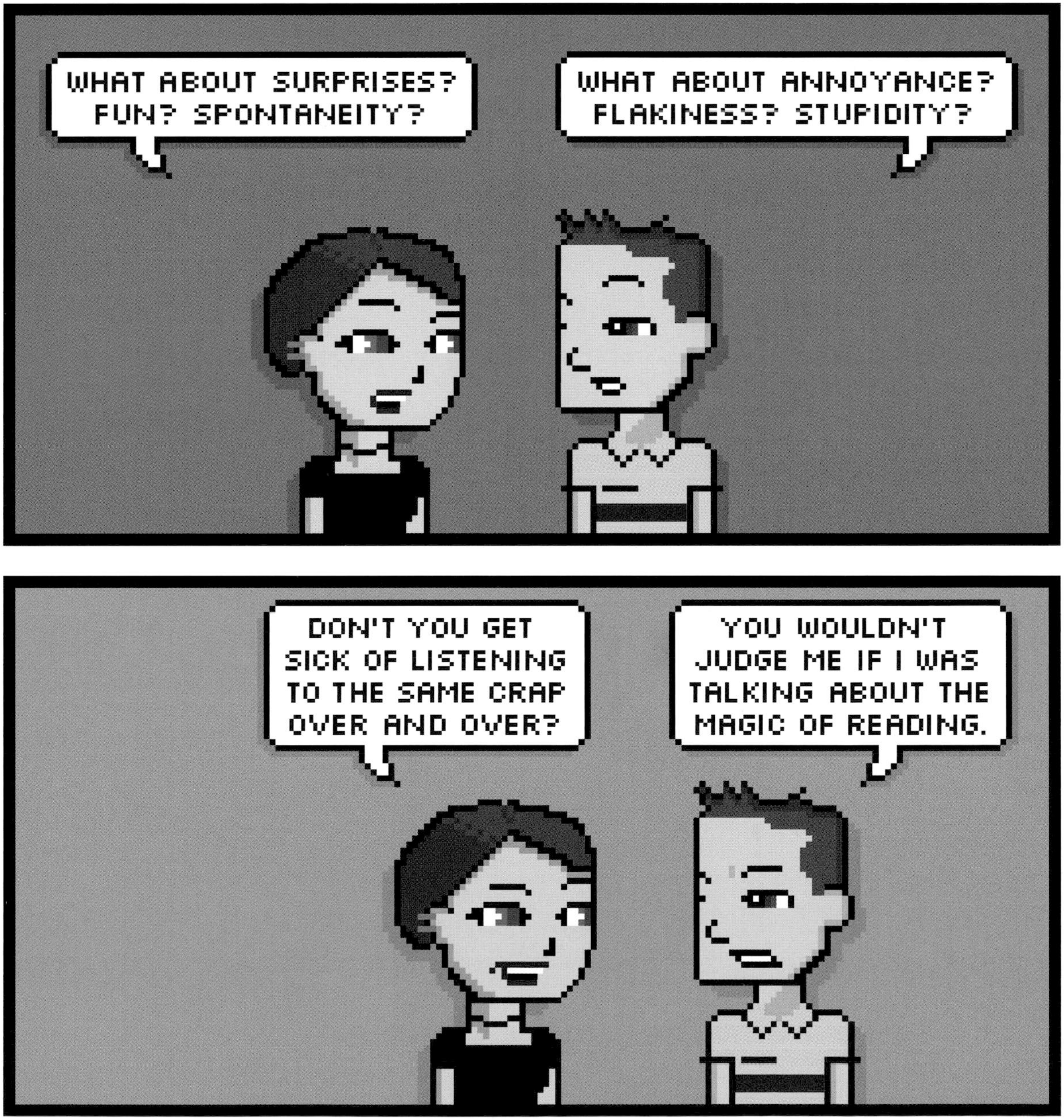
WHAT ABOUT SURPRISES? FUN? SPONTANEITY?
WHAT ABOUT ANNOYANCE? FLAKINESS? STUPIDITY?
DON'T YOU GET SICK OF LISTENING TO THE SAME CRAP OVER AND OVER?
YOU WOULDN'T JUDGE ME IF I WAS TALKING ABOUT THE MAGIC OF READING.

GIVING SIXTY-NINE A TEN

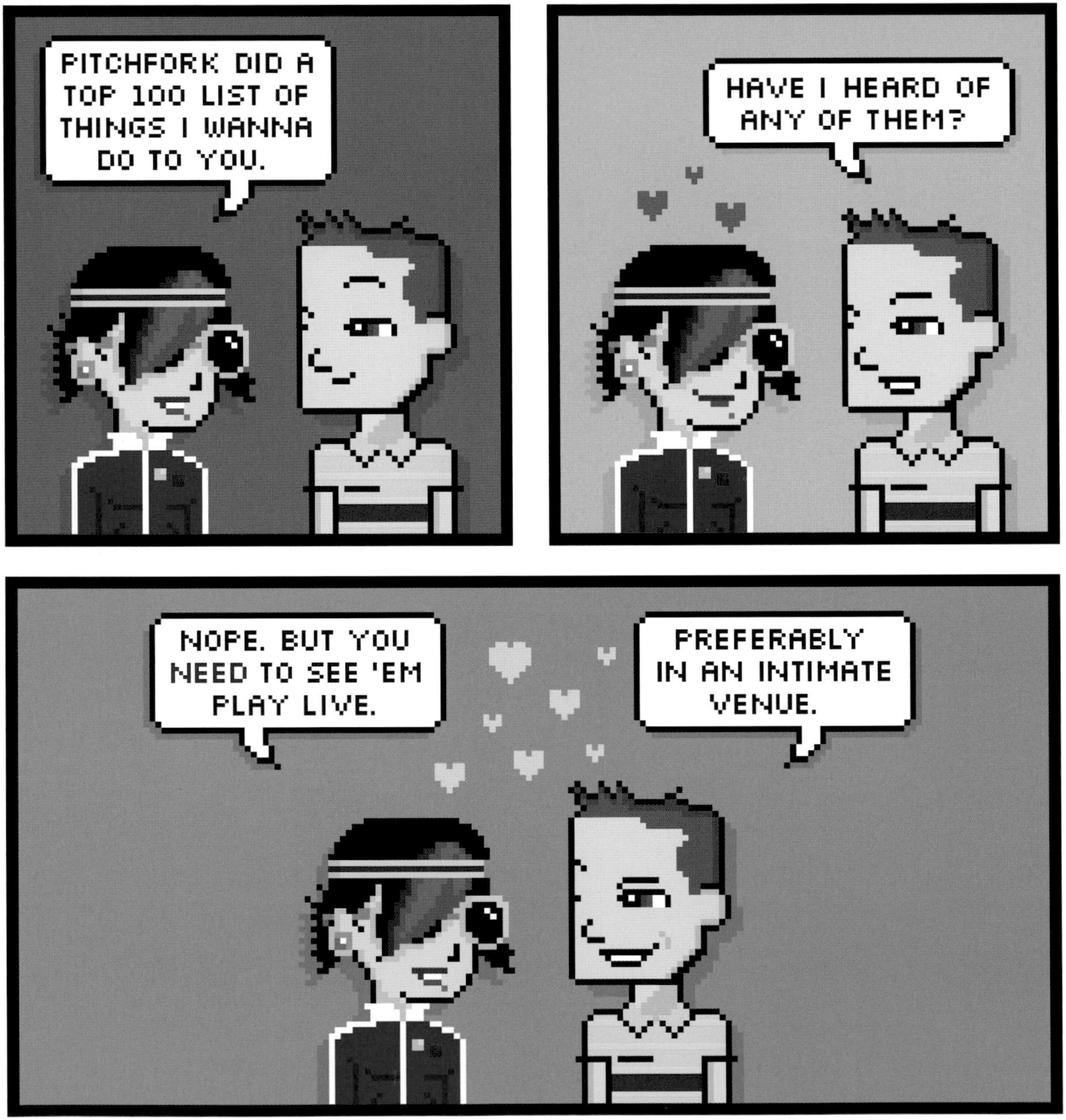

PITCHFORK DID A TOP 100 LIST OF THINGS I WANNA DO TO YOU.
HAVE I HEARD OF ANY OF THEM?
NOPE. BUT YOU NEED TO SEE 'EM PLAY LIVE.
PREFERABLY IN AN INTIMATE VENUE.

ANALOGUE ROLLING

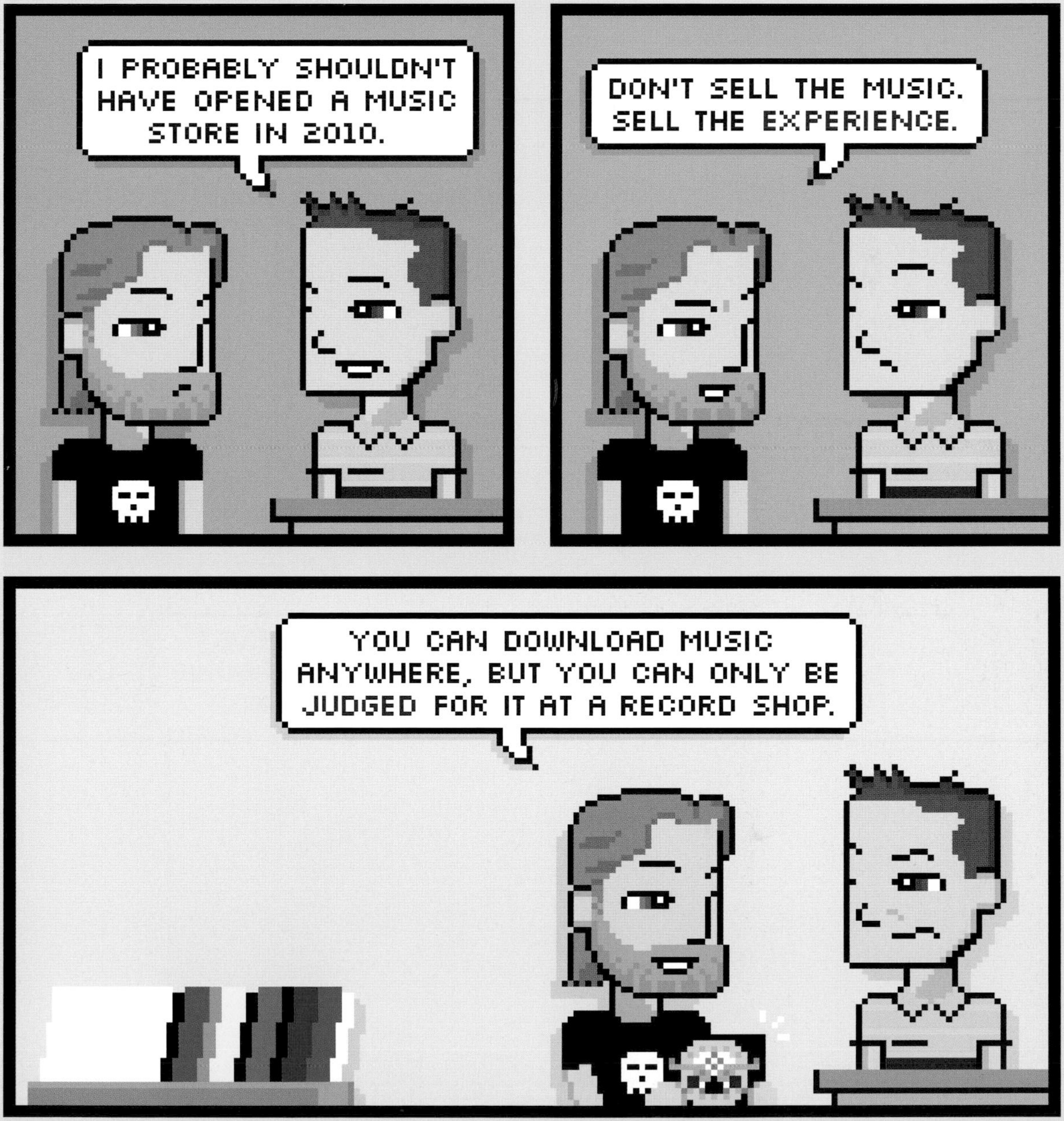
I PROBABLY SHOULDN'T HAVE OPENED A MUSIC STORE IN 2010.
DON'T SELL THE MUSIC. SELL THE EXPERIENCE.
YOU CAN DOWNLOAD MUSIC ANYWHERE, BUT YOU CAN ONLY BE JUDGED FOR IT AT A RECORD SHOP.

ACRONYMBLE

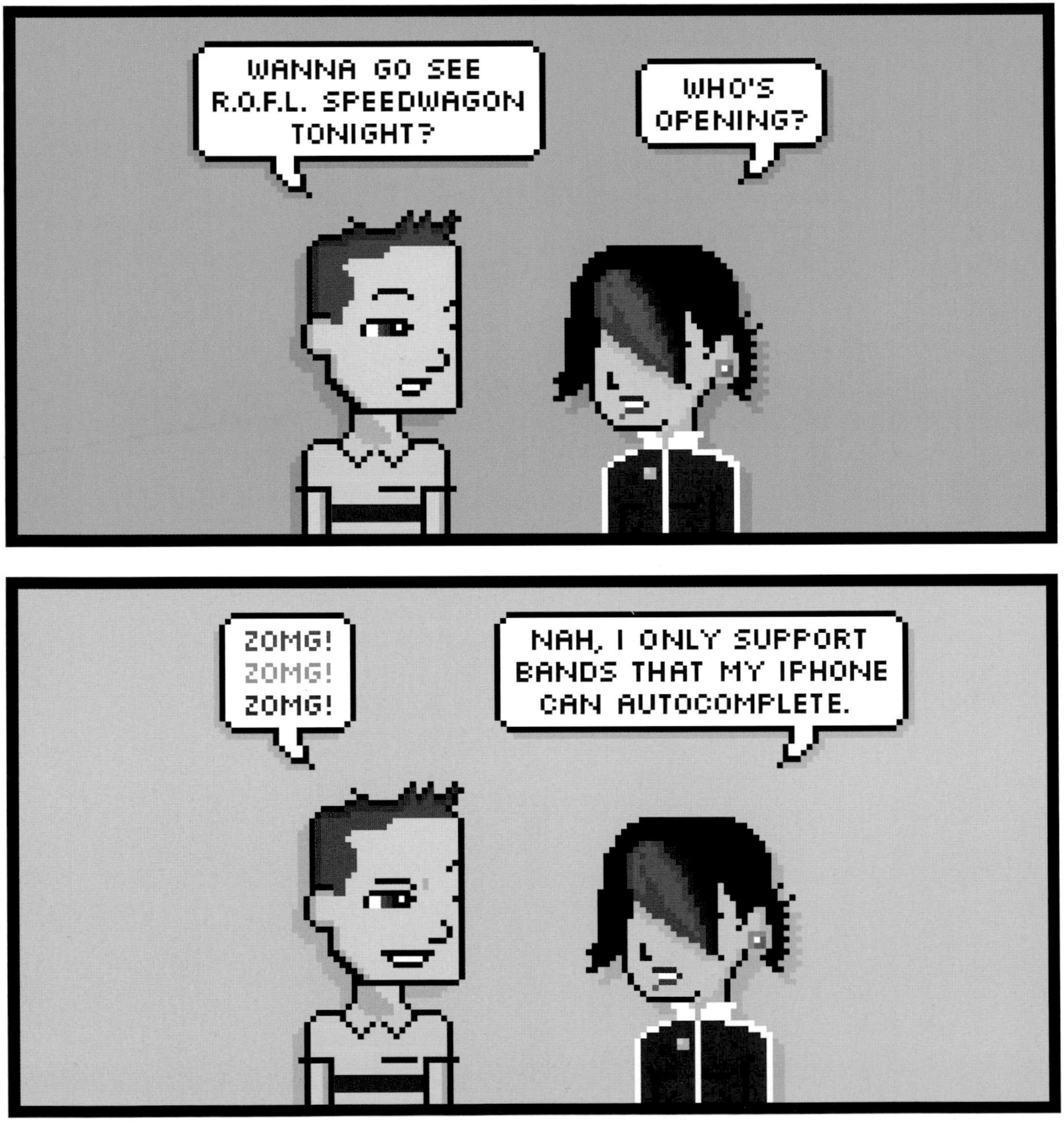
WANNA GO SEE R.O.F.L. SPEEDWAGON TONIGHT?
WHO'S OPENING?
ZOMG! ZOMG! ZOMG!
NAH, I ONLY SUPPORT BANDS THAT MY IPHONE CAN AUTOCOMPLETE.

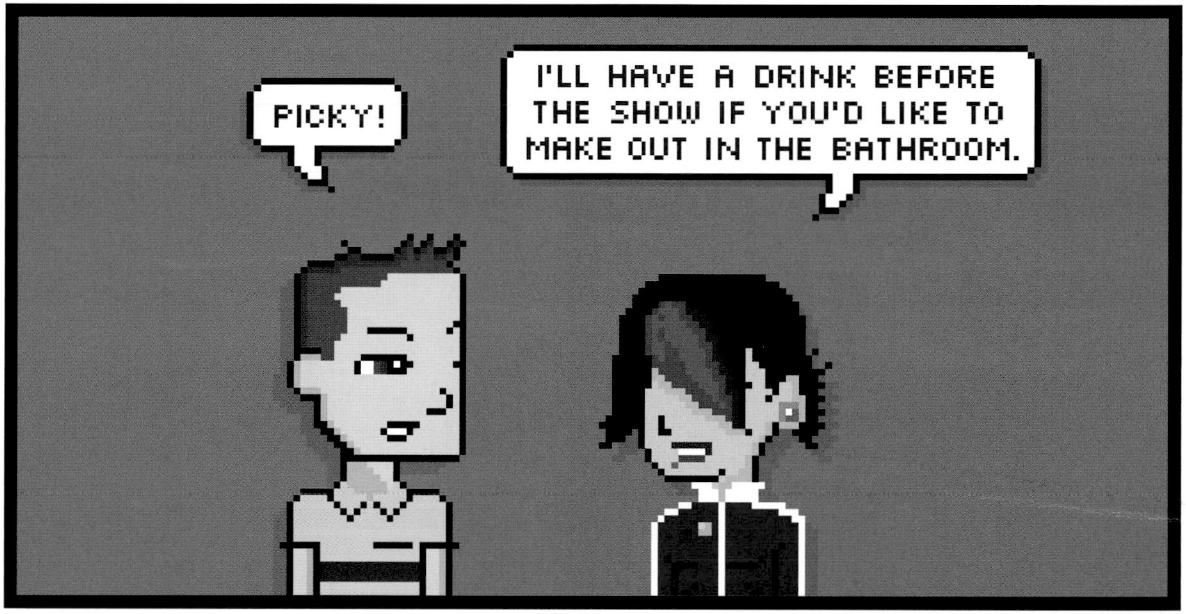
PICKY!
I'LL HAVE A DRINK BEFORE THE SHOW IF YOU'D LIKE TO MAKE OUT IN THE BATHROOM.

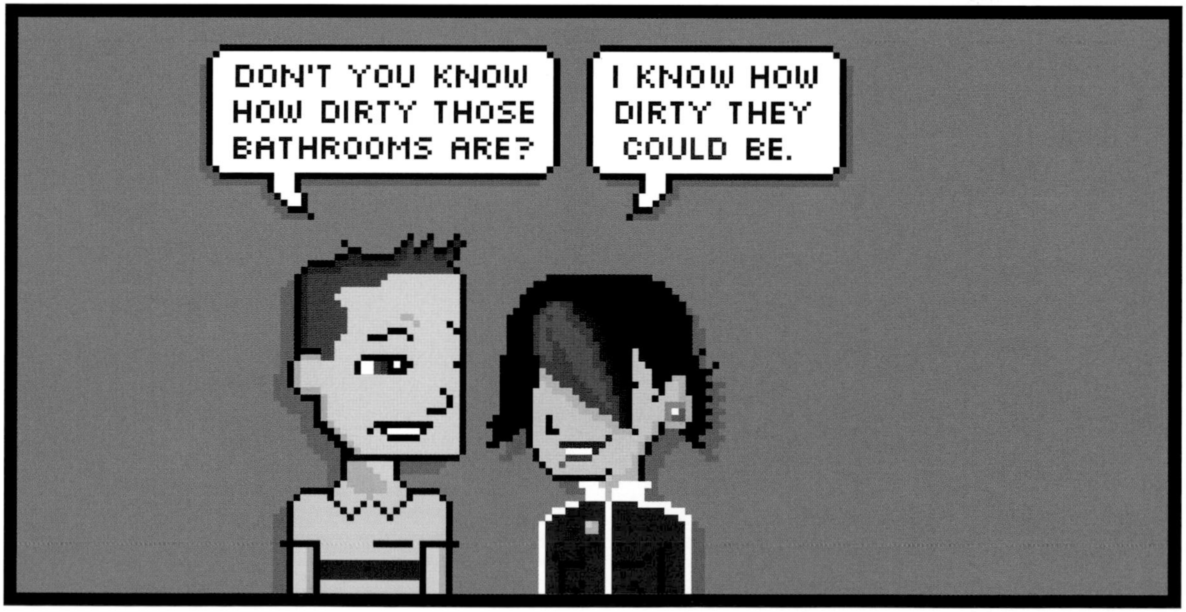
DON'T YOU KNOW HOW DIRTY THOSE BATHROOMS ARE?
I KNOW HOW DIRTY THEY COULD BE.

RECESSIVE TRAITS

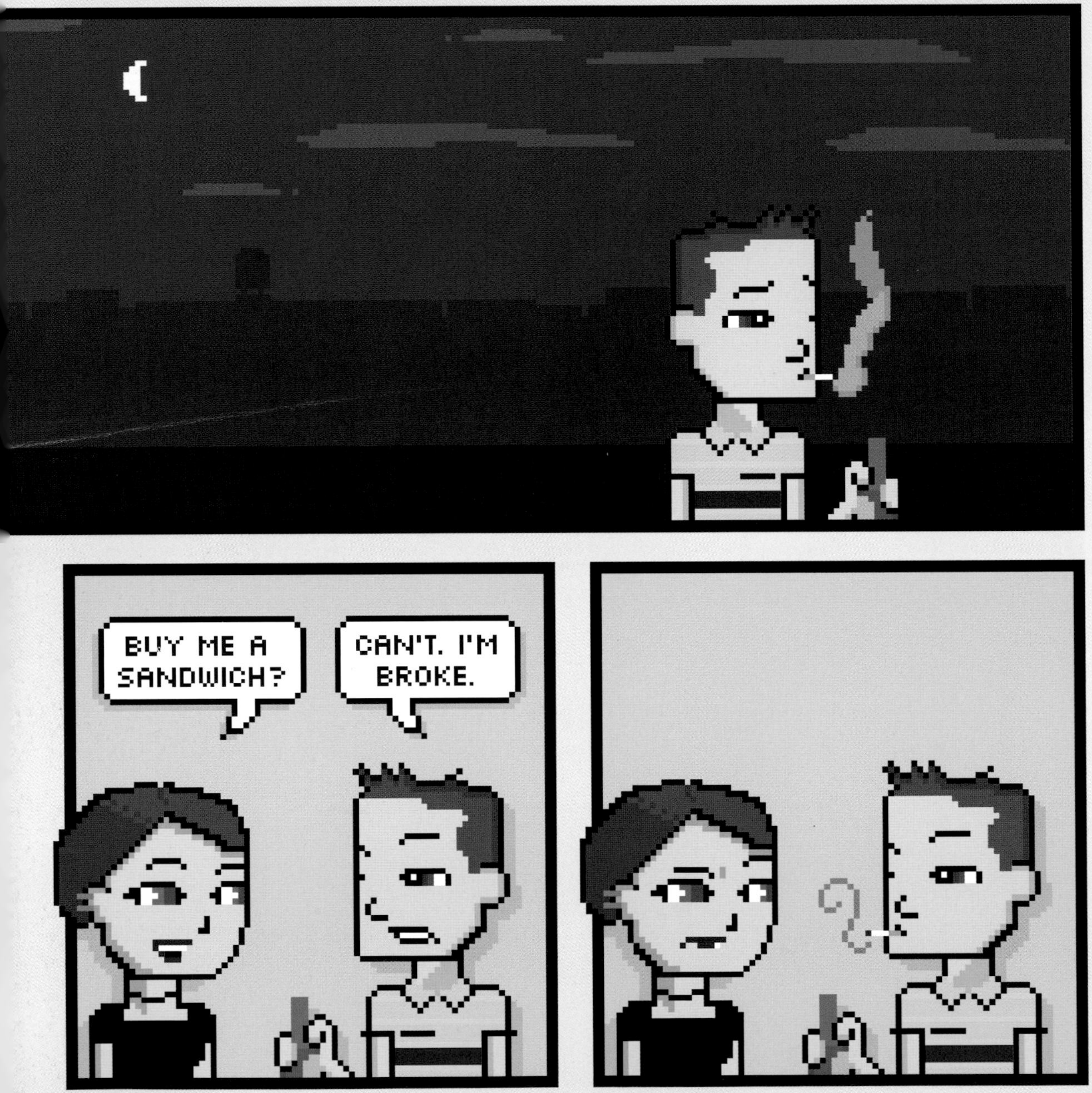
BUY ME A SANDWICH?
CAN'T. I'M BROKE.

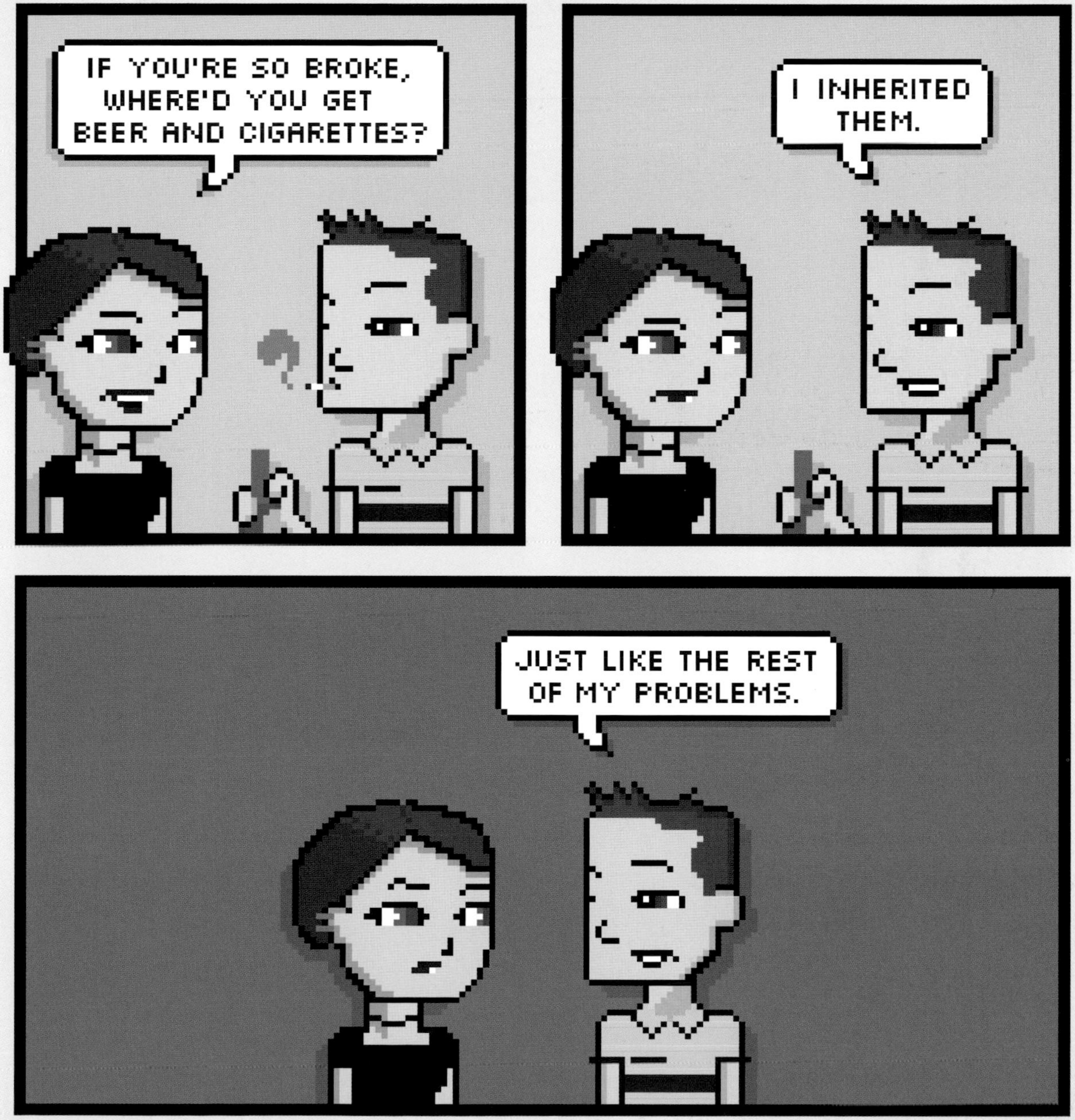
IF YOU'RE SO BROKE, WHERE'D YOU GET BEER AND CIGARETTES?
I INHERITED THEM.
JUST LIKE THE REST OF MY PROBLEMS.

THE UNSILENT MINORITY

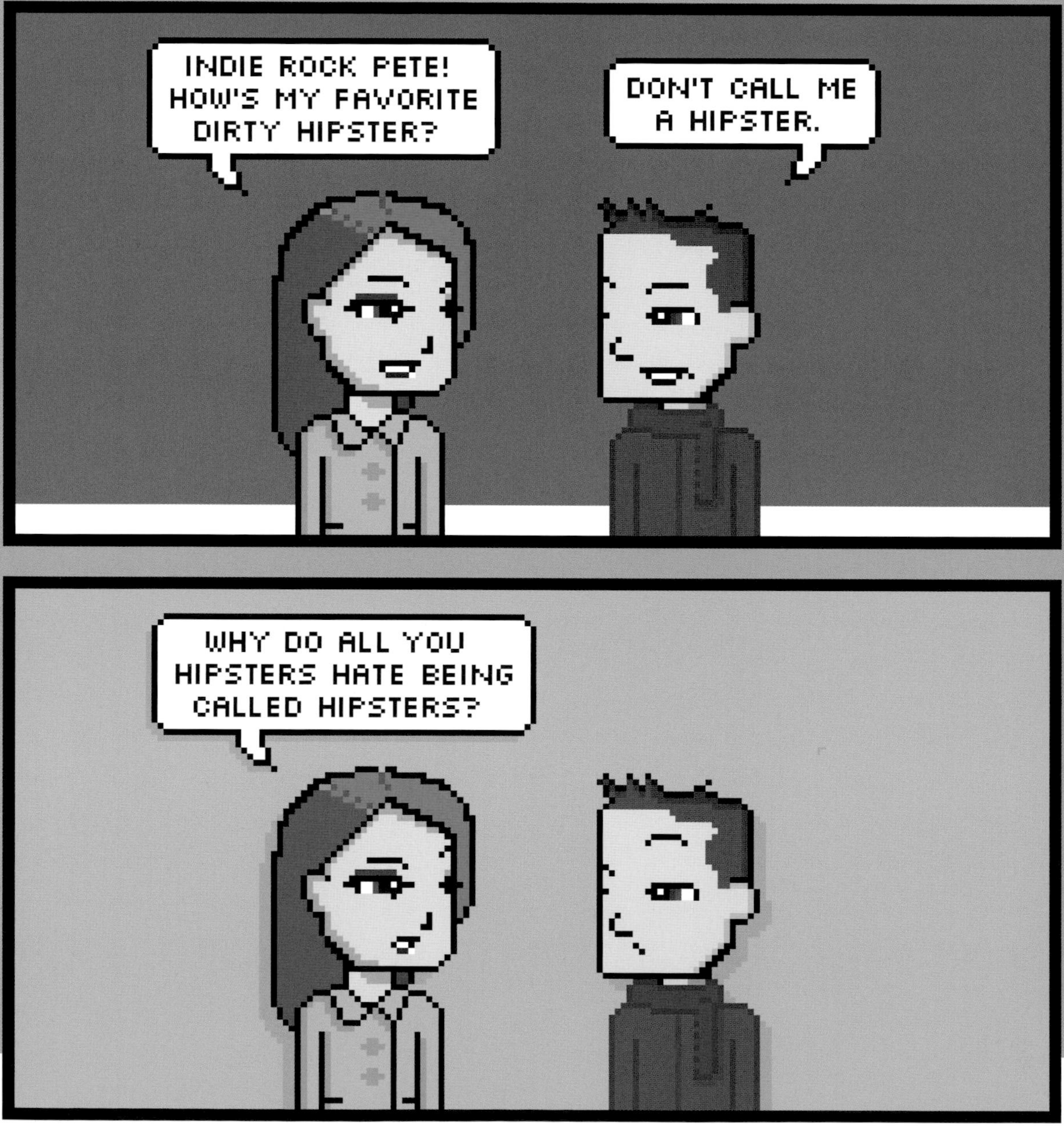
INDIE ROCK PETE! HOW'S MY FAVORITE DIRTY HIPSTER?
DON'T CALL ME A HIPSTER.
WHY DO ALL YOU HIPSTERS HATE BEING CALLED HIPSTERS?

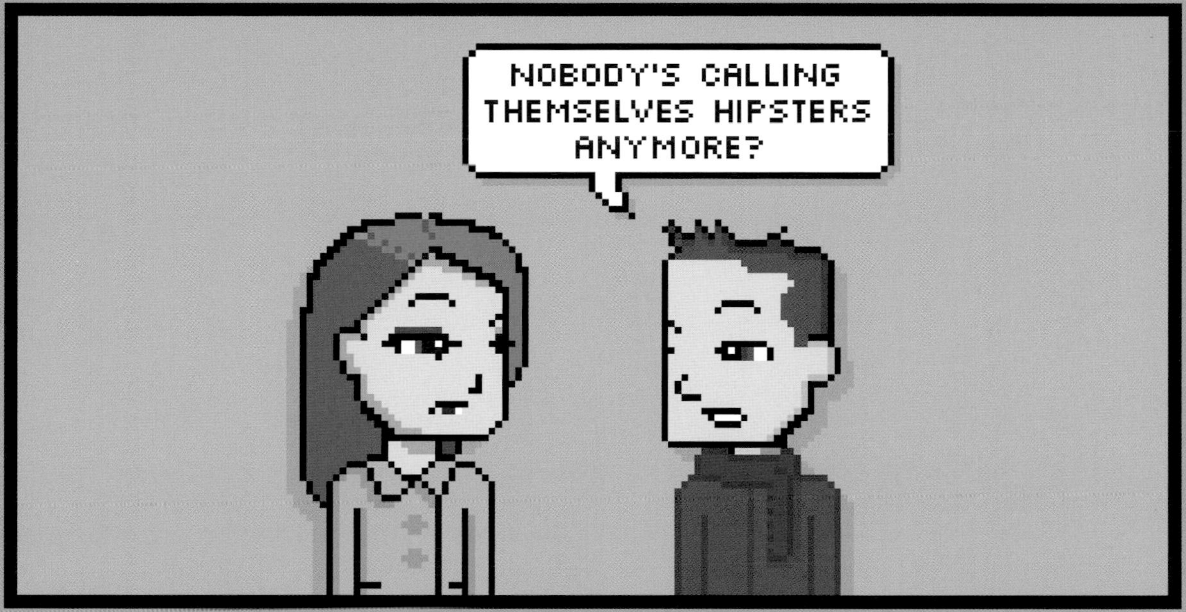
NOBODY'S CALLING THEMSELVES HIPSTERS ANYMORE?

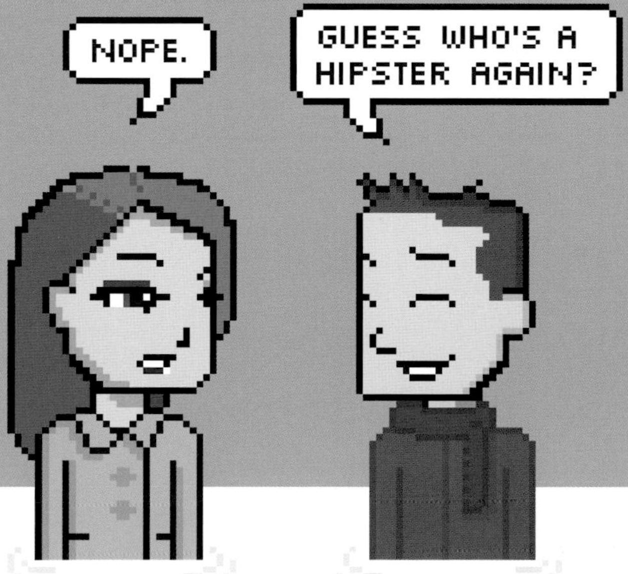
NOPE.
GUESS WHO'S A HIPSTER AGAIN?

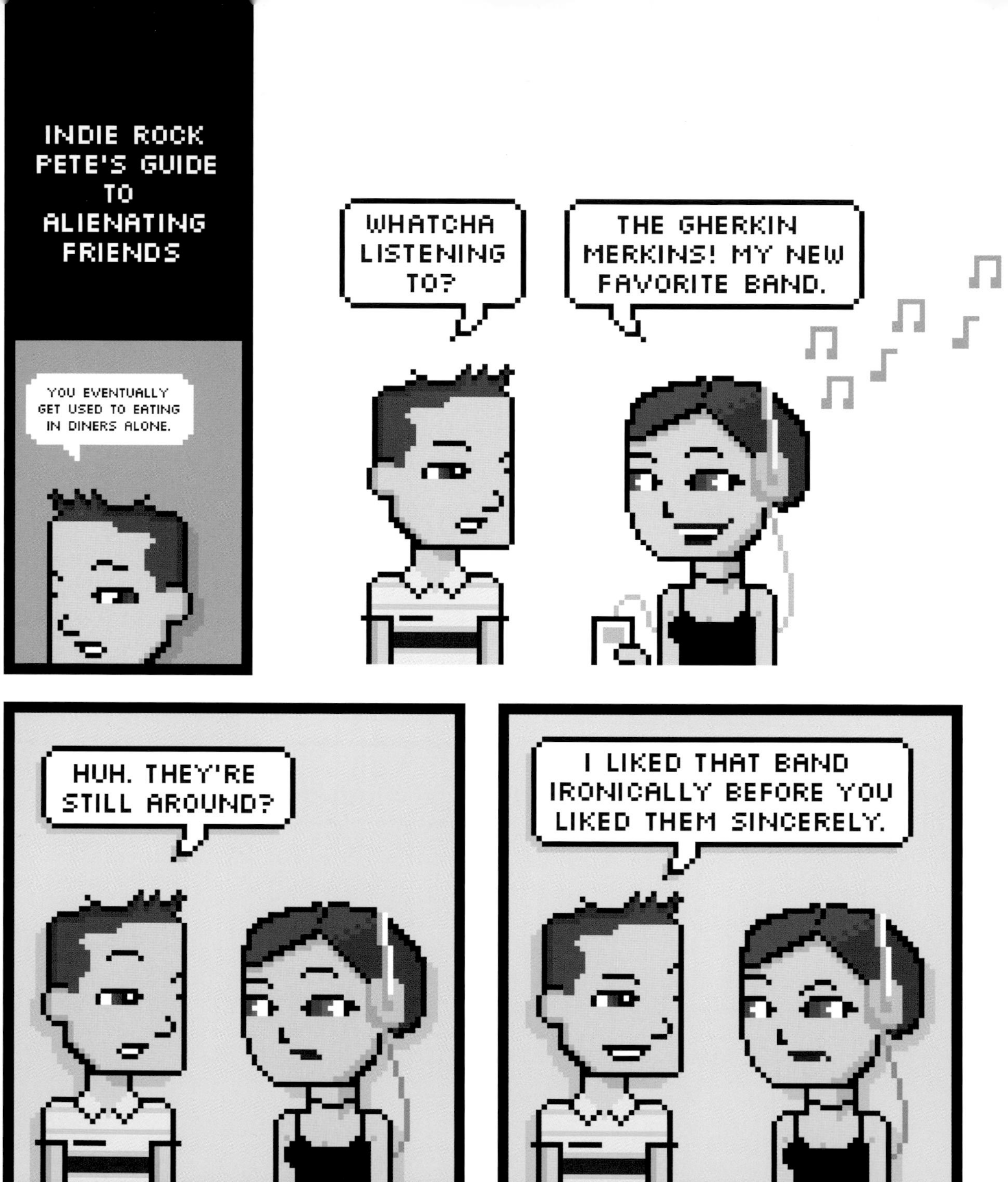
INDIE ROCK PETE'S GUIDE TO ALIENATING FRIENDS
YOU EVENTUALLY GET USED TO EATING IN DINERS ALONE.
WHATCHA LISTENING TO?
THE GHERKIN MERKINS! MY NEW FAVORITE BAND.
HUH. THEY'RE STILL AROUND?
I LIKED THAT BAND IRONICALLY BEFORE YOU LIKED THEM SINCERELY.

ROBBLEROUSERS

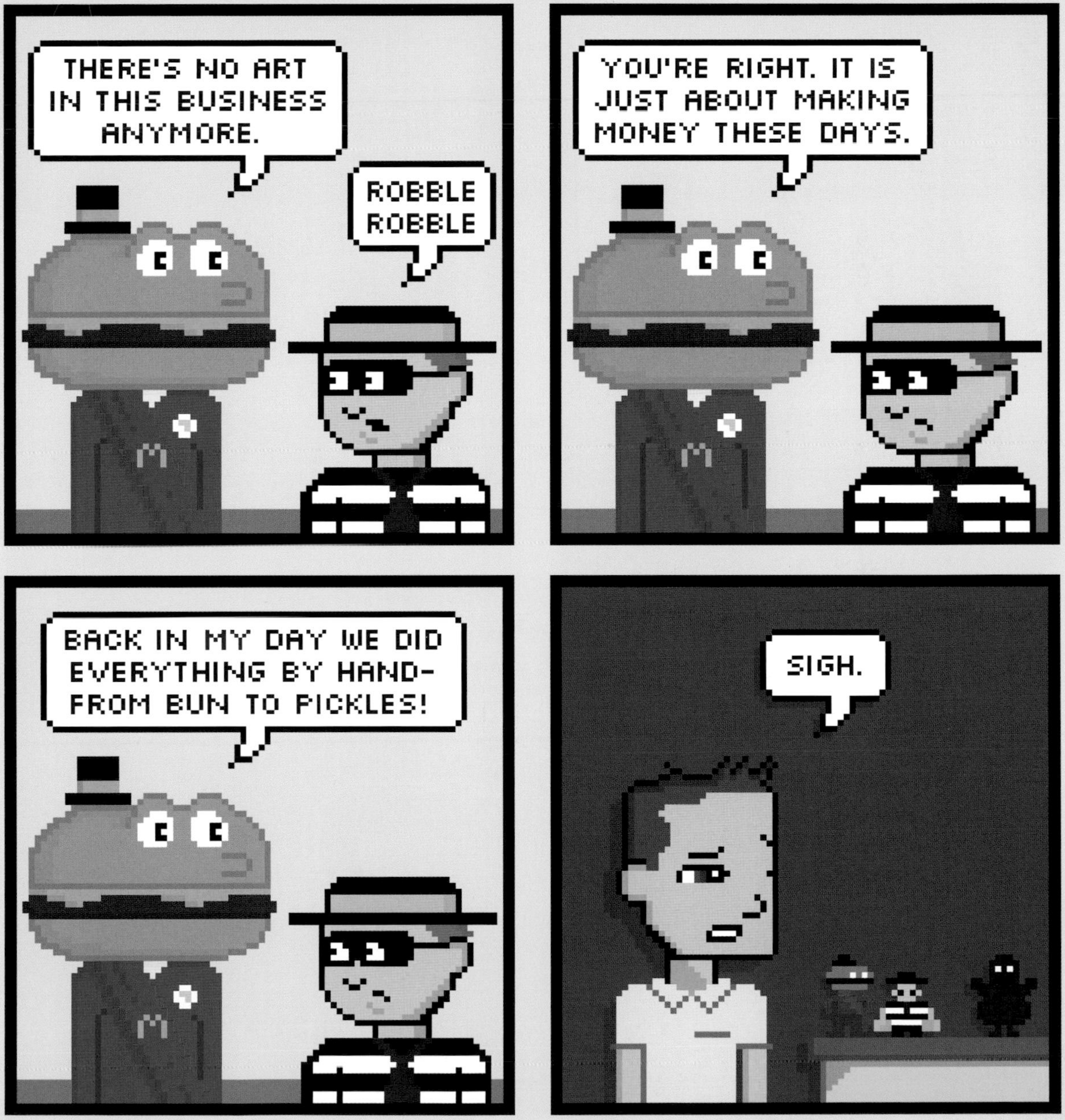
THERE'S NO ART IN THIS BUSINESS ANYMORE.
ROBBLE ROBBLE
YOU'RE RIGHT. IT IS JUST ABOUT MAKING MONEY THESE DAYS.
BACK IN MY DAY WE DID EVERYTHING BY HAND- FROM BUN TO PICKLES!
SIGH.

WHO IS THE FAIREST OF THIS MARKET VALUE?

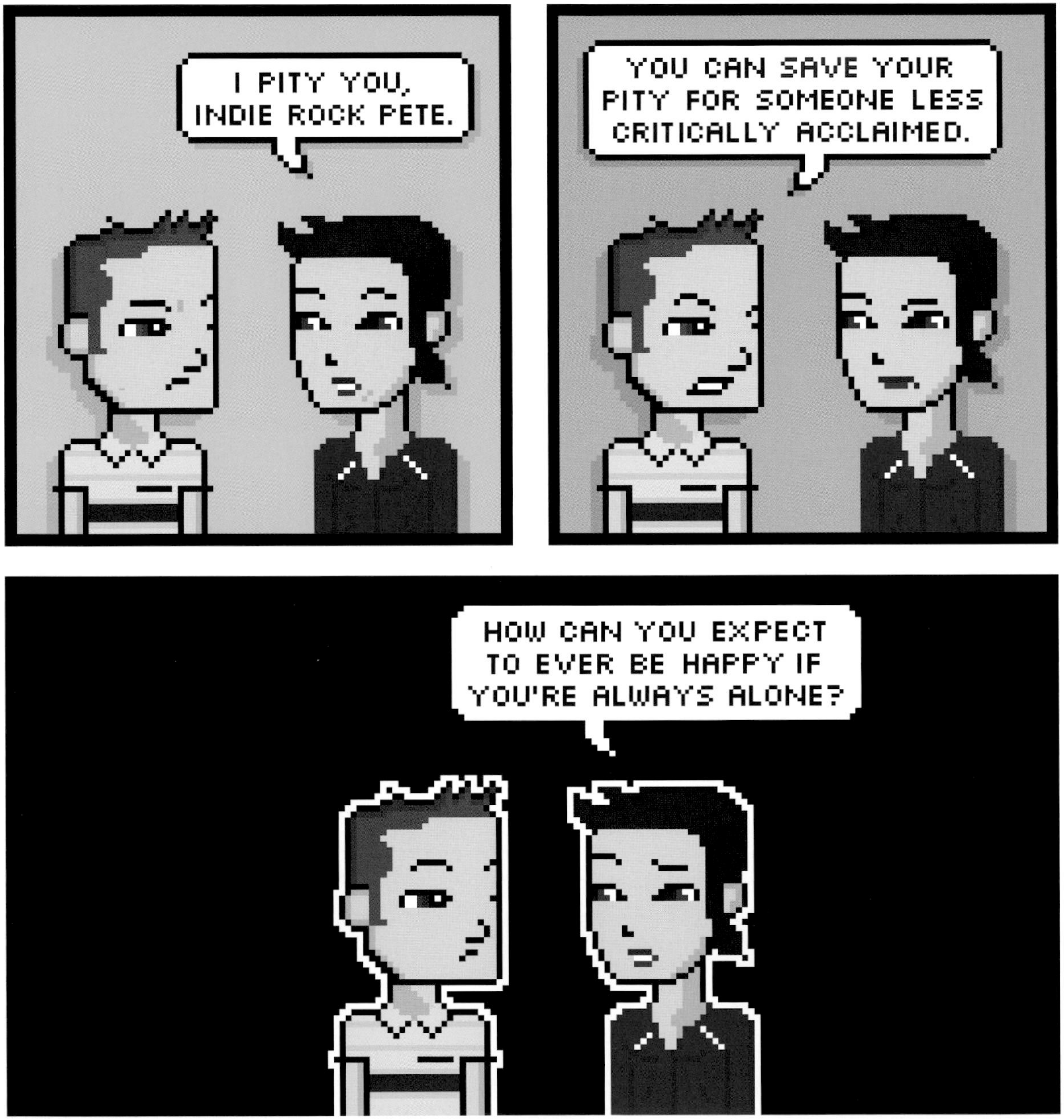
I PITY YOU, INDIE ROCK PETE.
YOU CAN SAVE YOUR PITY FOR SOMEONE LESS CRITICALLY ACCLAIMED.
HOW CAN YOU EXPECT TO EVER BE HAPPY IF YOU'RE ALWAYS ALONE?

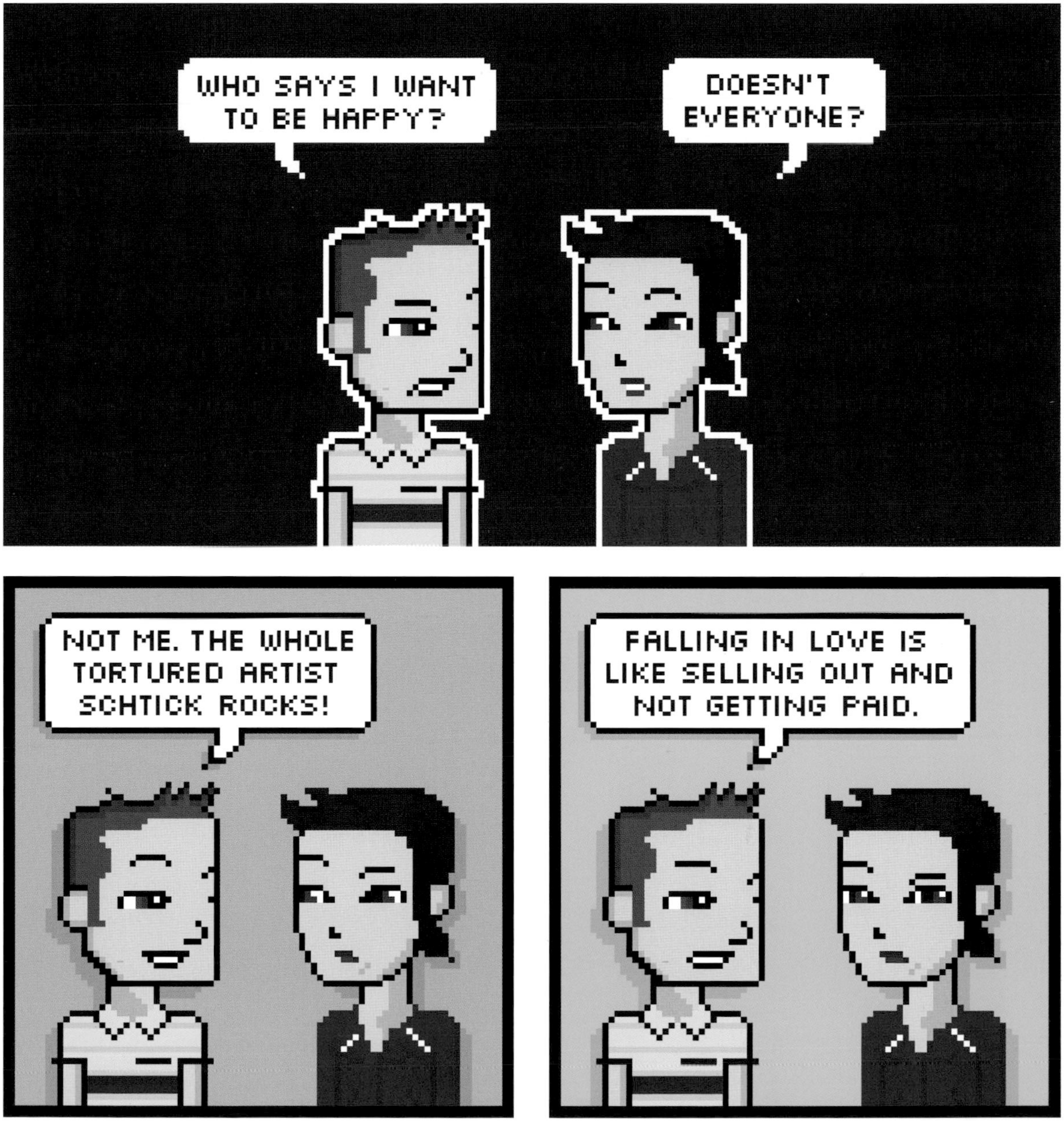
WHO SAYS I WANT TO BE HAPPY?
DOESN'T EVERYONE?
NOT ME. THE WHOLE TORTURED ARTIST SCHTICK ROCKS!
FALLING IN LOVE IS LIKE SELLING OUT AND NOT GETTING PAID.

GOLD MEDALIST

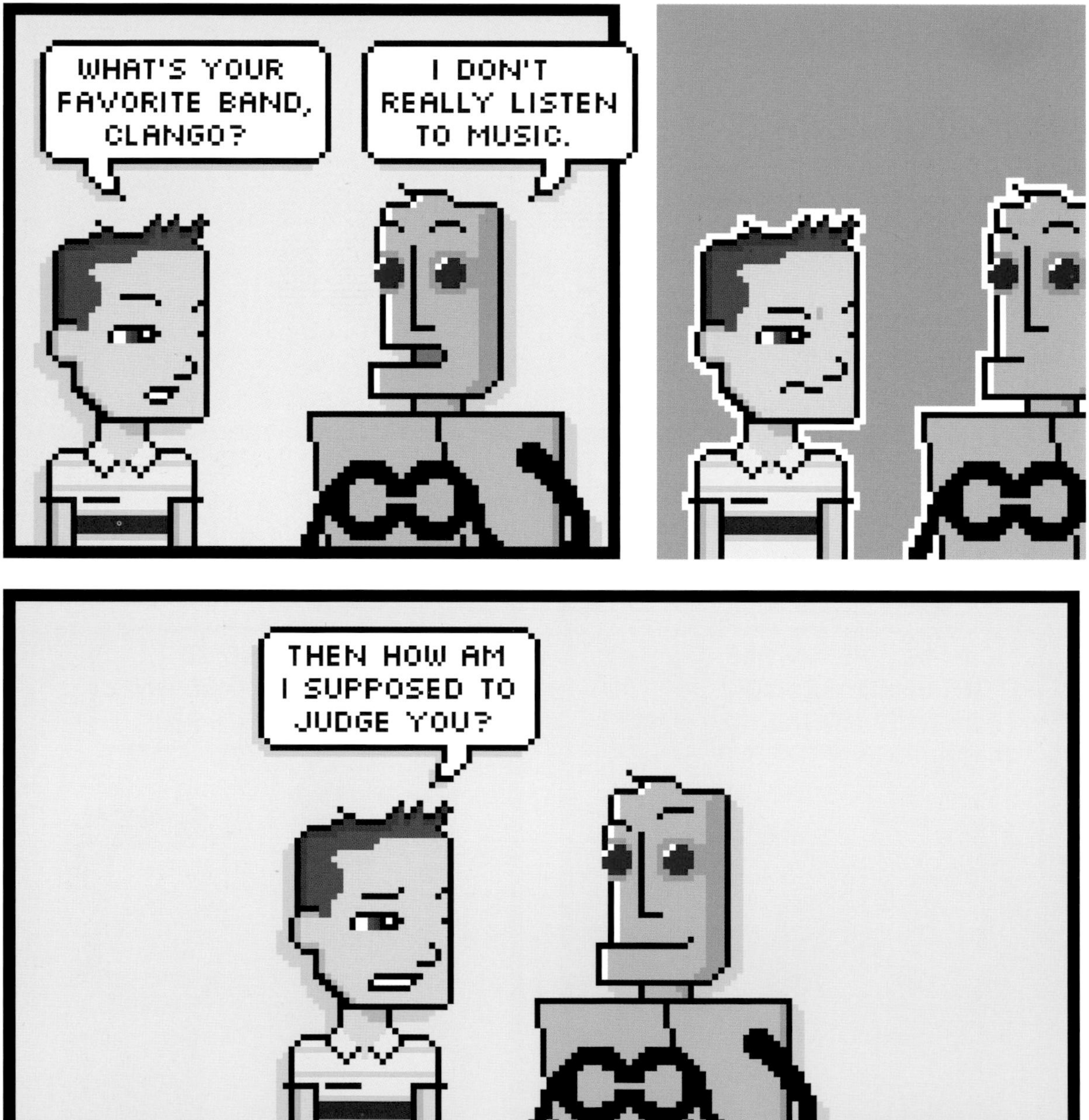
WHAT'S YOUR FAVORITE BAND, CLANGO?
I DON'T REALLY LISTEN TO MUSIC.
THEN HOW AM I SUPPOSED TO JUDGE YOU?

TRANSACTION FEES

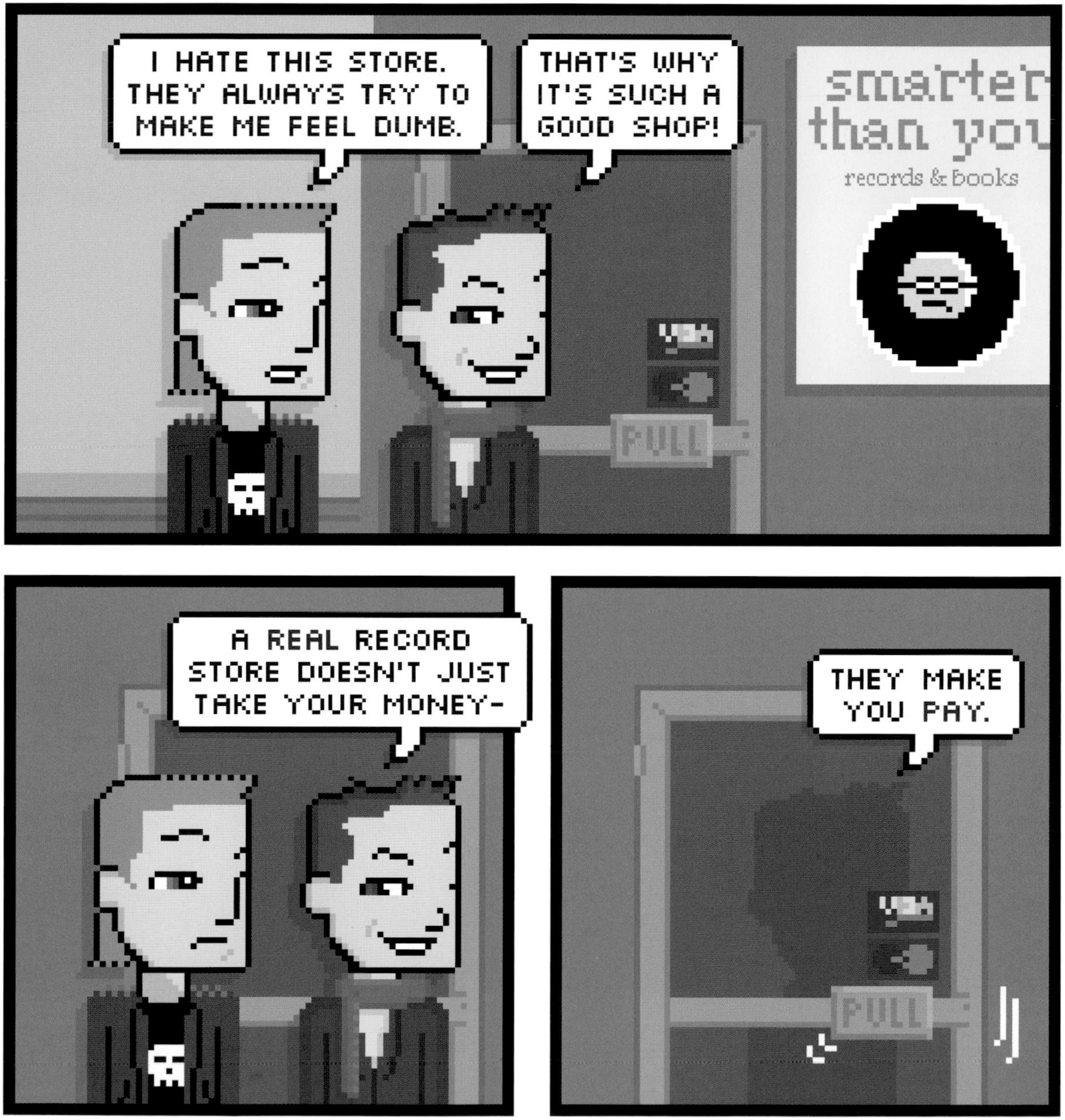
I HATE THIS STORE. THEY ALWAYS TRY TO MAKE ME FEEL DUMB.
THAT'S WHY IT'S SUCH A GOOD SHOP!
smarter than you
records & books
PULL
A REAL RECORD STORE DOESN'T JUST TAKE YOUR MONEY-
THEY MAKE YOU PAY.
PULL

ICE BURN

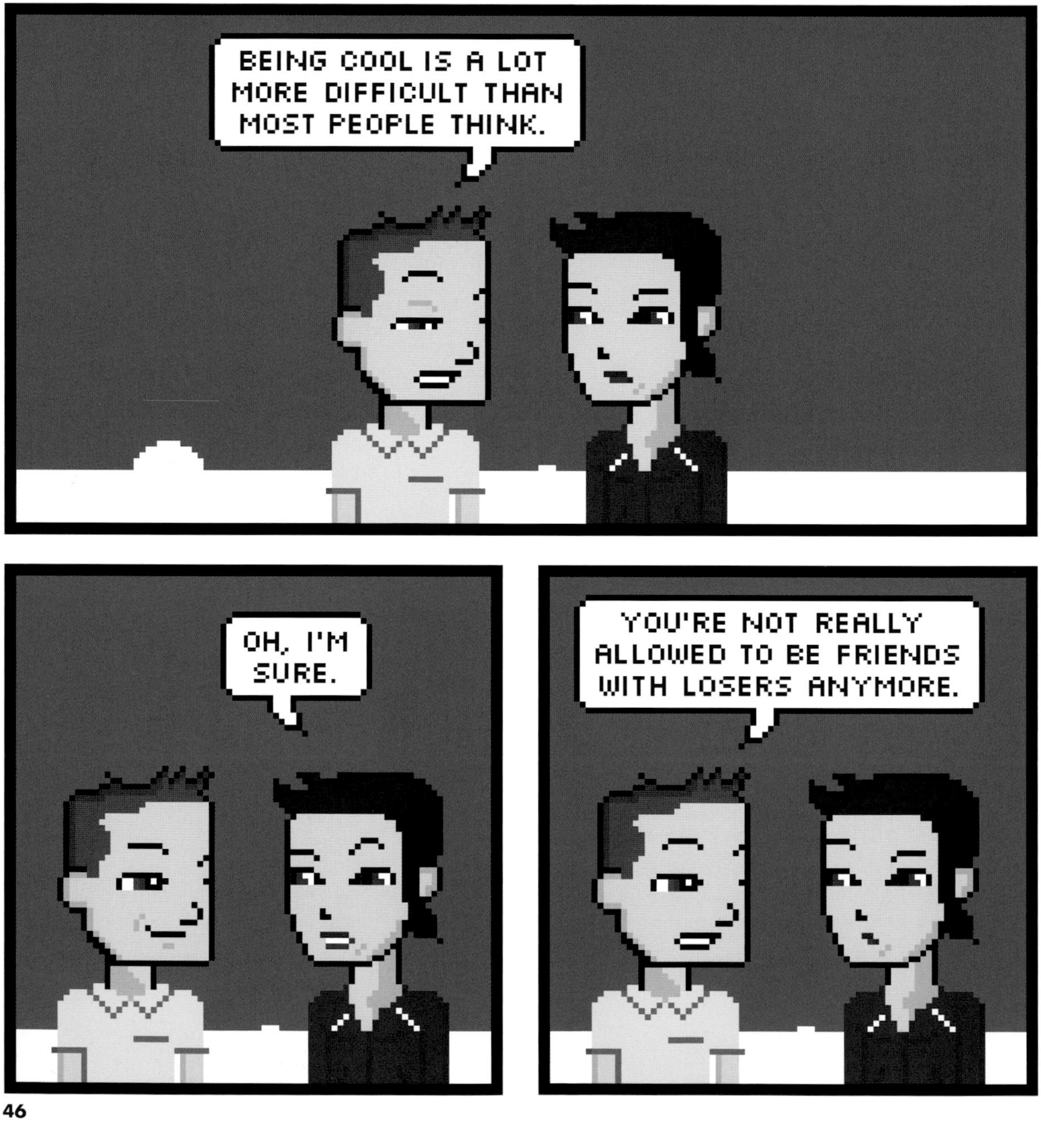
BEING COOL IS A LOT MORE DIFFICULT THAN MOST PEOPLE THINK.
OH, I'M SURE.
YOU'RE NOT REALLY ALLOWED TO BE FRIENDS WITH LOSERS ANYMORE.

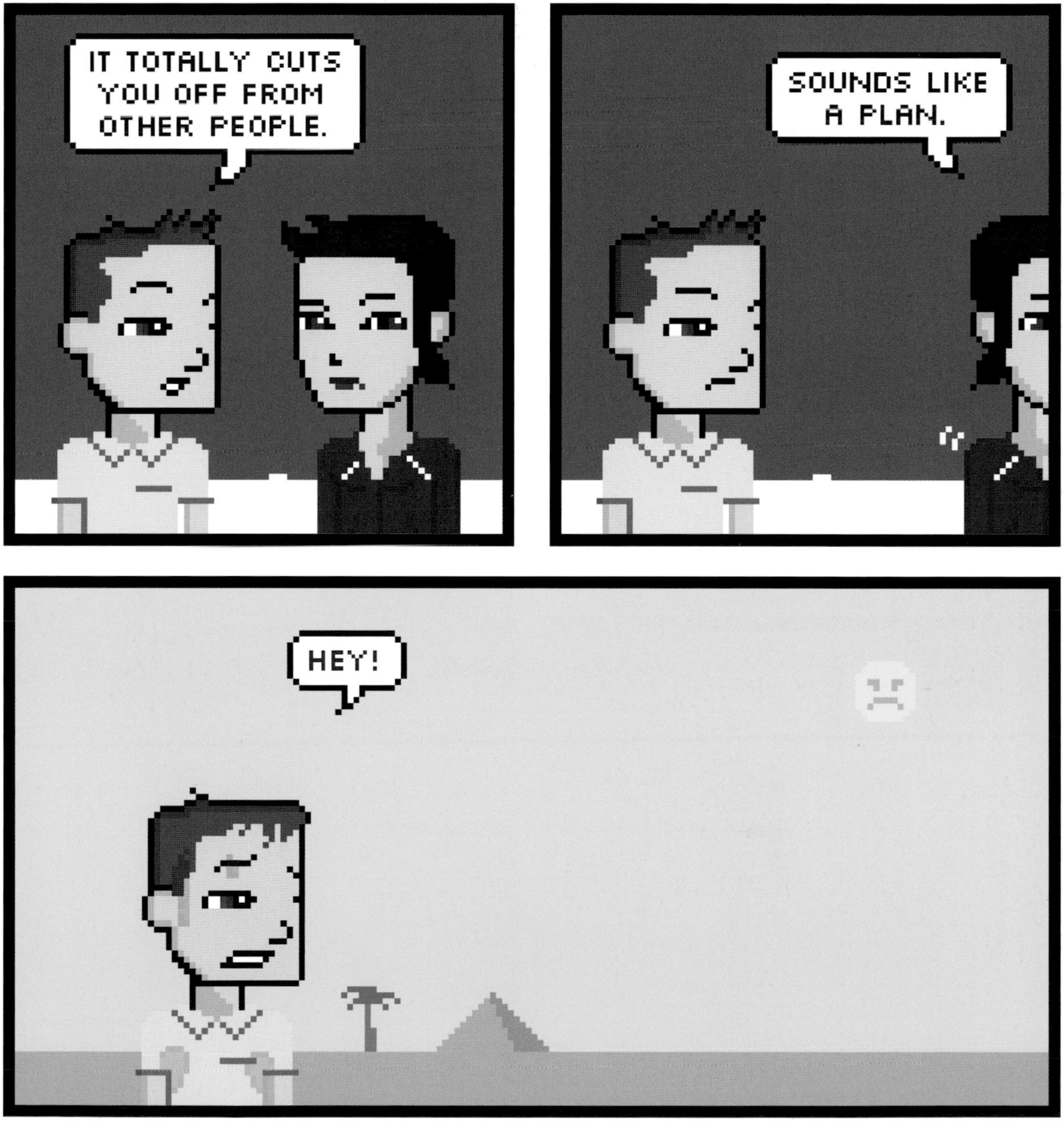
IT TOTALLY CUTS YOU OFF FROM OTHER PEOPLE.
SOUNDS LIKE A PLAN.
HEY!

COPYCAT CRIMES

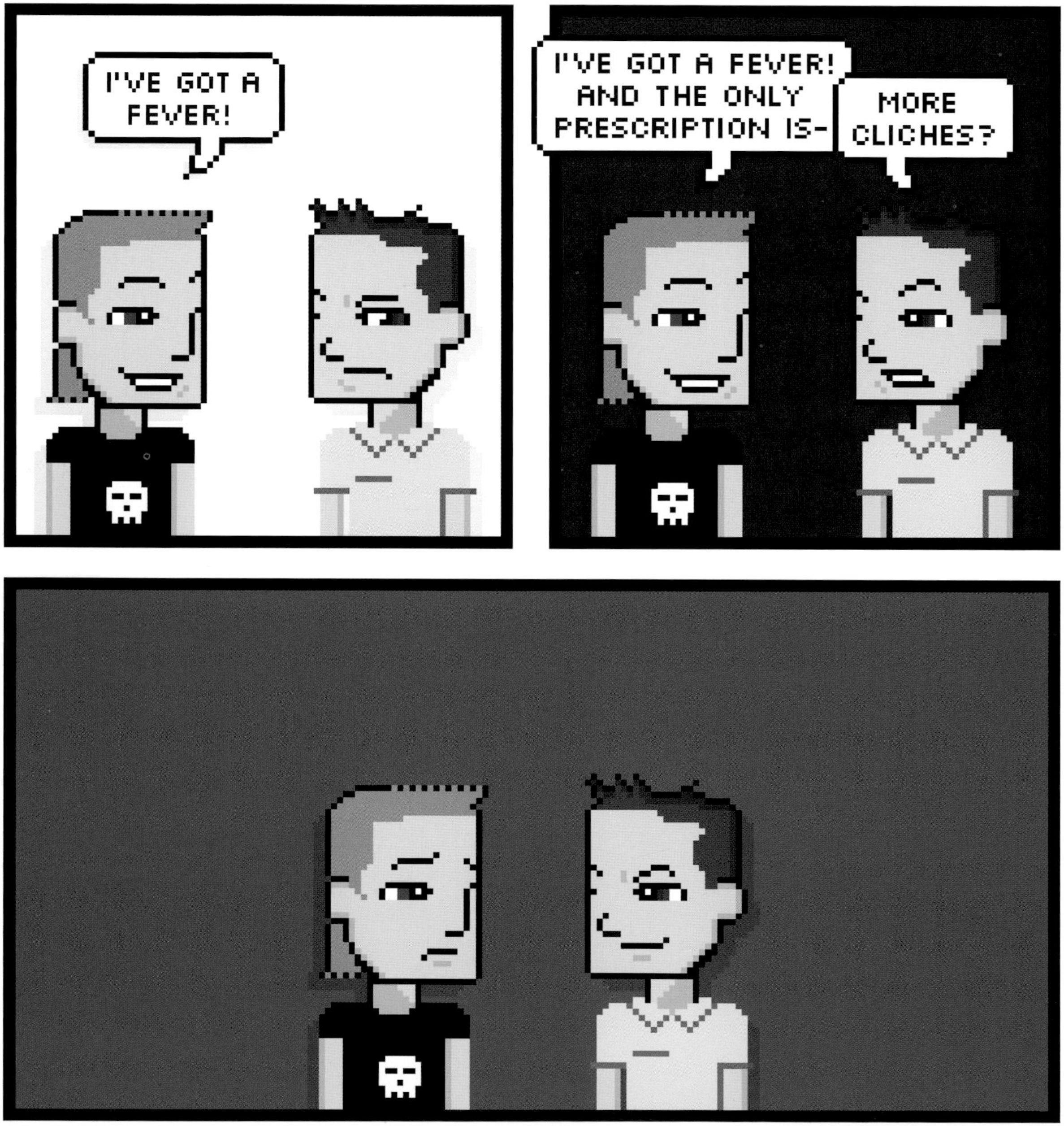
I'VE GOT A FEVER!
I'VE GOT A FEVER! AND THE ONLY PRESCRIPTION IS-
MORE CLICHES?

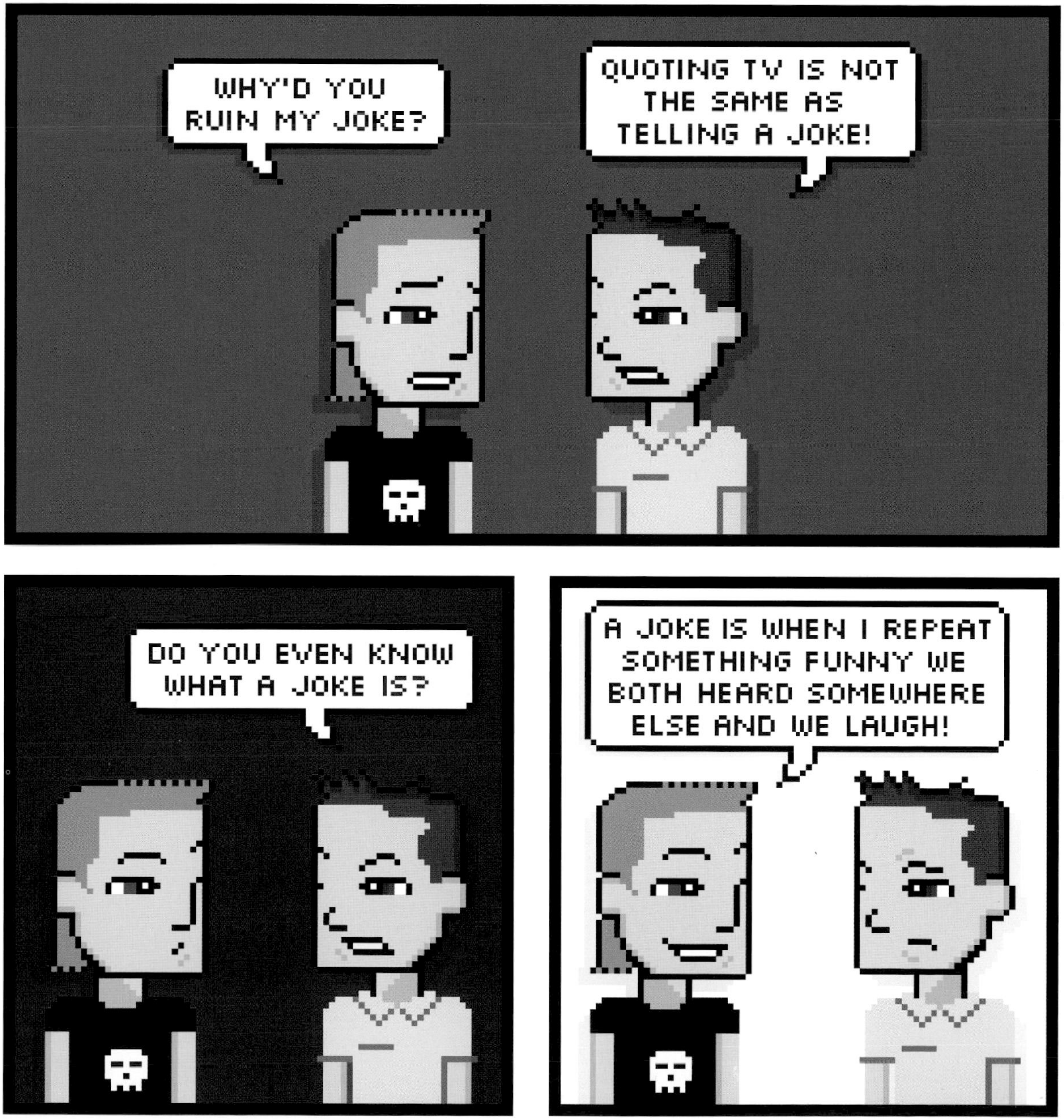
WHY'D YOU RUIN MY JOKE?
QUOTING TV IS NOT THE SAME AS TELLING A JOKE!
DO YOU EVEN KNOW WHAT A JOKE IS?
A JOKE IS WHEN I REPEAT SOMETHING FUNNY WE BOTH HEARD SOMEWHERE ELSE AND WE LAUGH!

TROJAN MAN WROTE THE LESSON PLAN

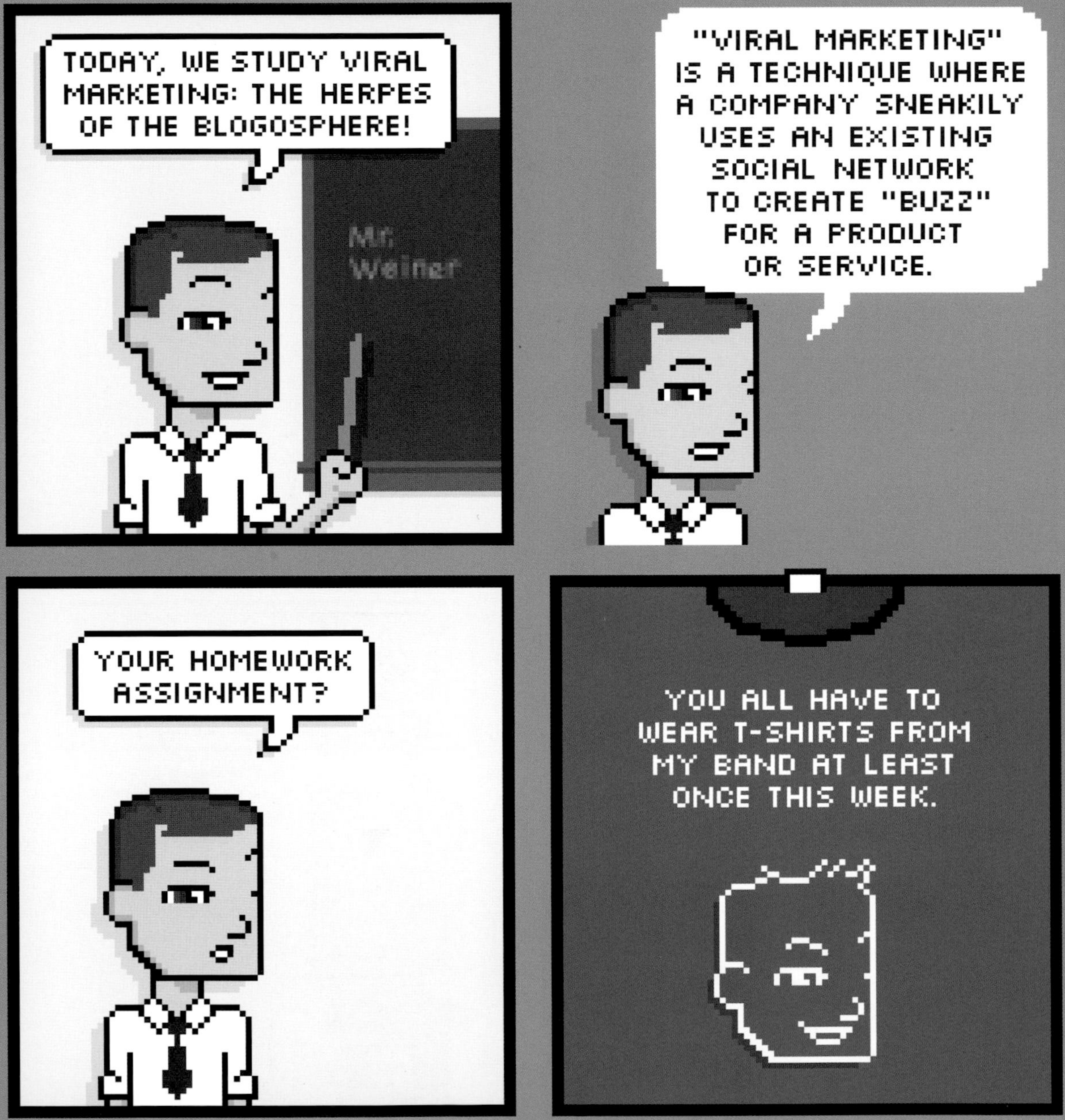
TODAY, WE STUDY VIRAL MARKETING: THE HERPES OF THE BLOGOSPHERE!
Mr. Weiner
"VIRAL MARKETING" IS A TECHNIQUE WHERE A COMPANY SNEAKILY USES AN EXISTING SOCIAL NETWORK TO CREATE "BUZZ" FOR A PRODUCT OR SERVICE.
YOUR HOMEWORK ASSIGNMENT?
YOU ALL HAVE TO WEAR T-SHIRTS FROM MY BAND AT LEAST ONCE THIS WEEK.

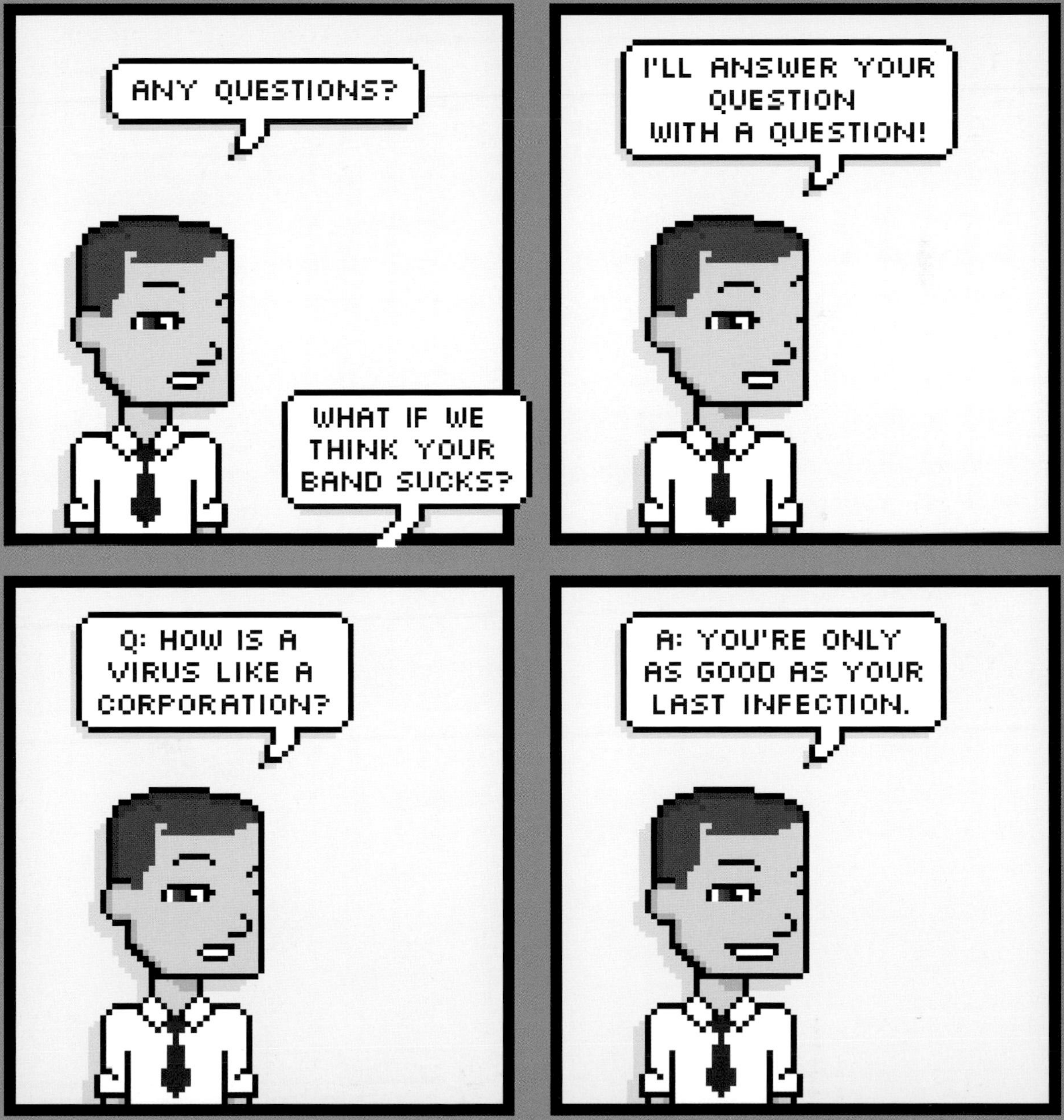
ANY QUESTIONS?
WHAT IF WE THINK YOUR BAND SUCKS?
I'LL ANSWER YOUR QUESTION WITH A QUESTION!
Q: HOW IS A VIRUS LIKE A CORPORATION?
A: YOU'RE ONLY AS GOOD AS YOUR LAST INFECTION.

NEVER TRUST ANYONE OVER 30

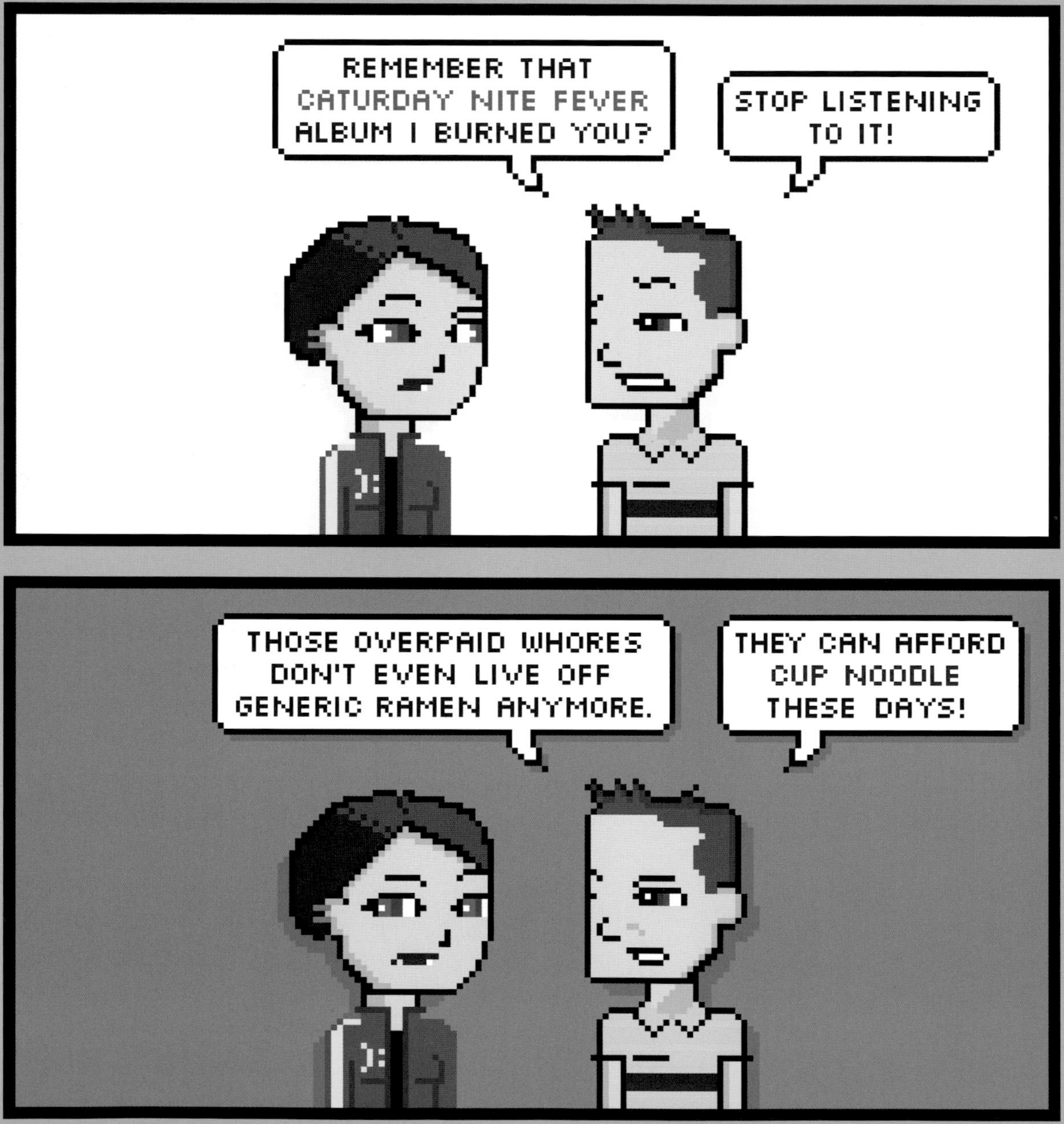
REMEMBER THAT CATURDAY NITE FEVER ALBUM I BURNED YOU?
STOP LISTENING TO IT!
THOSE OVERPAID WHORES DON'T EVEN LIVE OFF GENERIC RAMEN ANYMORE.
THEY CAN AFFORD CUP NOODLE THESE DAYS!

(PERCENT ABOVE THE POVERTY LINE)

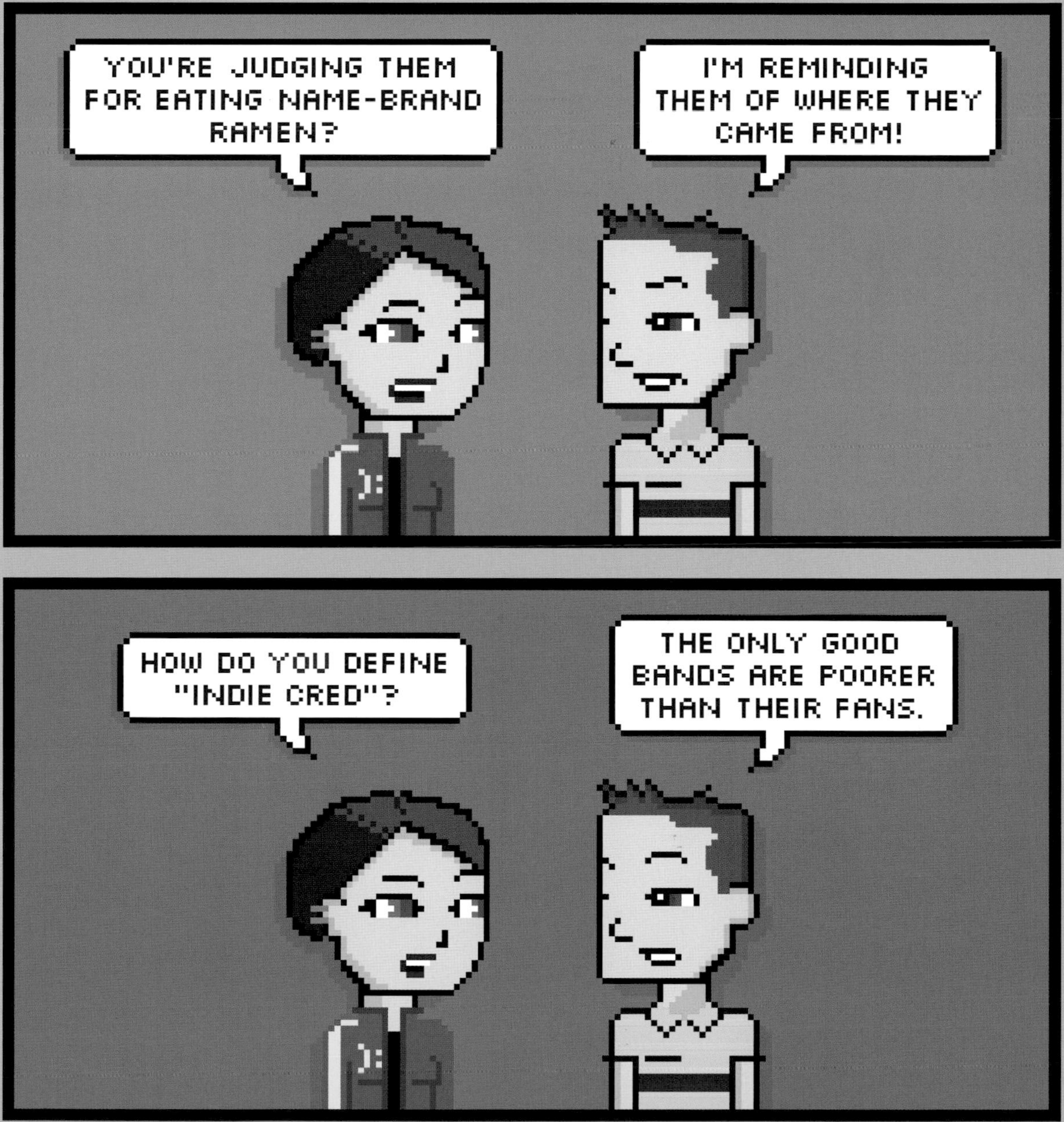
YOU'RE JUDGING THEM FOR EATING NAME-BRAND RAMEN?
I'M REMINDING THEM OF WHERE THEY CAME FROM!
HOW DO YOU DEFINE "INDIE CRED"?
THE ONLY GOOD BANDS ARE POORER THAN THEIR FANS.

FOR EVERY SEASON—BURN, BURN, BURN

NOBODY UNDERSTANDS ME.
YOU'RE A 45 RPM MAN IN A 33 RPM WORLD.

CLANGO, I'M SERIOUS!
I THINK THE WORD IS "HUMORLESS."

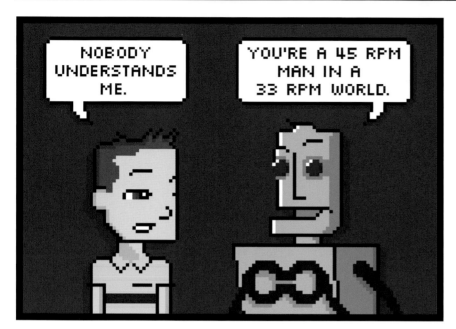

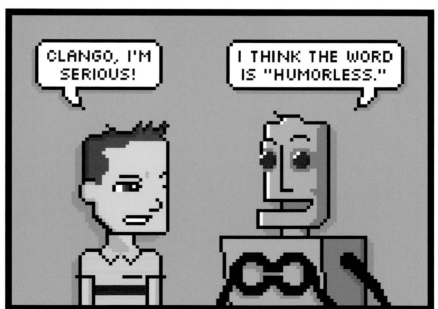

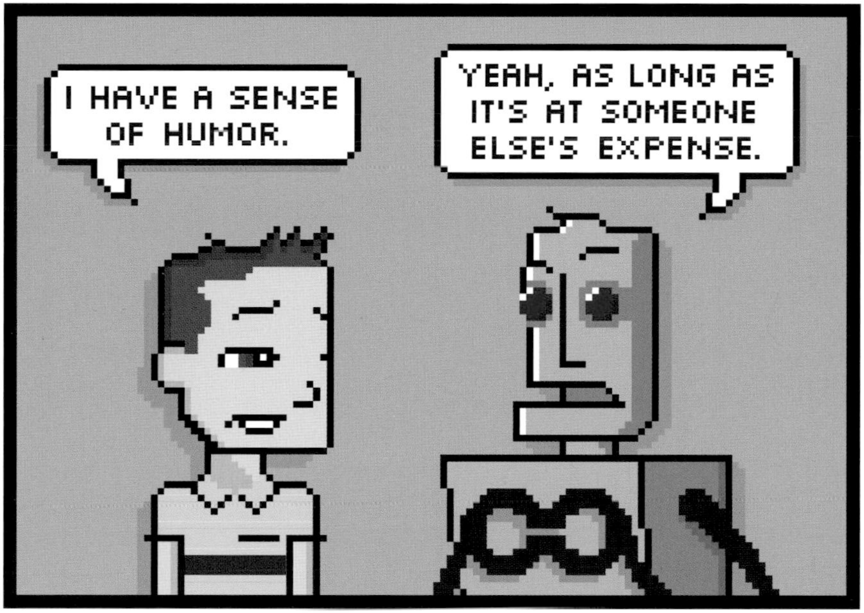
I HAVE A SENSE OF HUMOR.
YEAH, AS LONG AS IT'S AT SOMEONE ELSE'S EXPENSE.

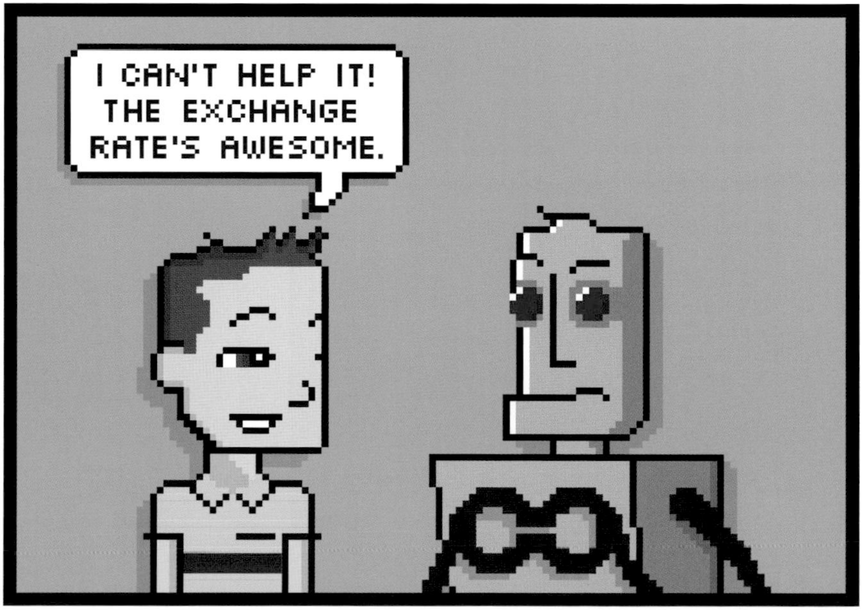
I CAN'T HELP IT! THE EXCHANGE RATE'S AWESOME.

IT'S THE GIFT THAT COUNTS

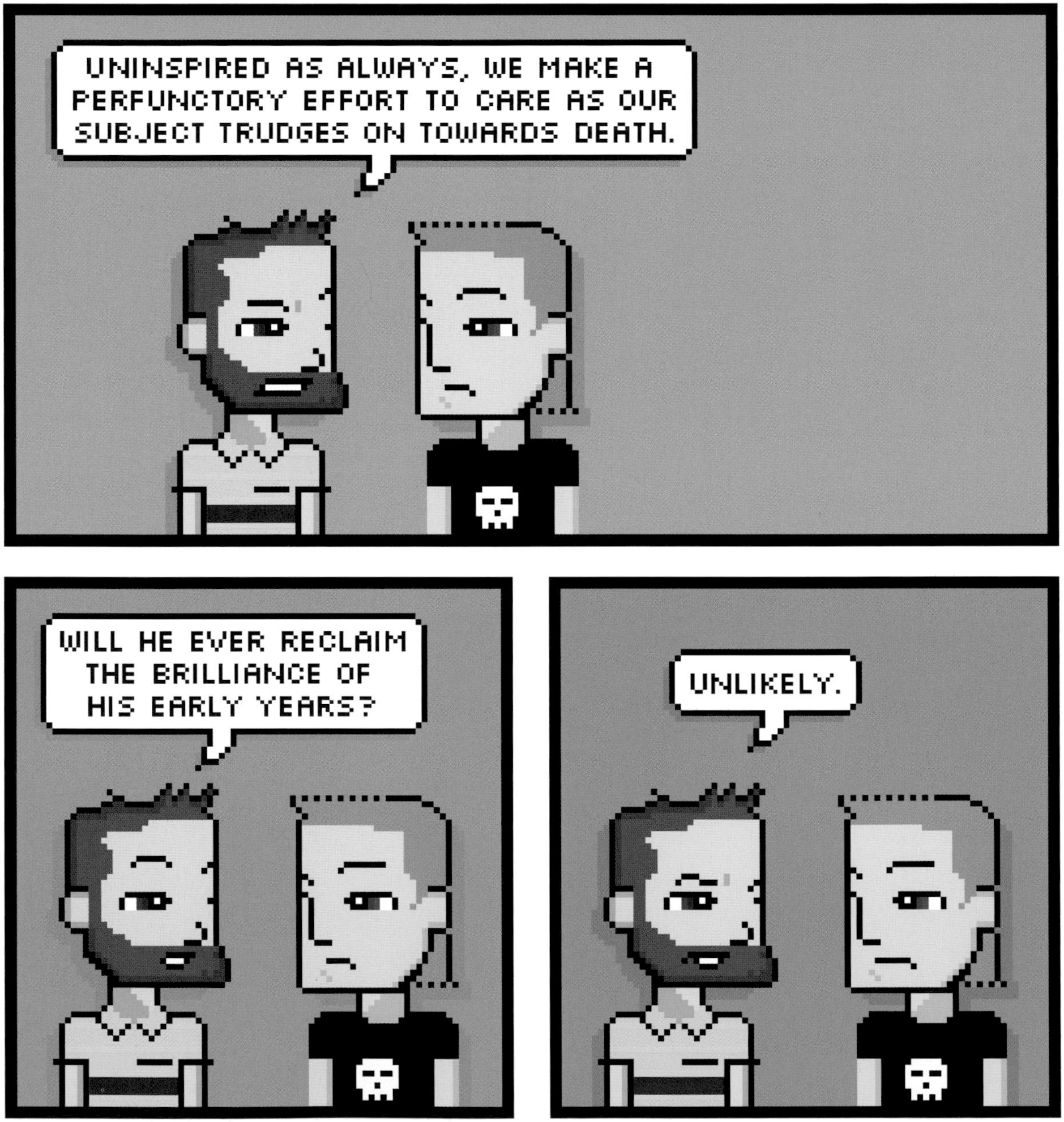
UNINSPIRED AS ALWAYS, WE MAKE A PERFUNCTORY EFFORT TO CARE AS OUR SUBJECT TRUDGES ON TOWARDS DEATH.
WILL HE EVER RECLAIM THE BRILLIANCE OF HIS EARLY YEARS?
UNLIKELY.

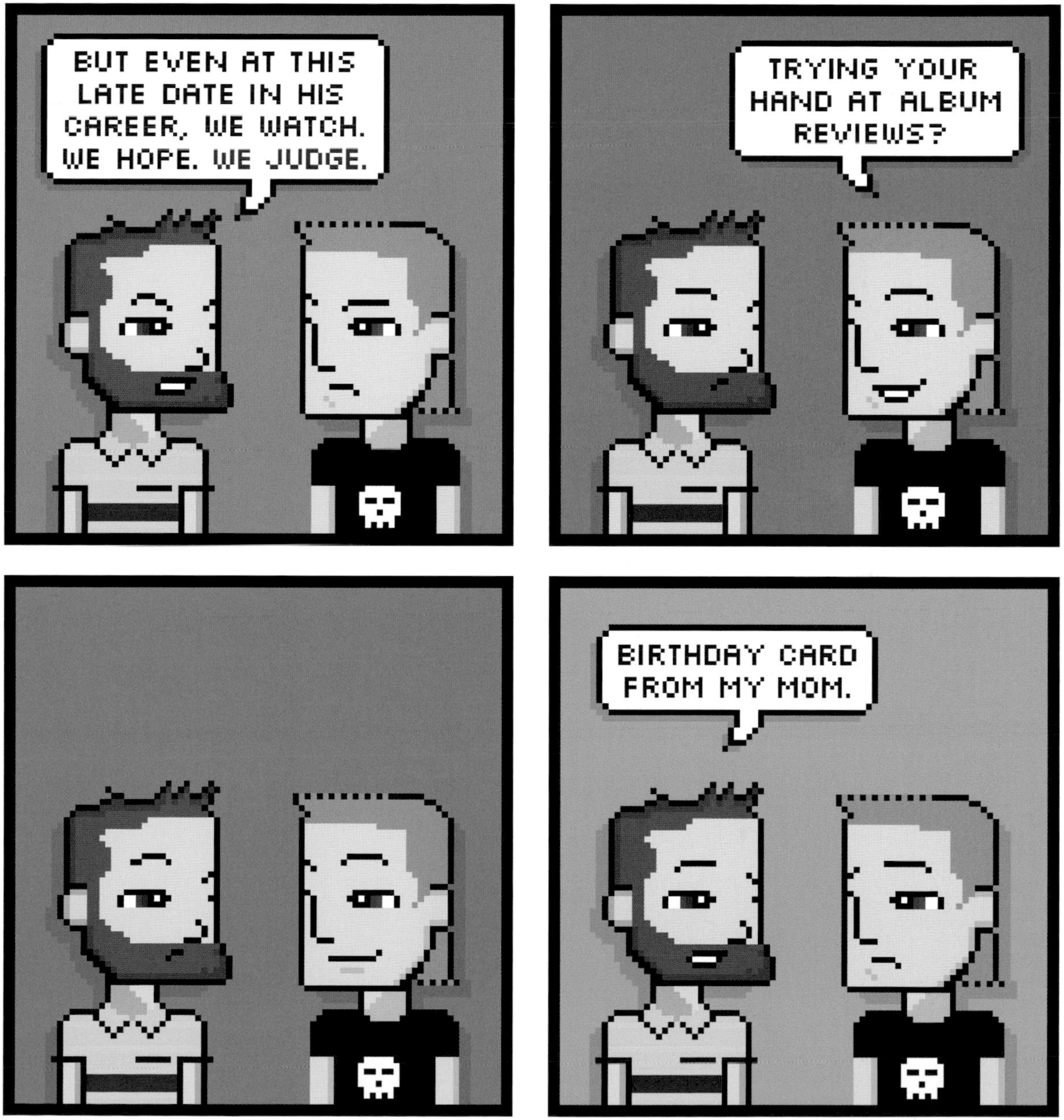
BUT EVEN AT THIS LATE DATE IN HIS CAREER, WE WATCH. WE HOPE. WE JUDGE.
TRYING YOUR HAND AT ALBUM REVIEWS?
BIRTHDAY CARD FROM MY MOM.

SILVER LINER

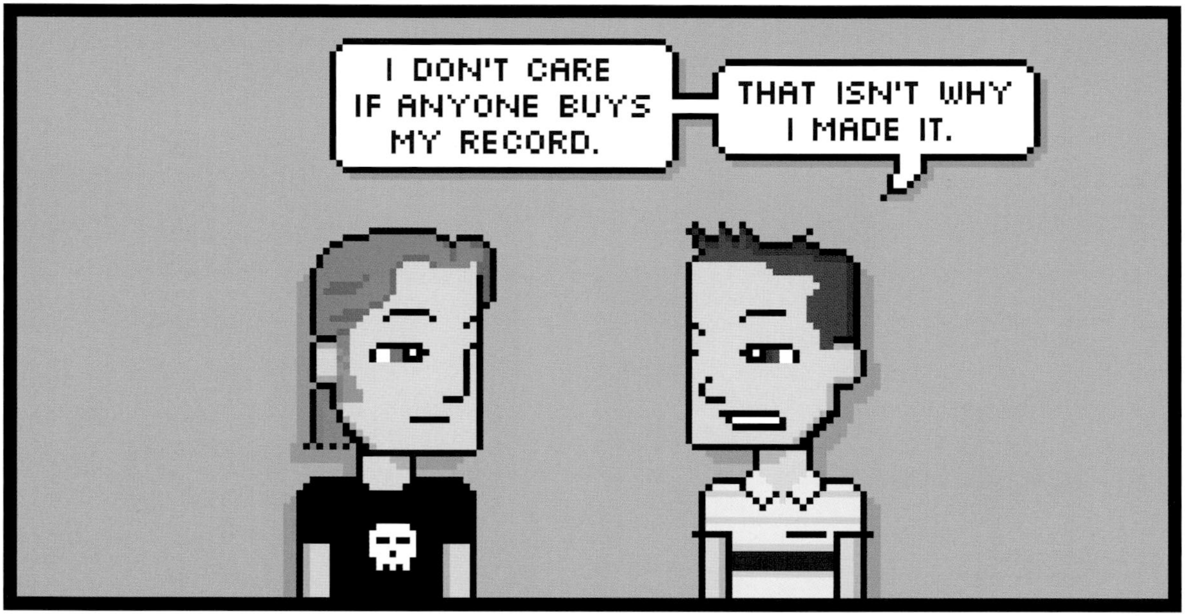
I DON'T CARE IF ANYONE BUYS MY RECORD.
THAT ISN'T WHY I MADE IT.

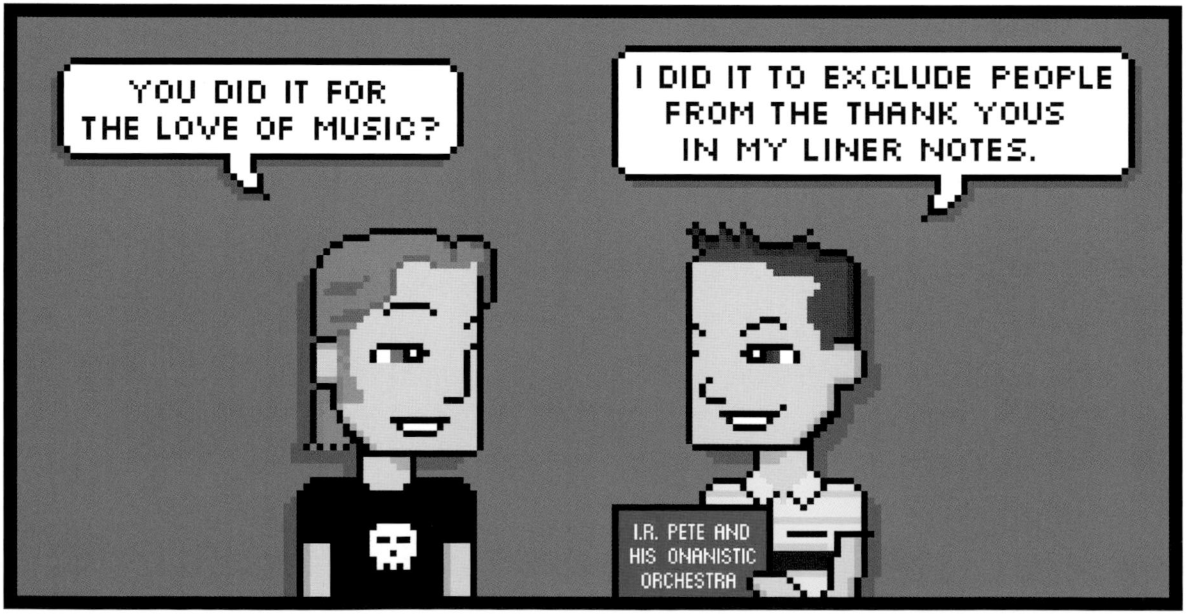
YOU DID IT FOR THE LOVE OF MUSIC?
I DID IT TO EXCLUDE PEOPLE FROM THE THANK YOUS IN MY LINER NOTES.
I.R. PETE AND HIS ONANISTIC ORCHESTRA

SELFISH-AWARENESS

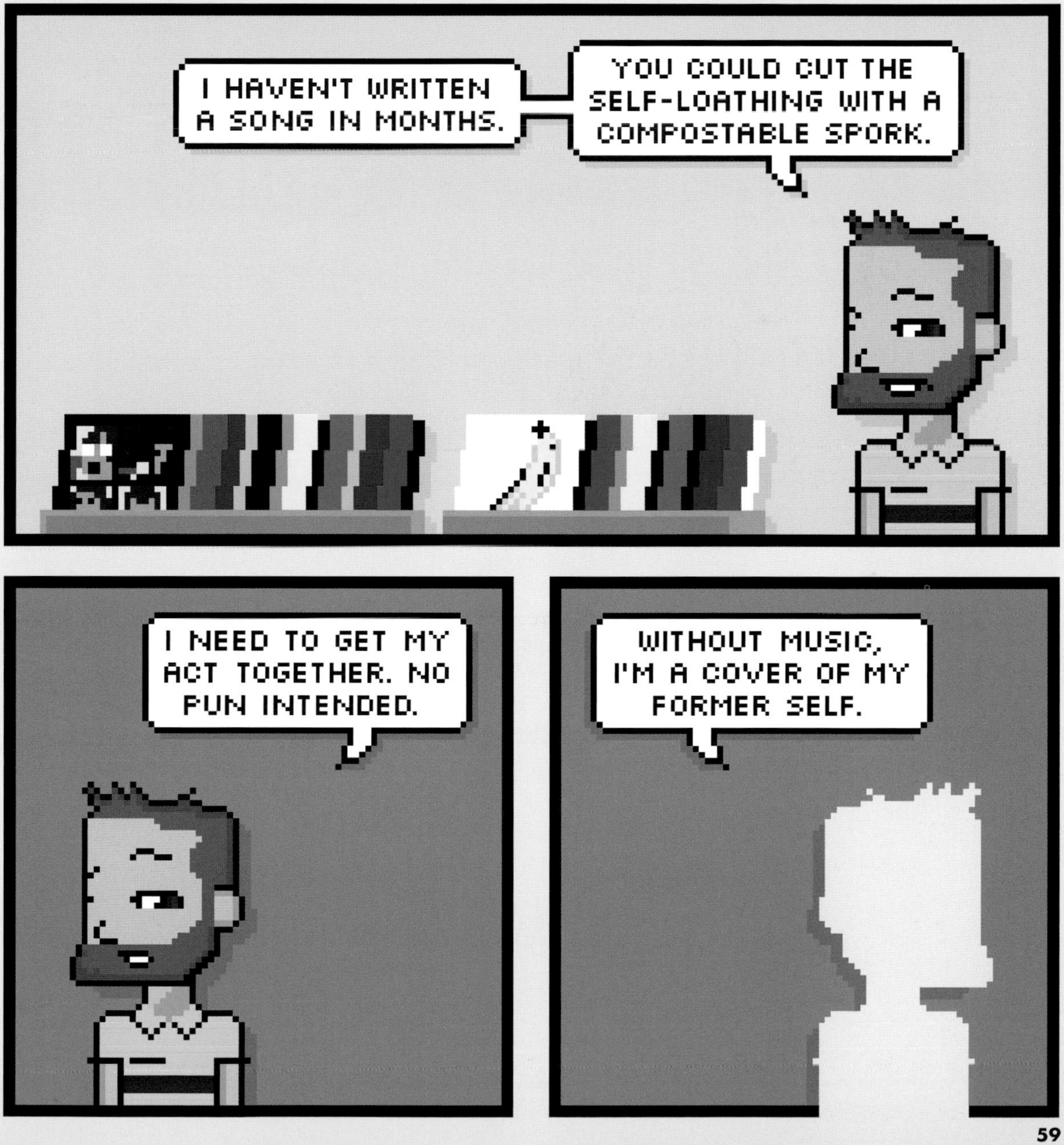
I HAVEN'T WRITTEN A SONG IN MONTHS.
YOU COULD CUT THE SELF-LOATHING WITH A COMPOSTABLE SPORK.
I NEED TO GET MY ACT TOGETHER. NO PUN INTENDED.
WITHOUT MUSIC, I'M A COVER OF MY FORMER SELF.

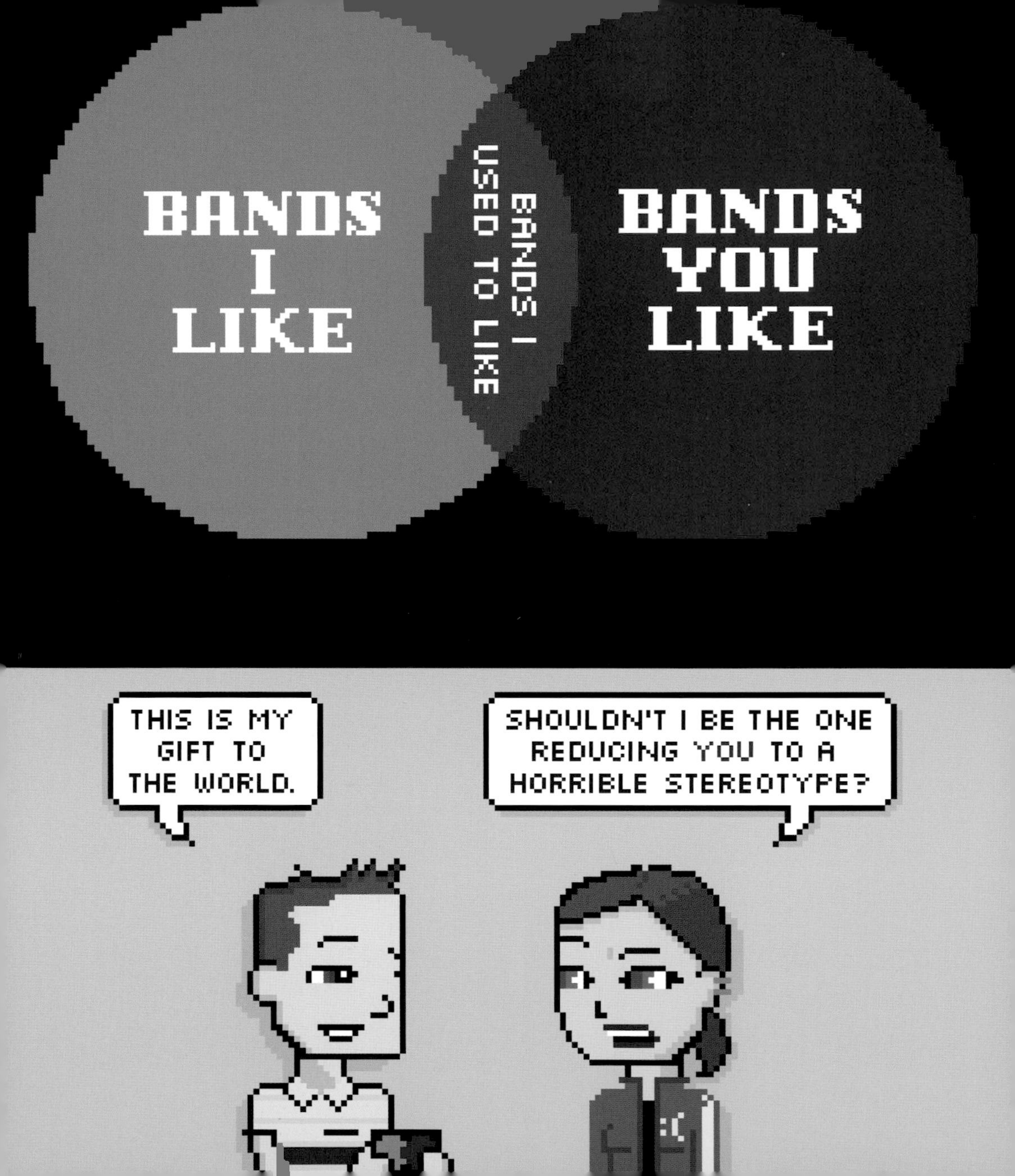
BANDS I LIKE
BANDS I USED TO LIKE
BANDS YOU LIKE
THIS IS MY GIFT TO THE WORLD.
SHOULDN'T I BE THE ONE REDUCING YOU TO A HORRIBLE STEREOTYPE?

PRE-LITISM

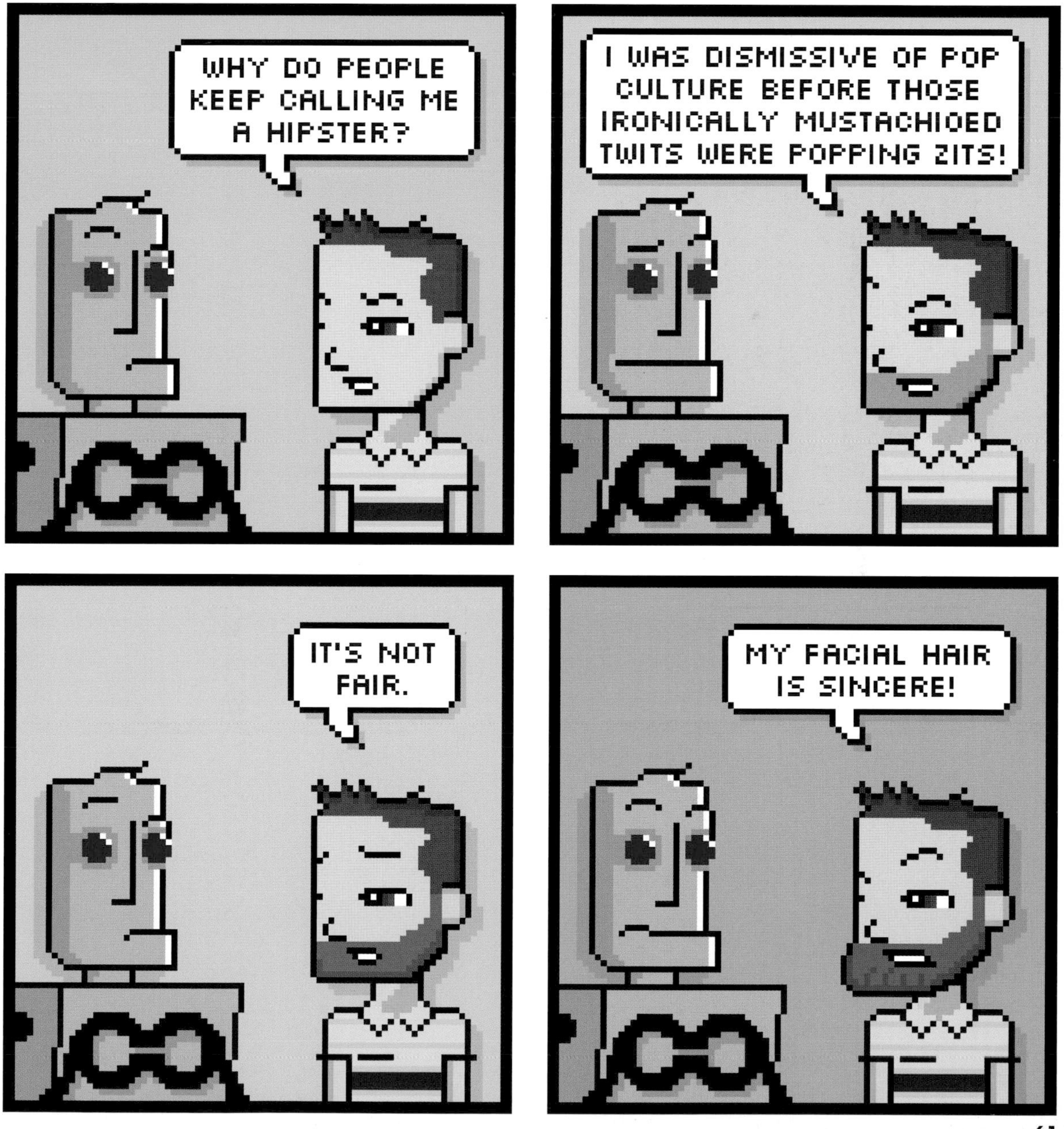
WHY DO PEOPLE KEEP CALLING ME A HIPSTER?
I WAS DISMISSIVE OF POP CULTURE BEFORE THOSE IRONICALLY MUSTACHIOED TWITS WERE POPPING ZITS!
IT'S NOT FAIR.
MY FACIAL HAIR IS SINCERE!

TAG-TEAM OF RIVALS

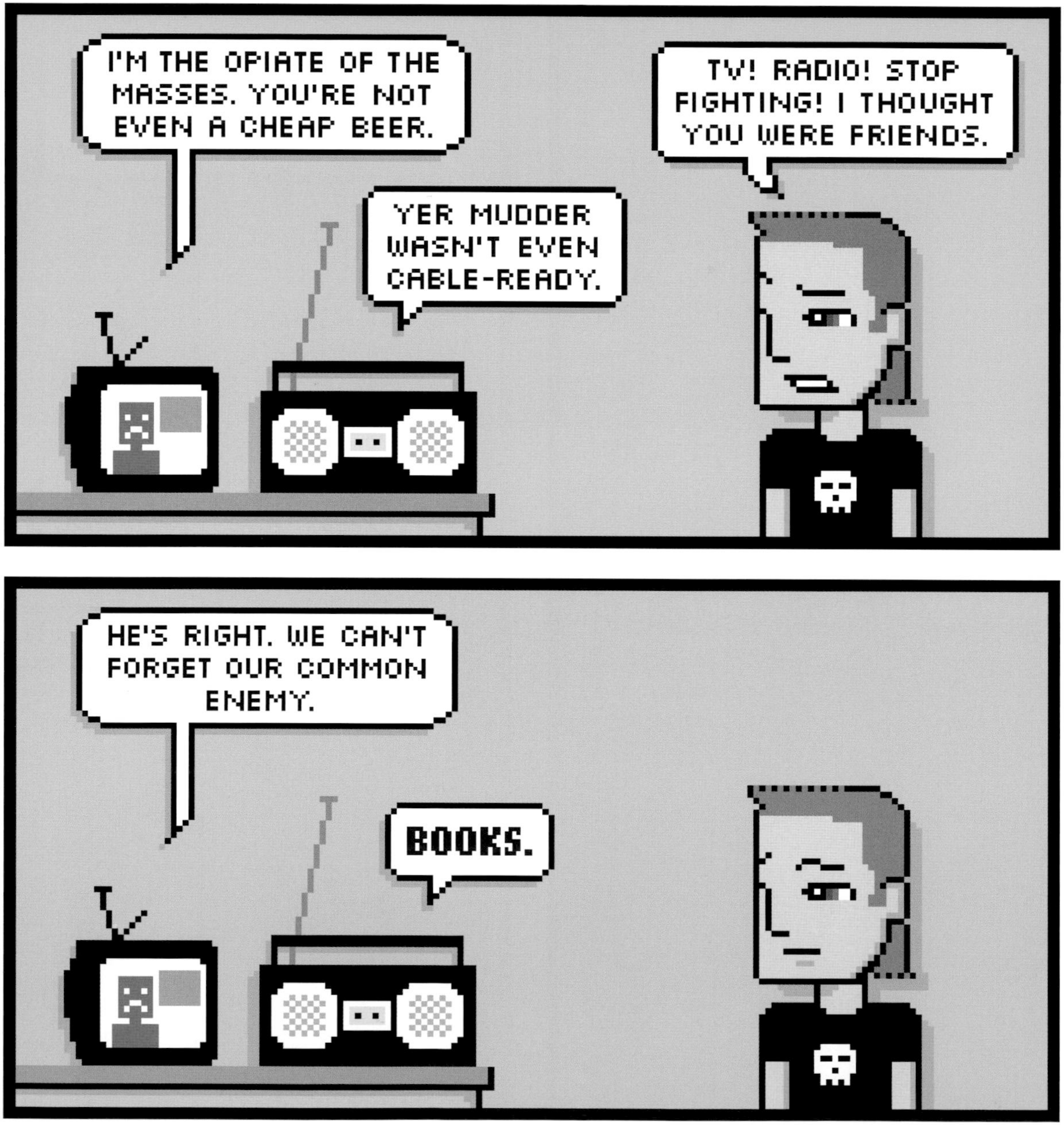
I'M THE OPIATE OF THE MASSES. YOU'RE NOT EVEN A CHEAP BEER.
YER MUDDER WASN'T EVEN CABLE-READY.
TV! RADIO! STOP FIGHTING! I THOUGHT YOU WERE FRIENDS.
HE'S RIGHT. WE CAN'T FORGET OUR COMMON ENEMY.
BOOKS.

IT'LL BE THERE WHEN YOU'RE READY

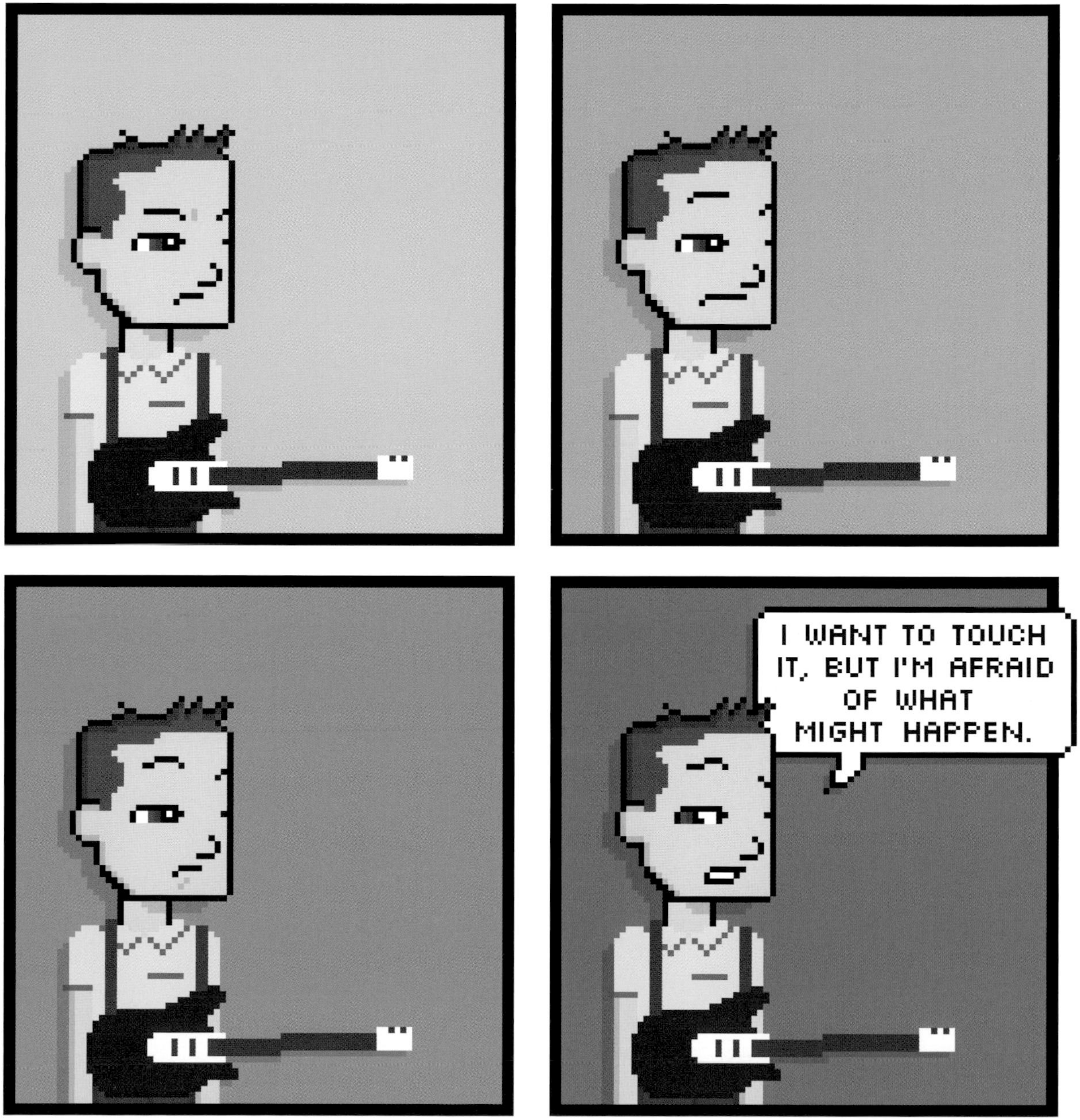
I WANT TO TOUCH IT, BUT I'M AFRAID OF WHAT MIGHT HAPPEN.

CHICKENS AND GOLDEN EGGS

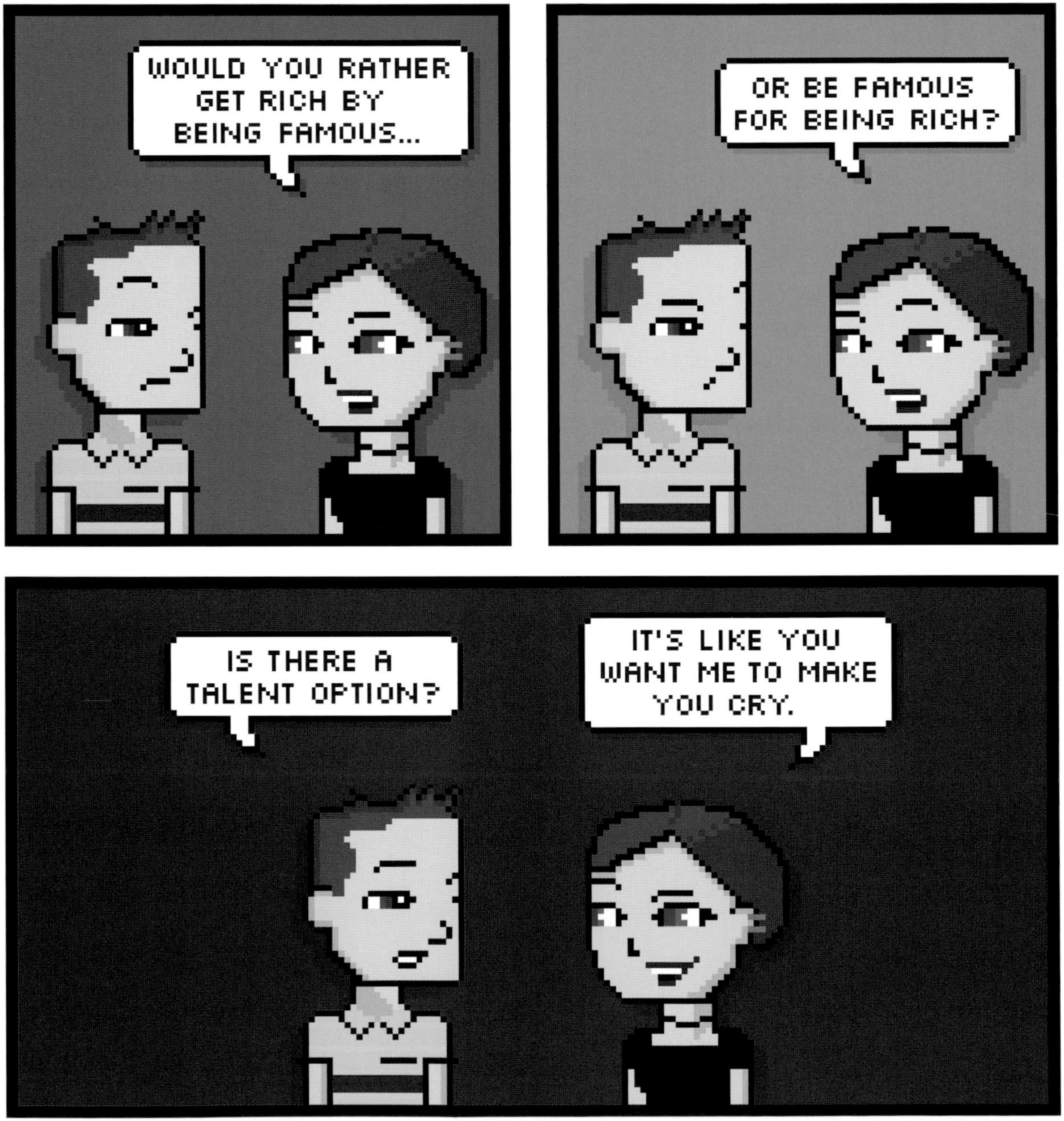
WOULD YOU RATHER GET RICH BY BEING FAMOUS...
OR BE FAMOUS FOR BEING RICH?
IS THERE A TALENT OPTION?
IT'S LIKE YOU WANT ME TO MAKE YOU CRY.

TONNAGE

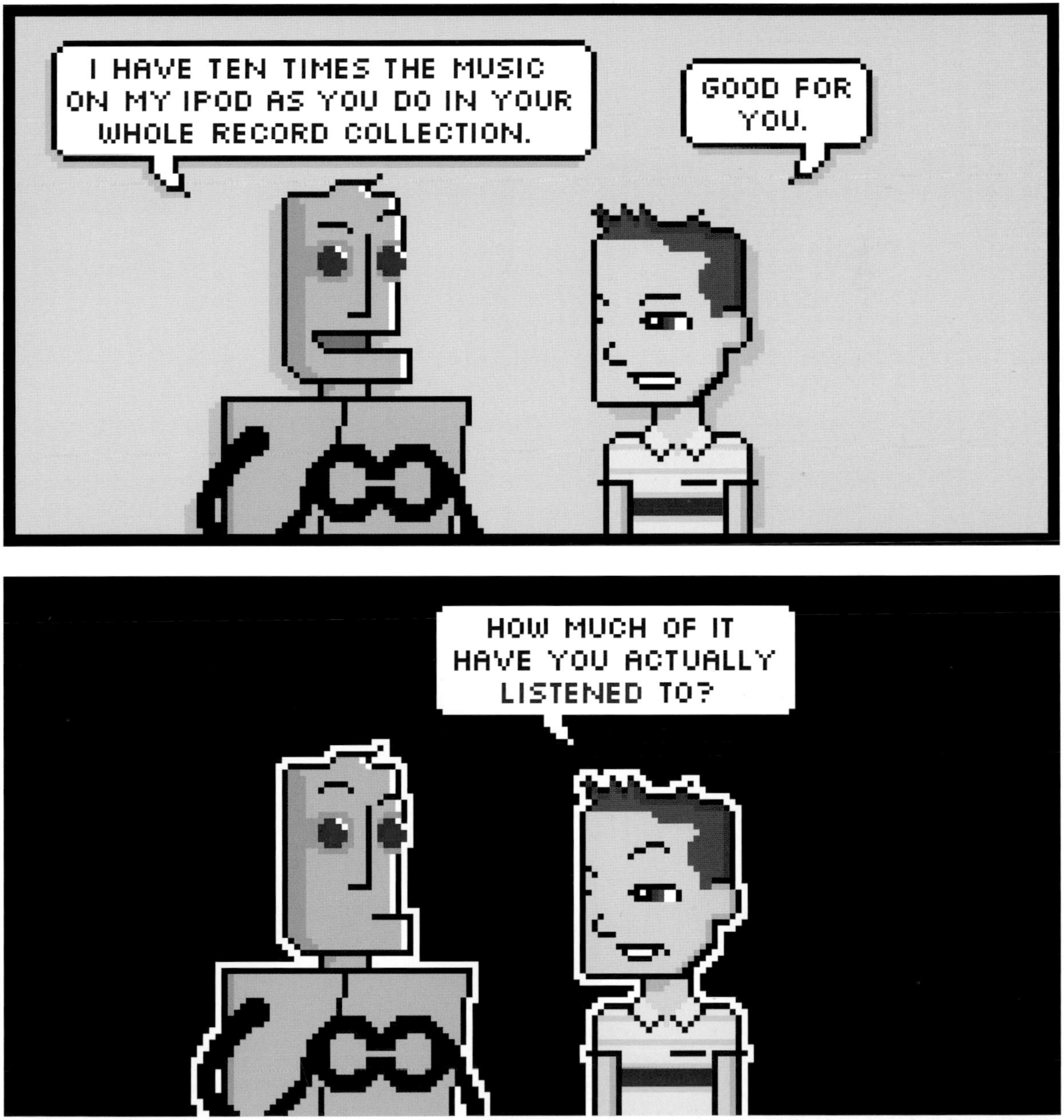
I HAVE TEN TIMES THE MUSIC ON MY IPOD AS YOU DO IN YOUR WHOLE RECORD COLLECTION.
GOOD FOR YOU.
HOW MUCH OF IT HAVE YOU ACTUALLY LISTENED TO?

BACK AND FORTH, IN AND OUT

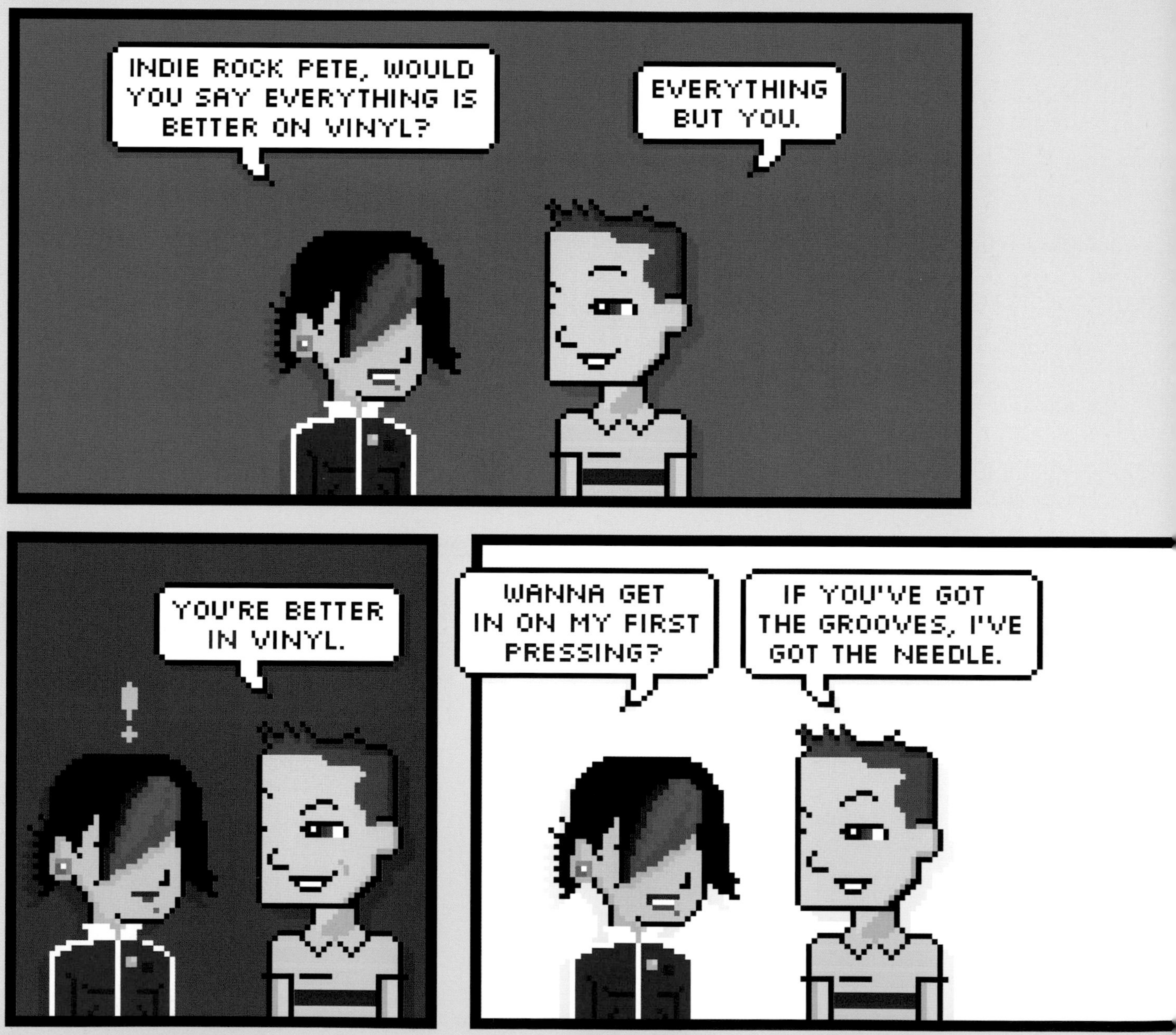

INDIE ROCK PETE, WOULD YOU SAY EVERYTHING IS BETTER ON VINYL?
EVERYTHING BUT YOU.
YOU'RE BETTER IN VINYL.
!
WANNA GET IN ON MY FIRST PRESSING?
IF YOU'VE GOT THE GROOVES, I'VE GOT THE NEEDLE.

IF THERE'S A MORE ELABORATE MATING DANCE, IT INVOLVES BEAKS AND FEATHERS.

ENEMY OF THE CARROT

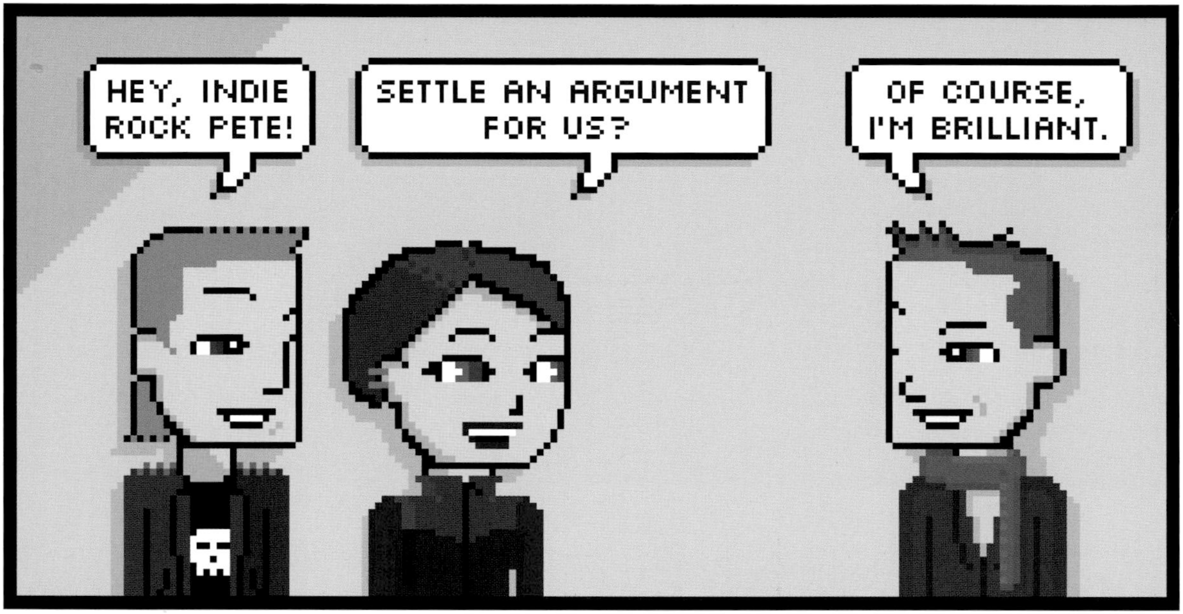
HEY, INDIE ROCK PETE!
SETTLE AN ARGUMENT FOR US?
OF COURSE, I'M BRILLIANT.

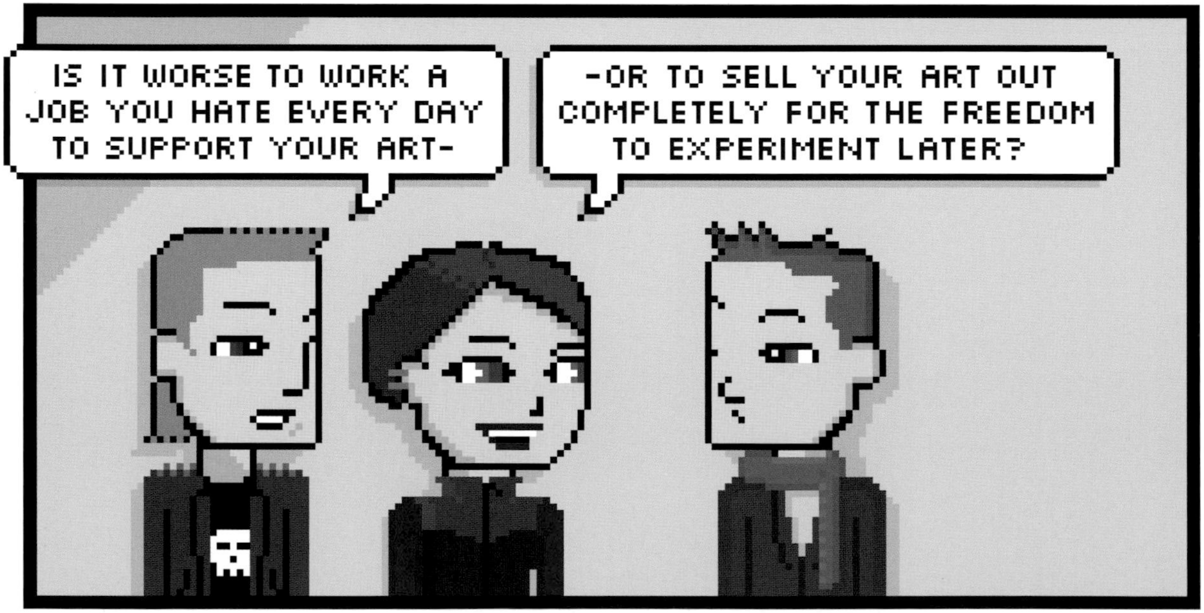
IS IT WORSE TO WORK A JOB YOU HATE EVERY DAY TO SUPPORT YOUR ART-
-OR TO SELL YOUR ART OUT COMPLETELY FOR THE FREEDOM TO EXPERIMENT LATER?

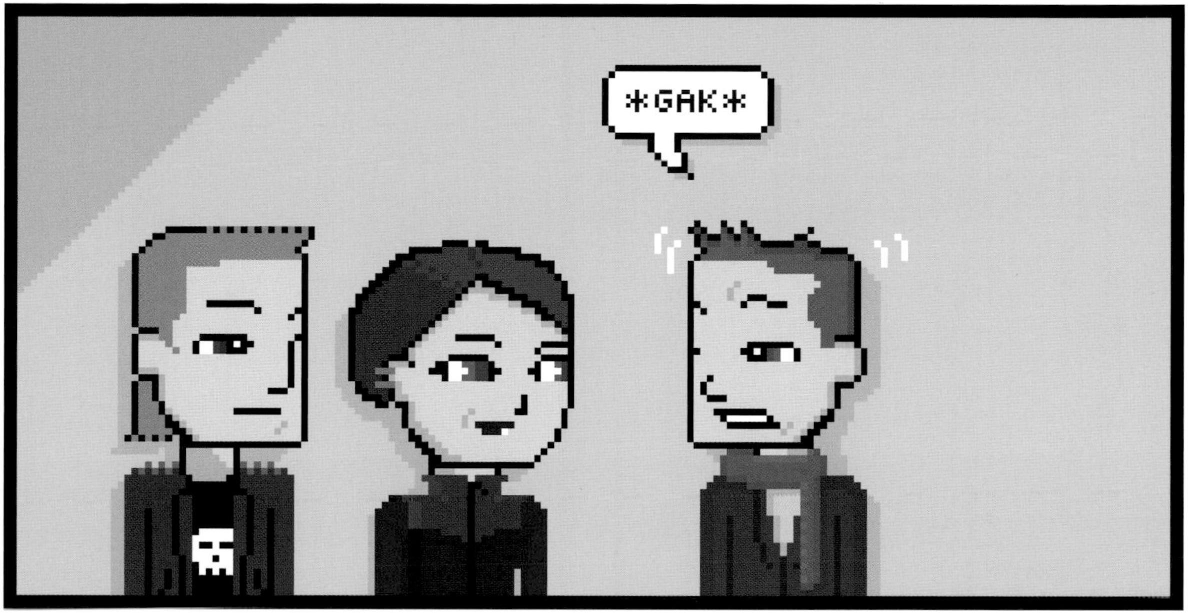
GAK

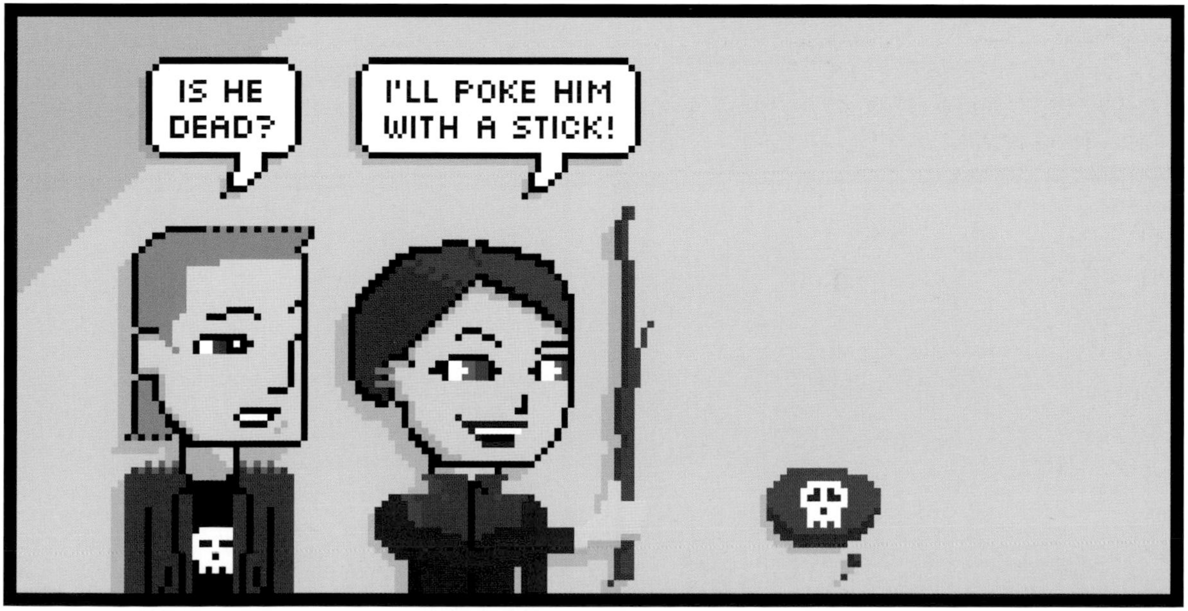
IS HE DEAD?
I'LL POKE HIM WITH A STICK!

LESS THAN ZERO

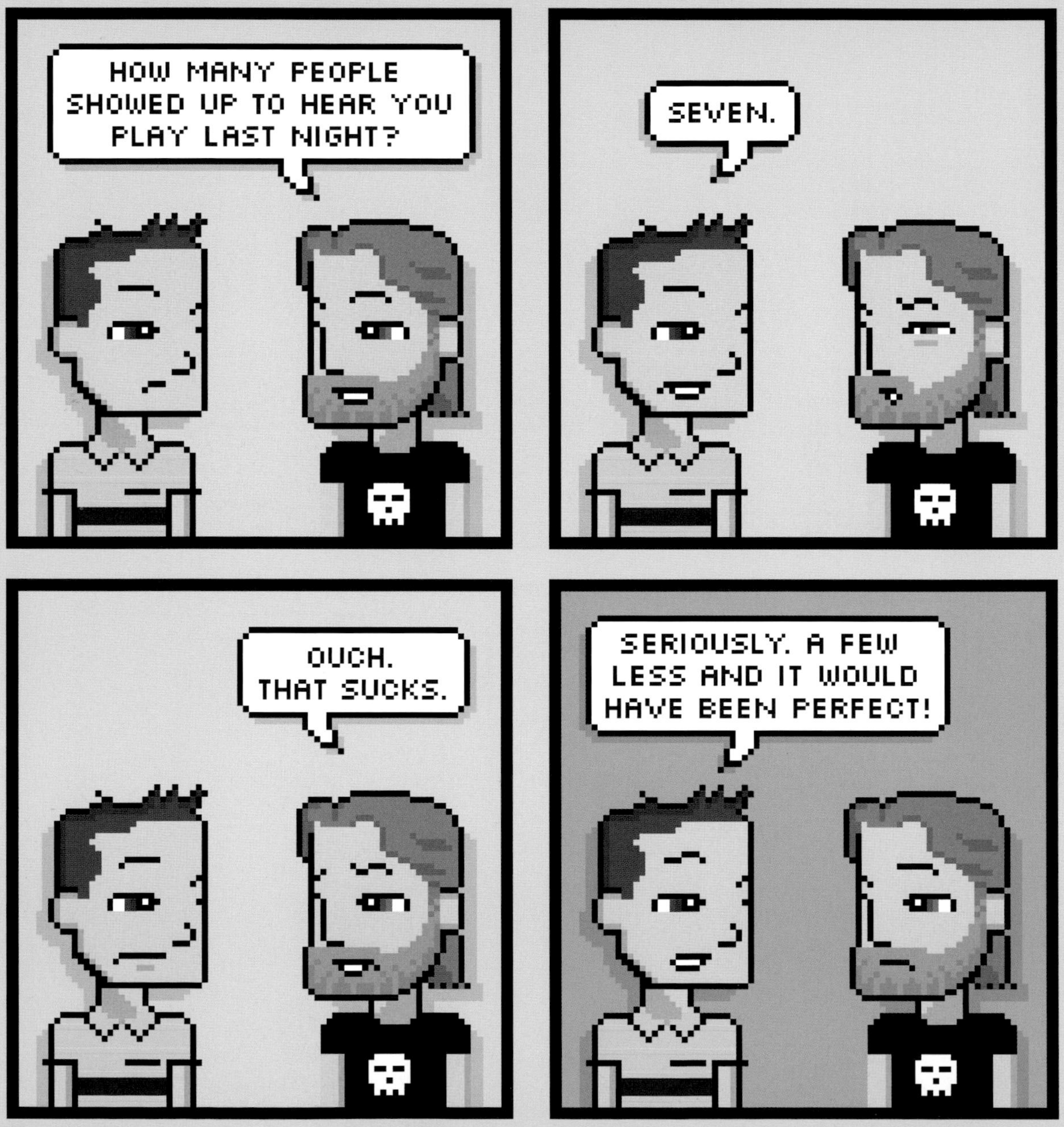
HOW MANY PEOPLE SHOWED UP TO HEAR YOU PLAY LAST NIGHT?
SEVEN.
OUCH. THAT SUCKS.
SERIOUSLY. A FEW LESS AND IT WOULD HAVE BEEN PERFECT!

BARRIERS TO ACCESS

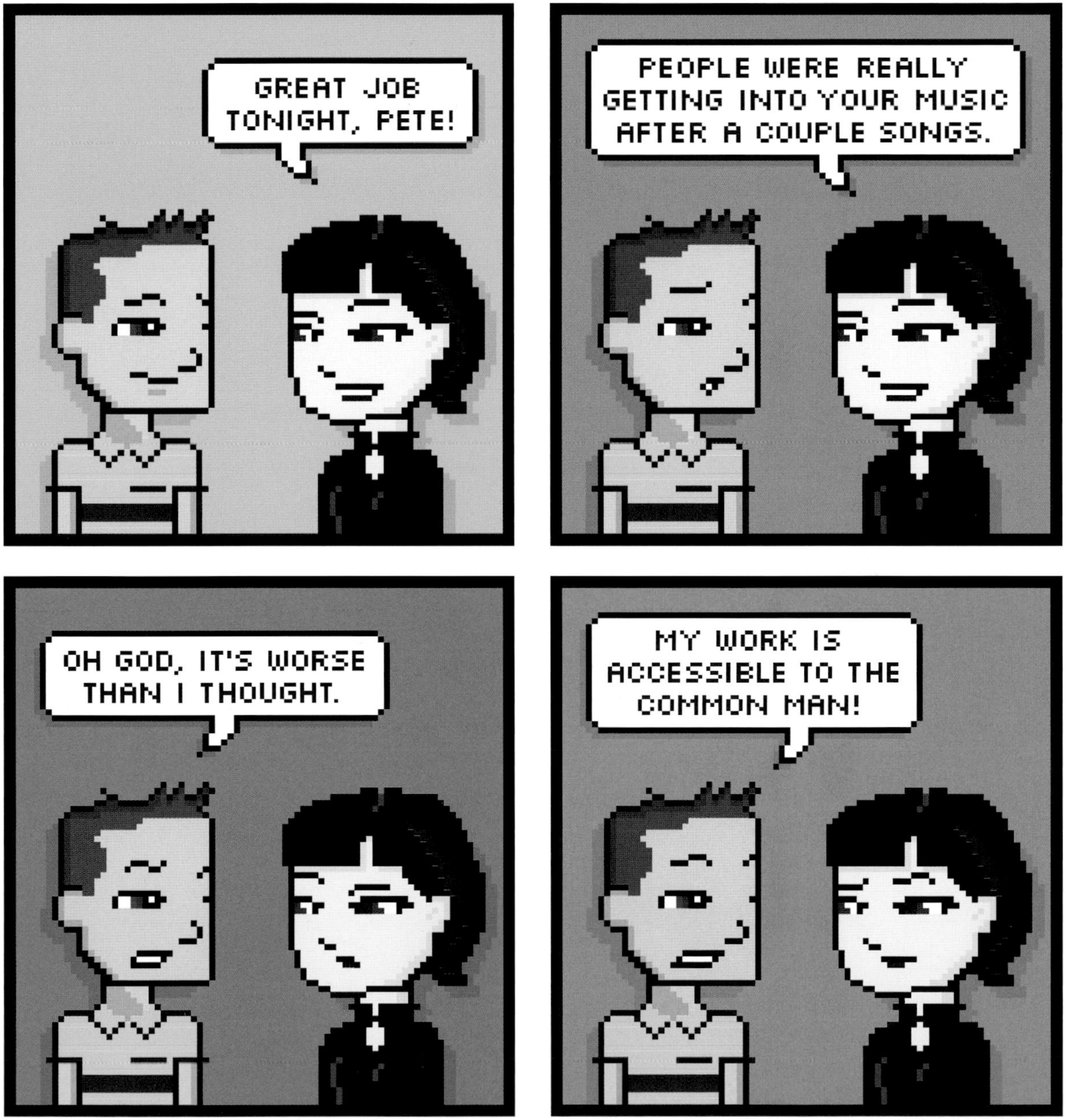
GREAT JOB TONIGHT, PETE!
PEOPLE WERE REALLY GETTING INTO YOUR MUSIC AFTER A COUPLE SONGS.
OH GOD, IT'S WORSE THAN I THOUGHT.
MY WORK IS ACCESSIBLE TO THE COMMON MAN!

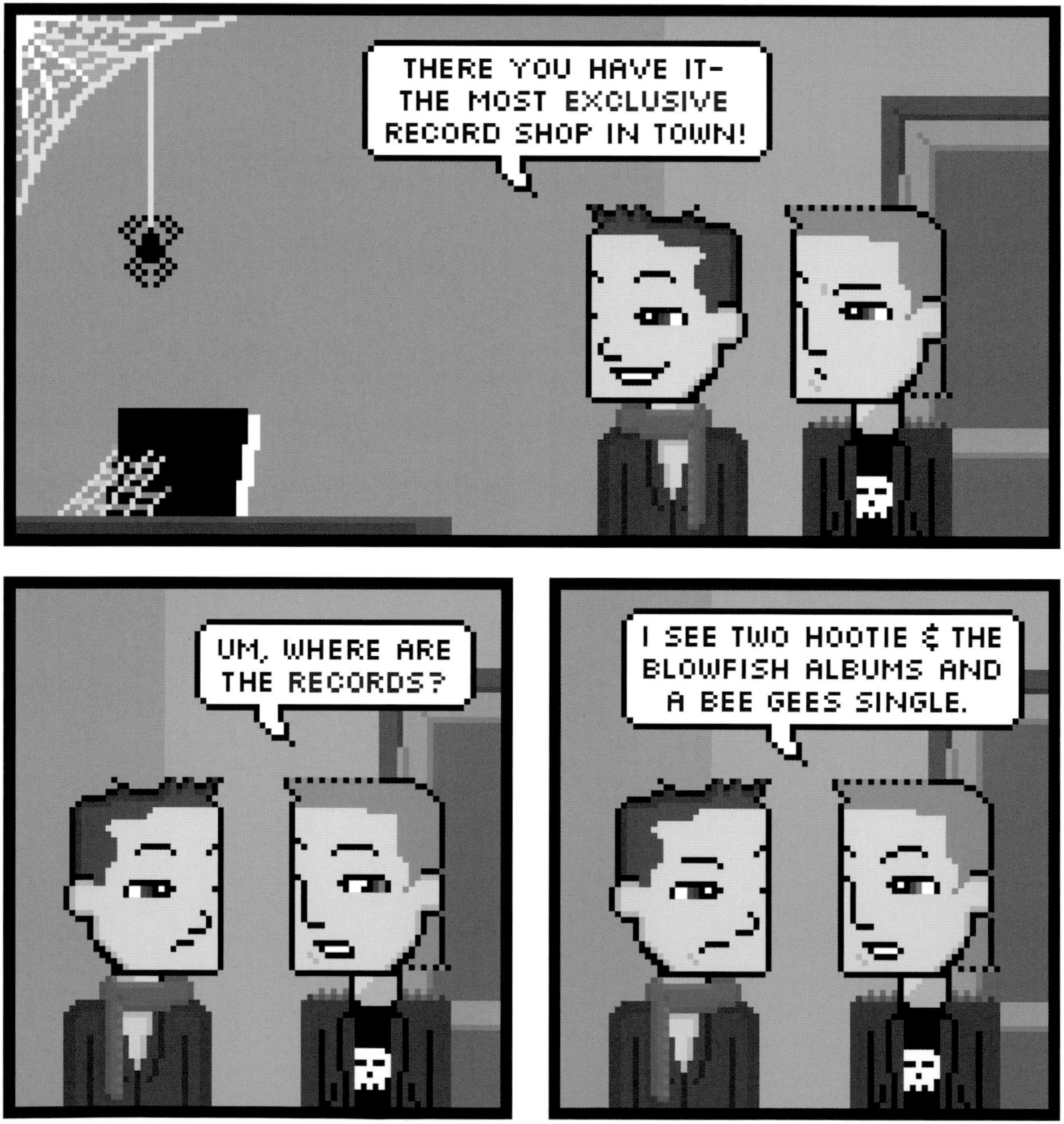
THERE YOU HAVE IT- THE MOST EXCLUSIVE RECORD SHOP IN TOWN!
UM, WHERE ARE THE RECORDS?
I SEE TWO HOOTIE & THE BLOWFISH ALBUMS AND A BEE GEES SINGLE.

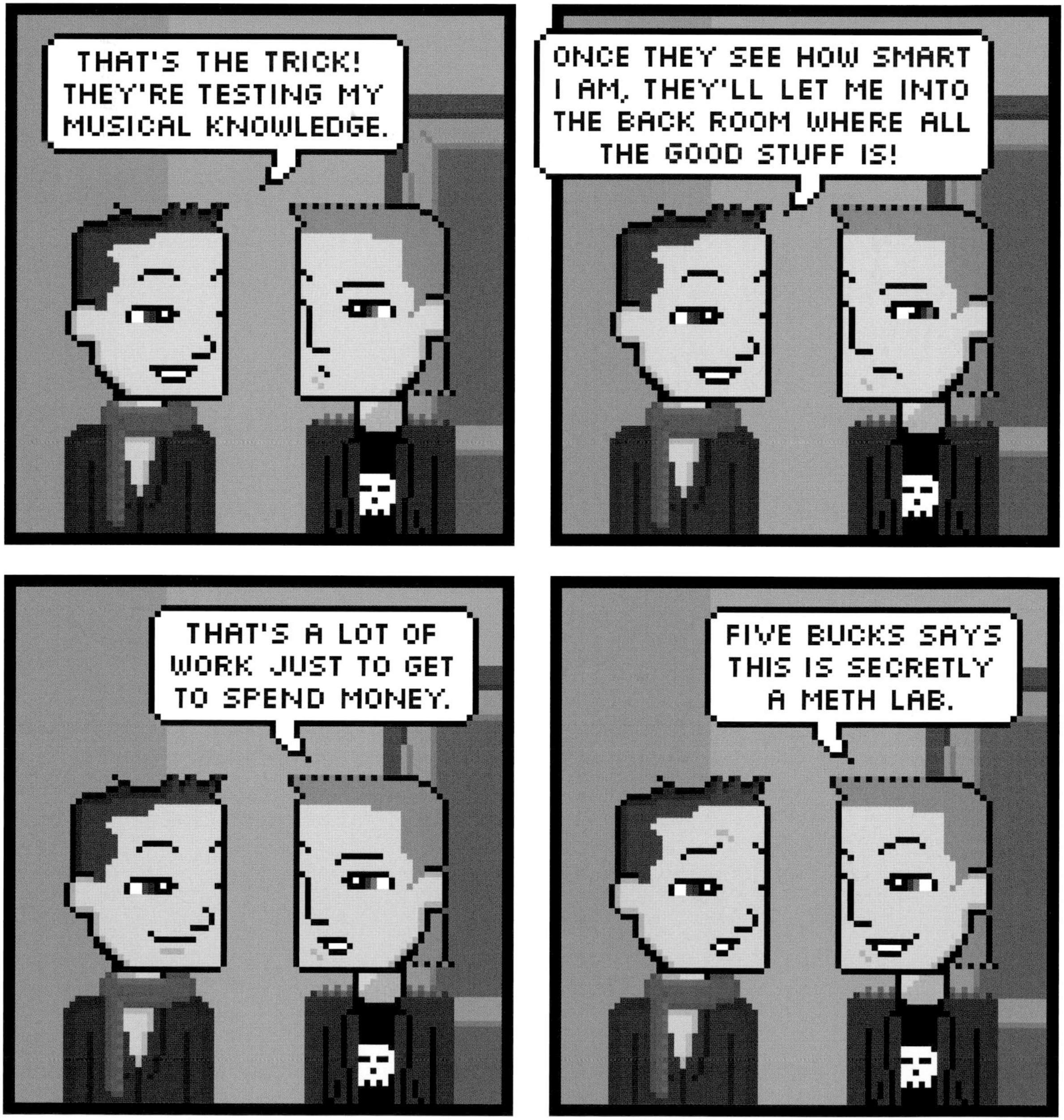
THAT'S THE TRICK! THEY'RE TESTING MY MUSICAL KNOWLEDGE.
ONCE THEY SEE HOW SMART I AM, THEY'LL LET ME INTO THE BACK ROOM WHERE ALL THE GOOD STUFF IS!
THAT'S A LOT OF WORK JUST TO GET TO SPEND MONEY.
FIVE BUCKS SAYS THIS IS SECRETLY A METH LAB.

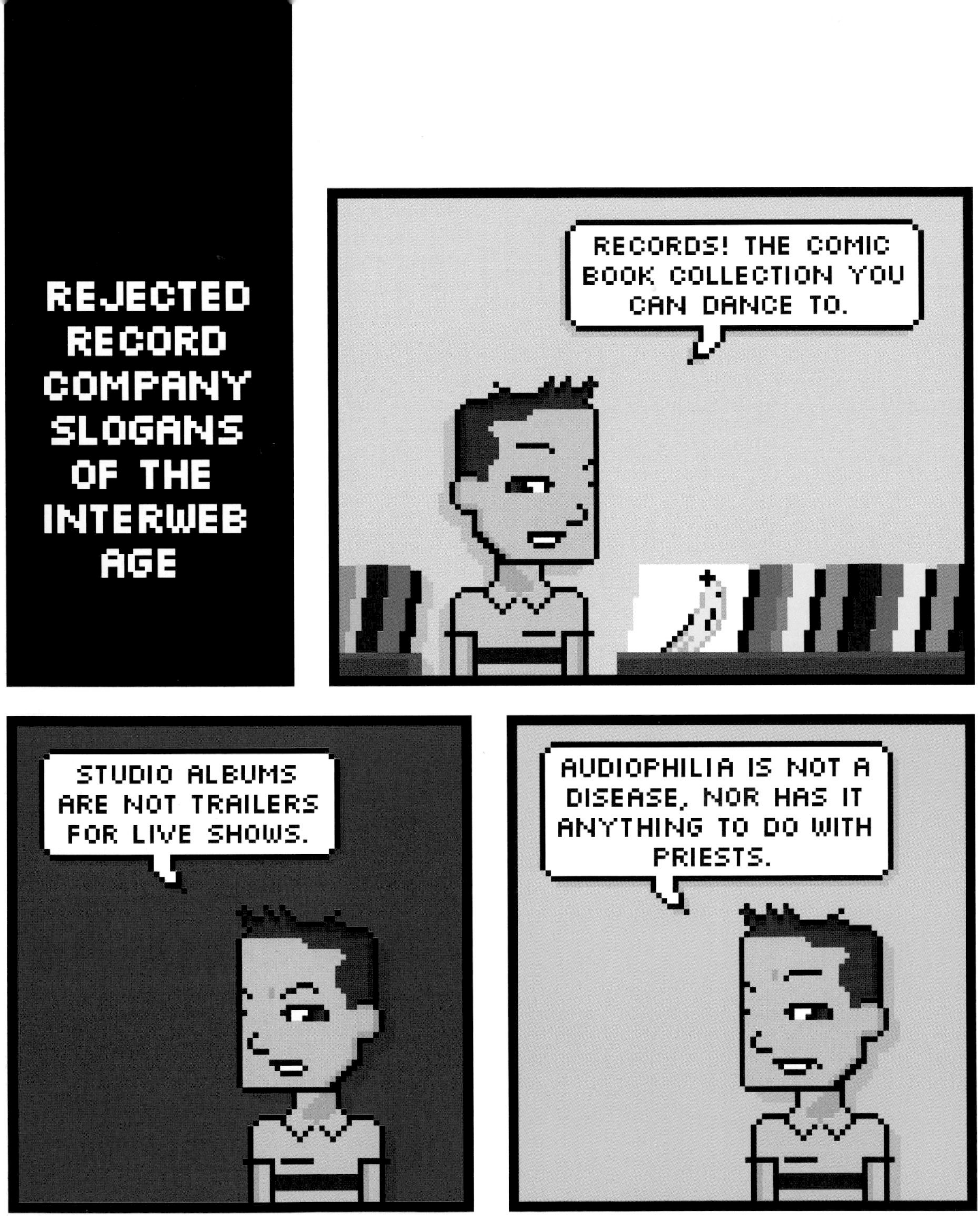
REJECTED RECORD COMPANY SLOGANS OF THE INTERWEB AGE
RECORDS! THE COMIC BOOK COLLECTION YOU CAN DANCE TO.
STUDIO ALBUMS ARE NOT TRAILERS FOR LIVE SHOWS.
AUDIOPHILIA IS NOT A DISEASE, NOR HAS IT ANYTHING TO DO WITH PRIESTS.

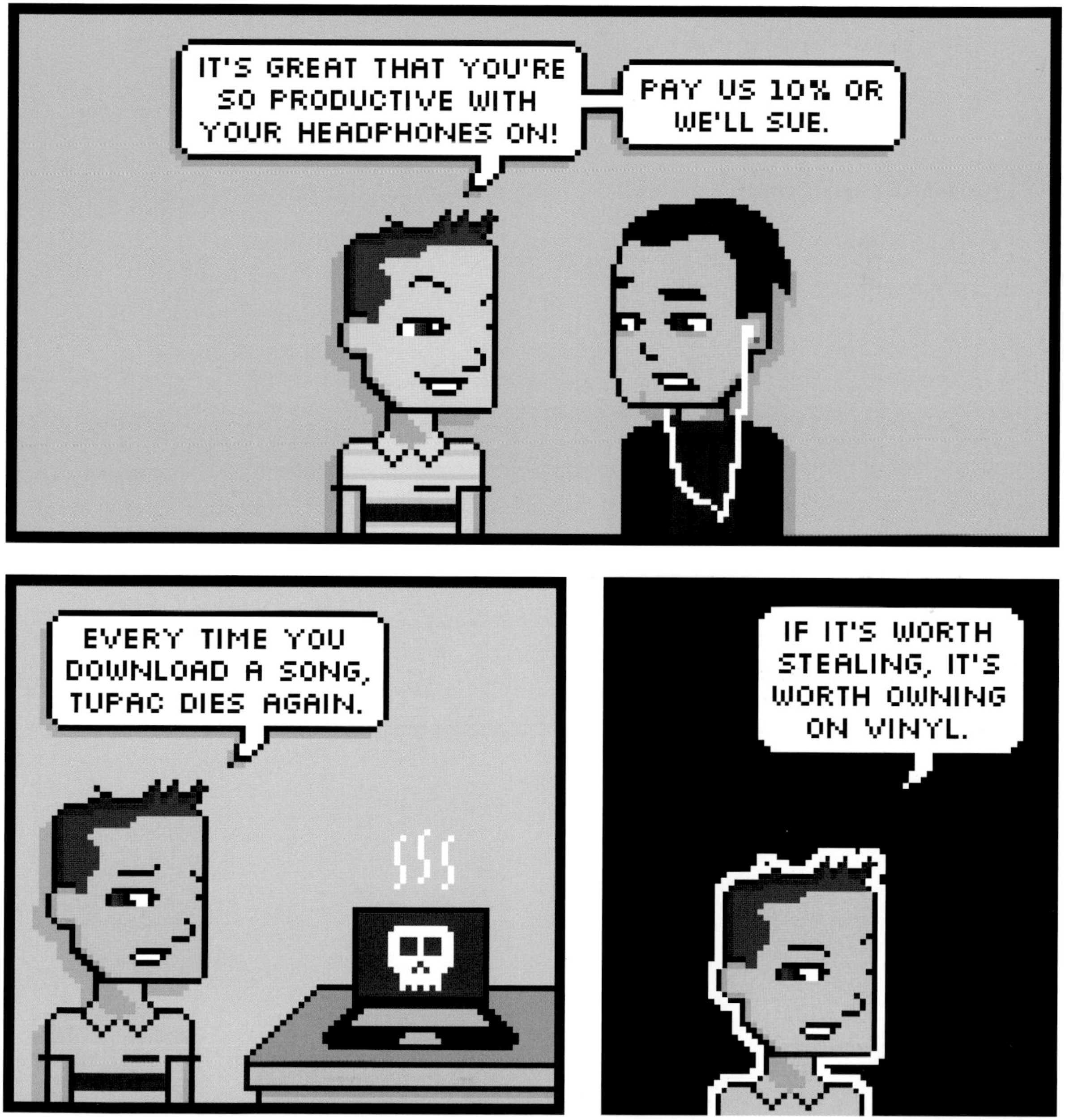
IT'S GREAT THAT YOU'RE SO PRODUCTIVE WITH YOUR HEADPHONES ON!
PAY US 10% OR WE'LL SUE.
EVERY TIME YOU DOWNLOAD A SONG, TUPAC DIES AGAIN.
IF IT'S WORTH STEALING, IT'S WORTH OWNING ON VINYL.

I ADMIT, I DID PAY FOR "WHIP SMART"

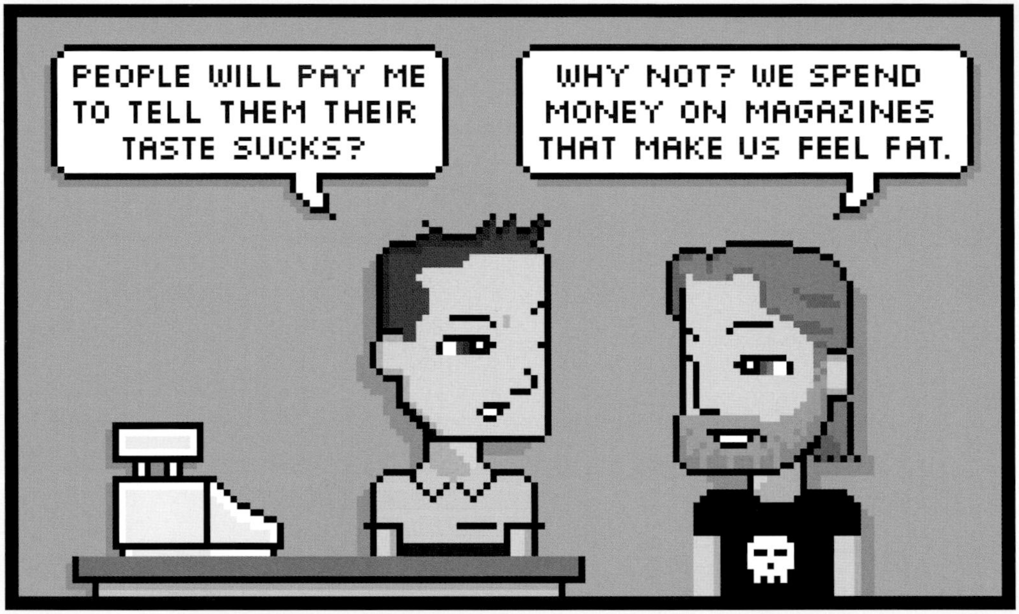
PEOPLE WILL PAY ME TO TELL THEM THEIR TASTE SUCKS?
WHY NOT? WE SPEND MONEY ON MAGAZINES THAT MAKE US FEEL FAT.

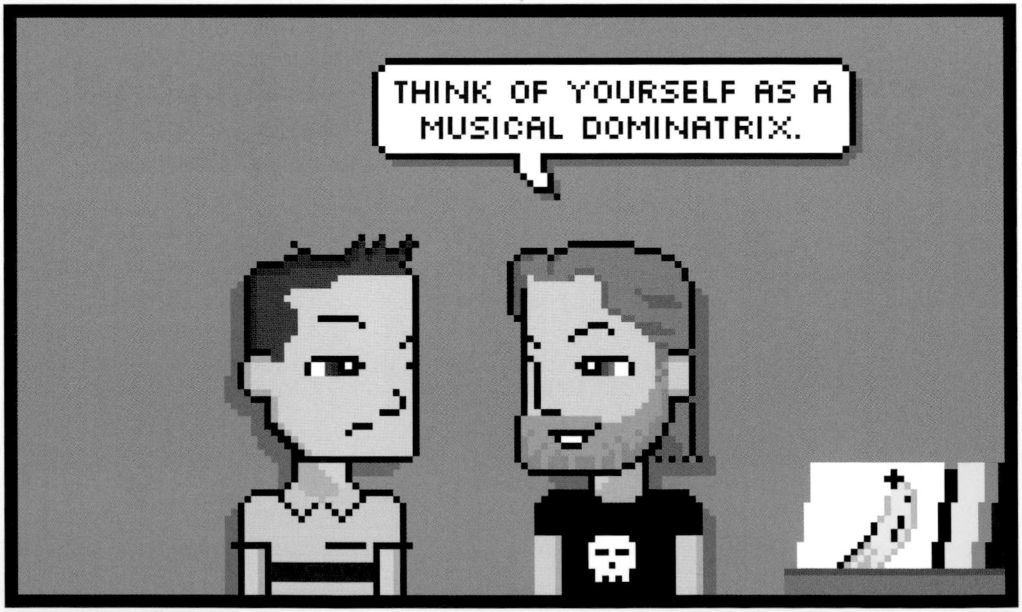
THINK OF YOURSELF AS A MUSICAL DOMINATRIX.

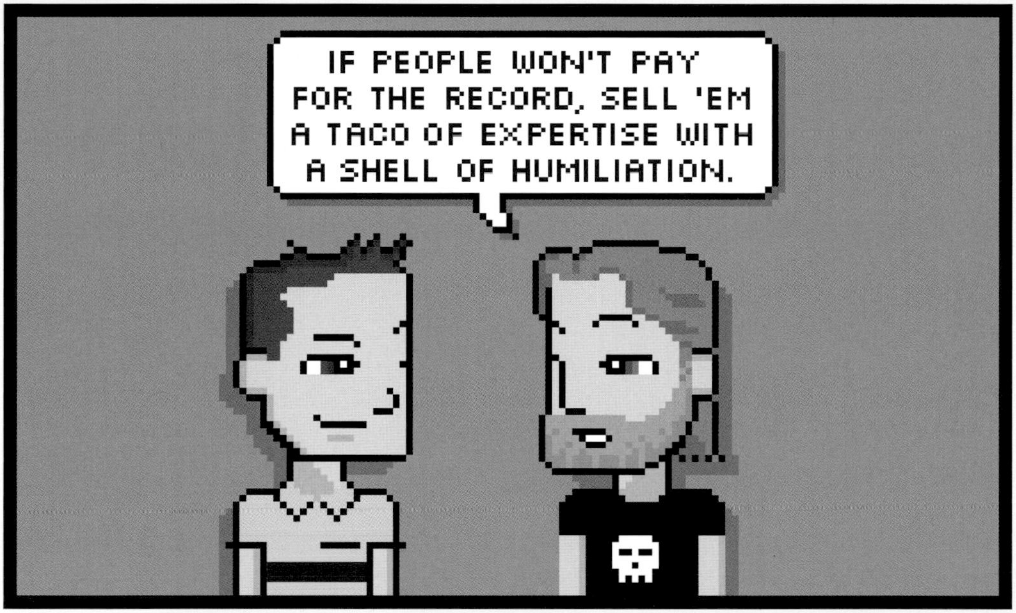
IF PEOPLE WON'T PAY FOR THE RECORD, SELL 'EM A TACO OF EXPERTISE WITH A SHELL OF HUMILIATION.

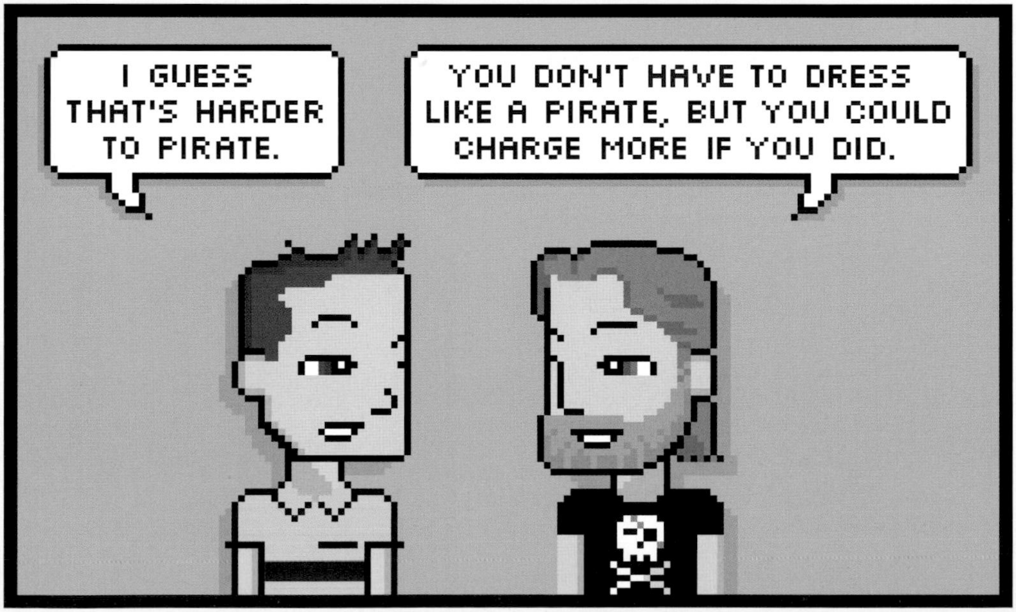
I GUESS THAT'S HARDER TO PIRATE.
YOU DON'T HAVE TO DRESS LIKE A PIRATE, BUT YOU COULD CHARGE MORE IF YOU DID.

JUST CHICKEN TO SEE IF YOU'RE PAYING EGGTENTION

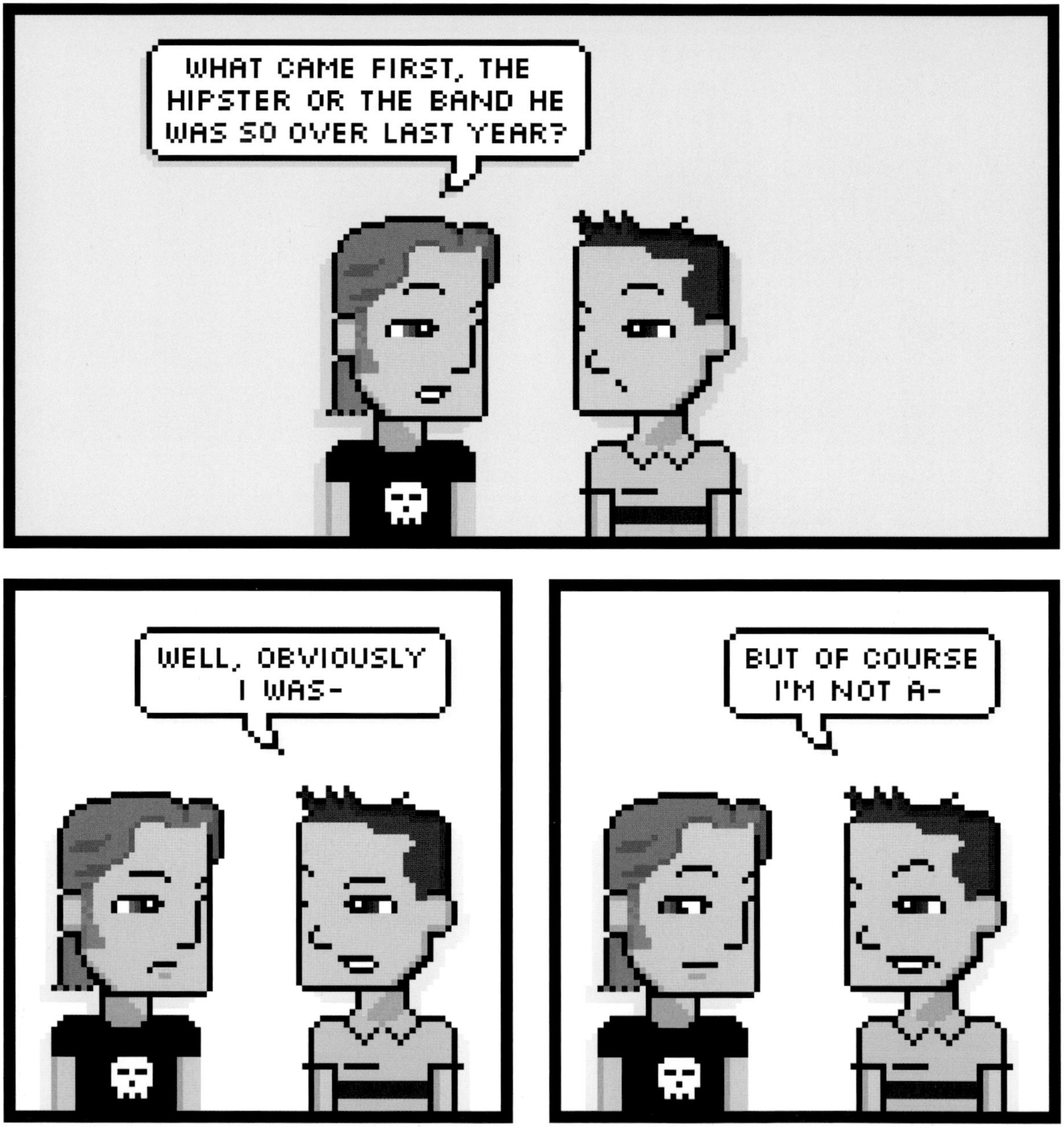
WHAT CAME FIRST, THE HIPSTER OR THE BAND HE WAS SO OVER LAST YEAR?
WELL, OBVIOUSLY I WAS-
BUT OF COURSE I'M NOT A-

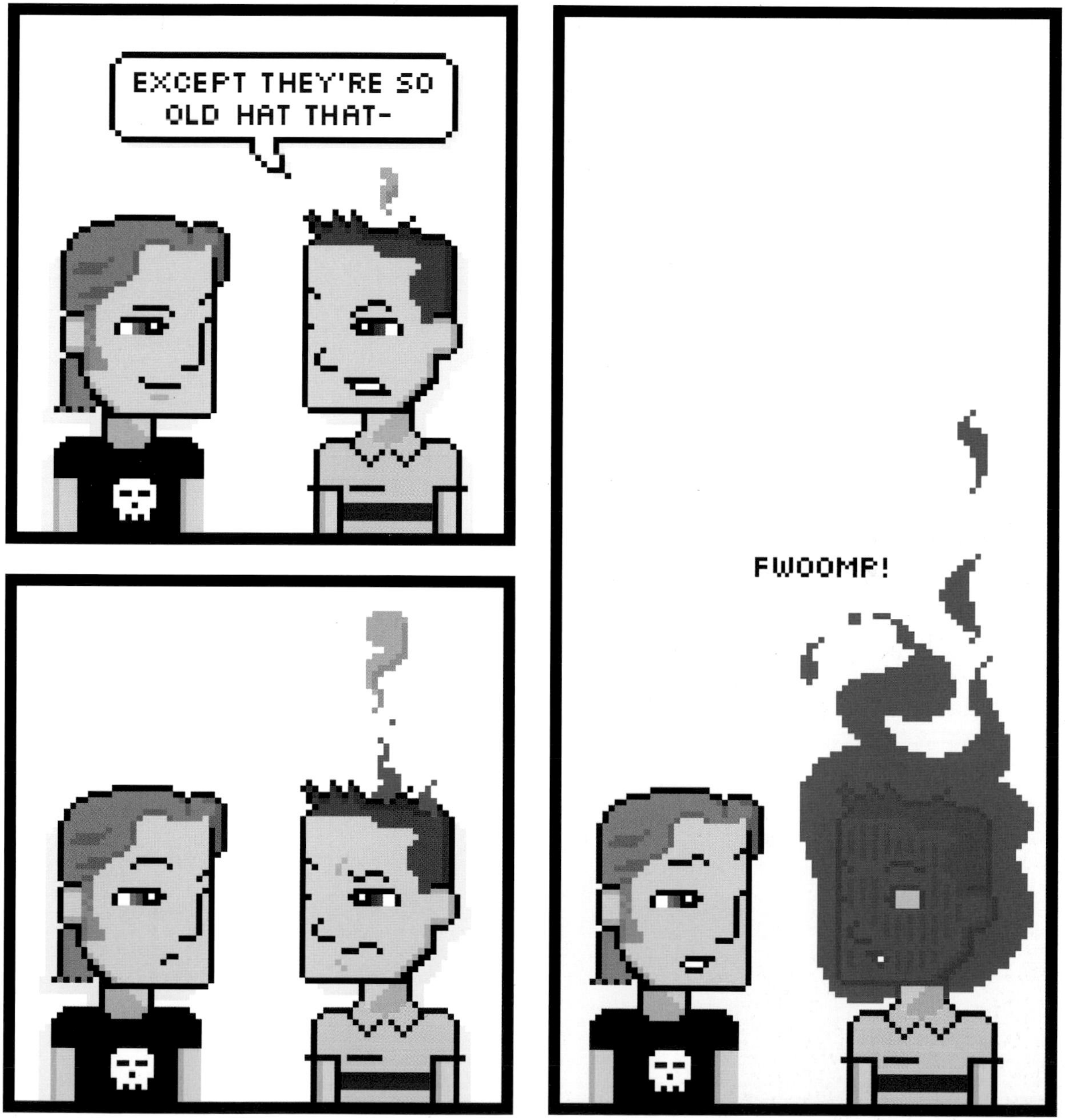
EXCEPT THEY'RE SO OLD HAT THAT-
FWOOMP!

ANTEDILUVIANNOYING

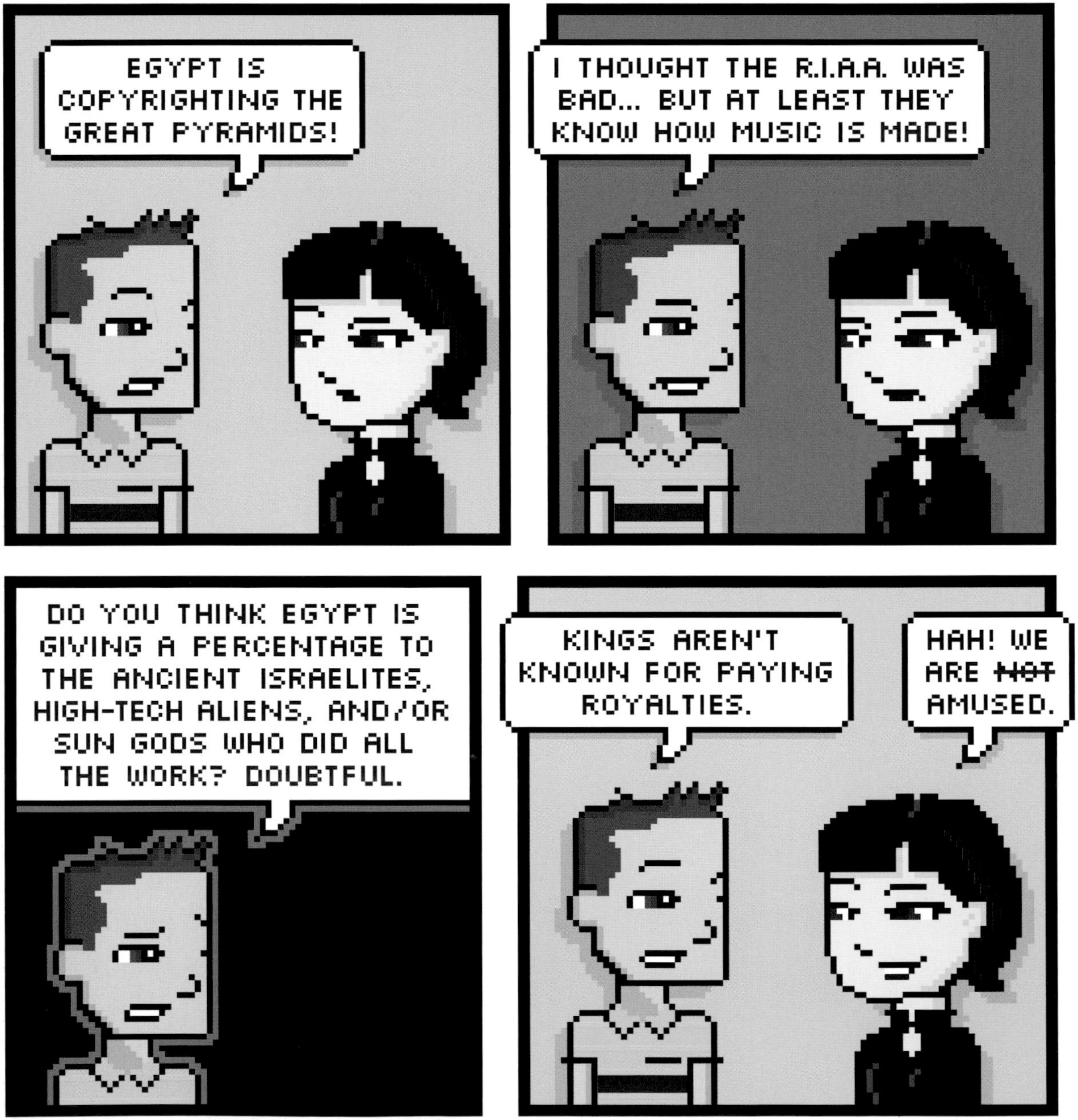

EGYPT IS COPYRIGHTING THE GREAT PYRAMIDS!
I THOUGHT THE R.I.A.A. WAS BAD... BUT AT LEAST THEY KNOW HOW MUSIC IS MADE!
DO YOU THINK EGYPT IS GIVING A PERCENTAGE TO THE ANCIENT ISRAELITES, HIGH-TECH ALIENS, AND/OR SUN GODS WHO DID ALL THE WORK? DOUBTFUL.
KINGS AREN'T KNOWN FOR PAYING ROYALTIES.
HAH! WE ARE ~~NOT~~ AMUSED.

LUXURIOUSLY YOURS

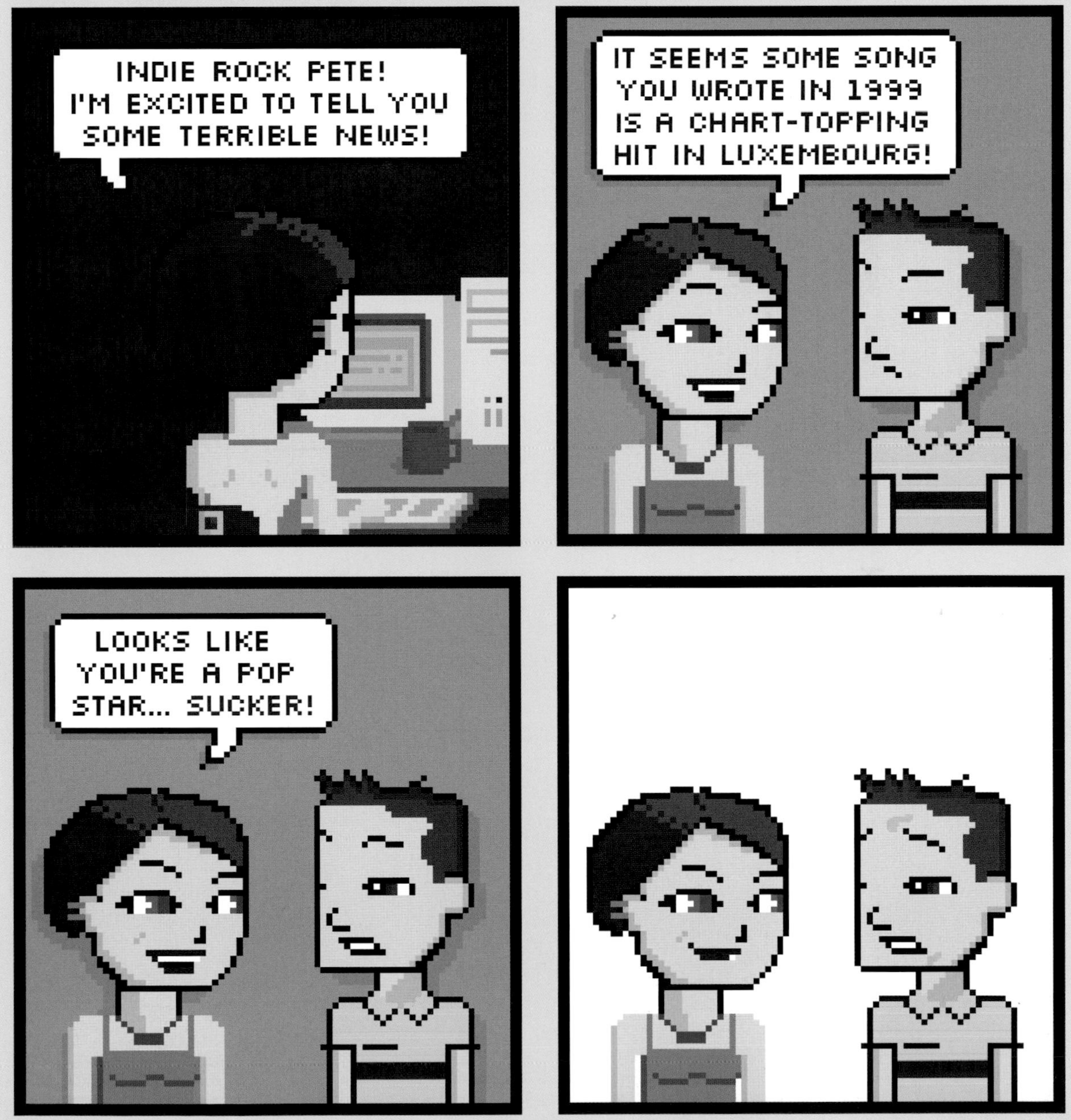
INDIE ROCK PETE! I'M EXCITED TO TELL YOU SOME TERRIBLE NEWS!
IT SEEMS SOME SONG YOU WROTE IN 1999 IS A CHART-TOPPING HIT IN LUXEMBOURG!
LOOKS LIKE YOU'RE A POP STAR... SUCKER!

LIMBER UP

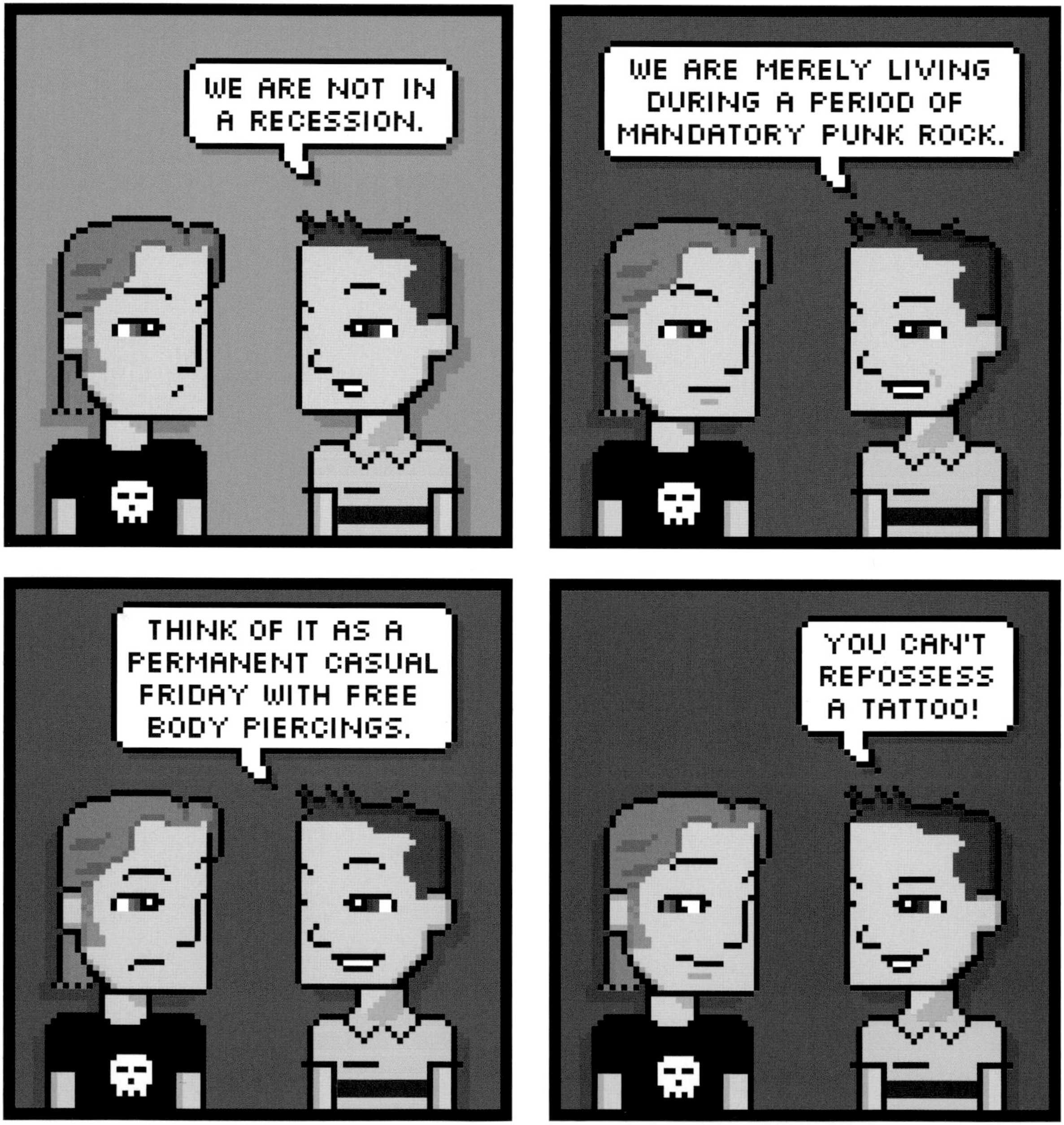
WE ARE NOT IN A RECESSION.
WE ARE MERELY LIVING DURING A PERIOD OF MANDATORY PUNK ROCK.
THINK OF IT AS A PERMANENT CASUAL FRIDAY WITH FREE BODY PIERCINGS.
YOU CAN'T REPOSSESS A TATTOO!

THE TRUTH LESS VARNISHED

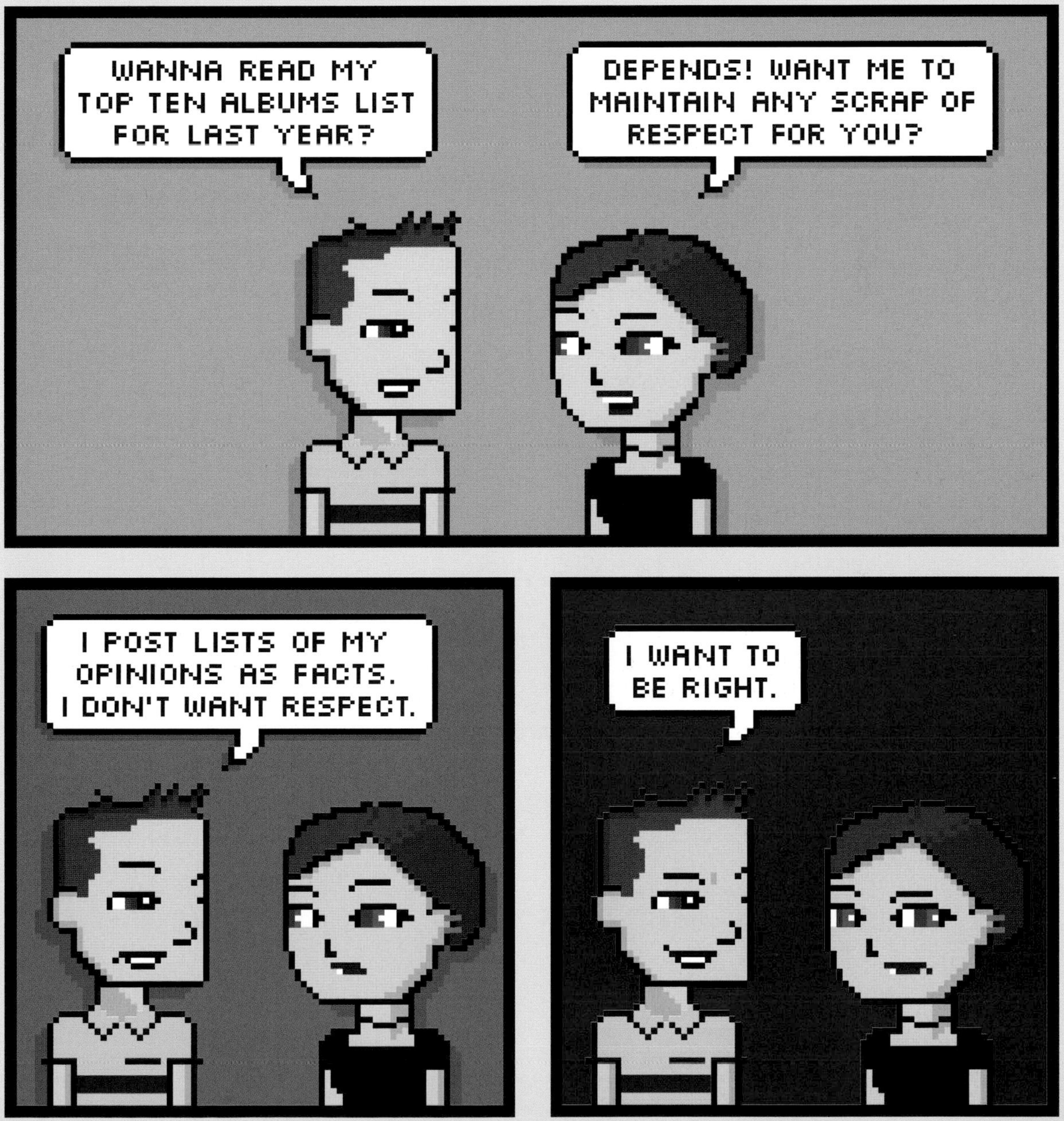
WANNA READ MY TOP TEN ALBUMS LIST FOR LAST YEAR?
DEPENDS! WANT ME TO MAINTAIN ANY SCRAP OF RESPECT FOR YOU?
I POST LISTS OF MY OPINIONS AS FACTS. I DON'T WANT RESPECT.
I WANT TO BE RIGHT.

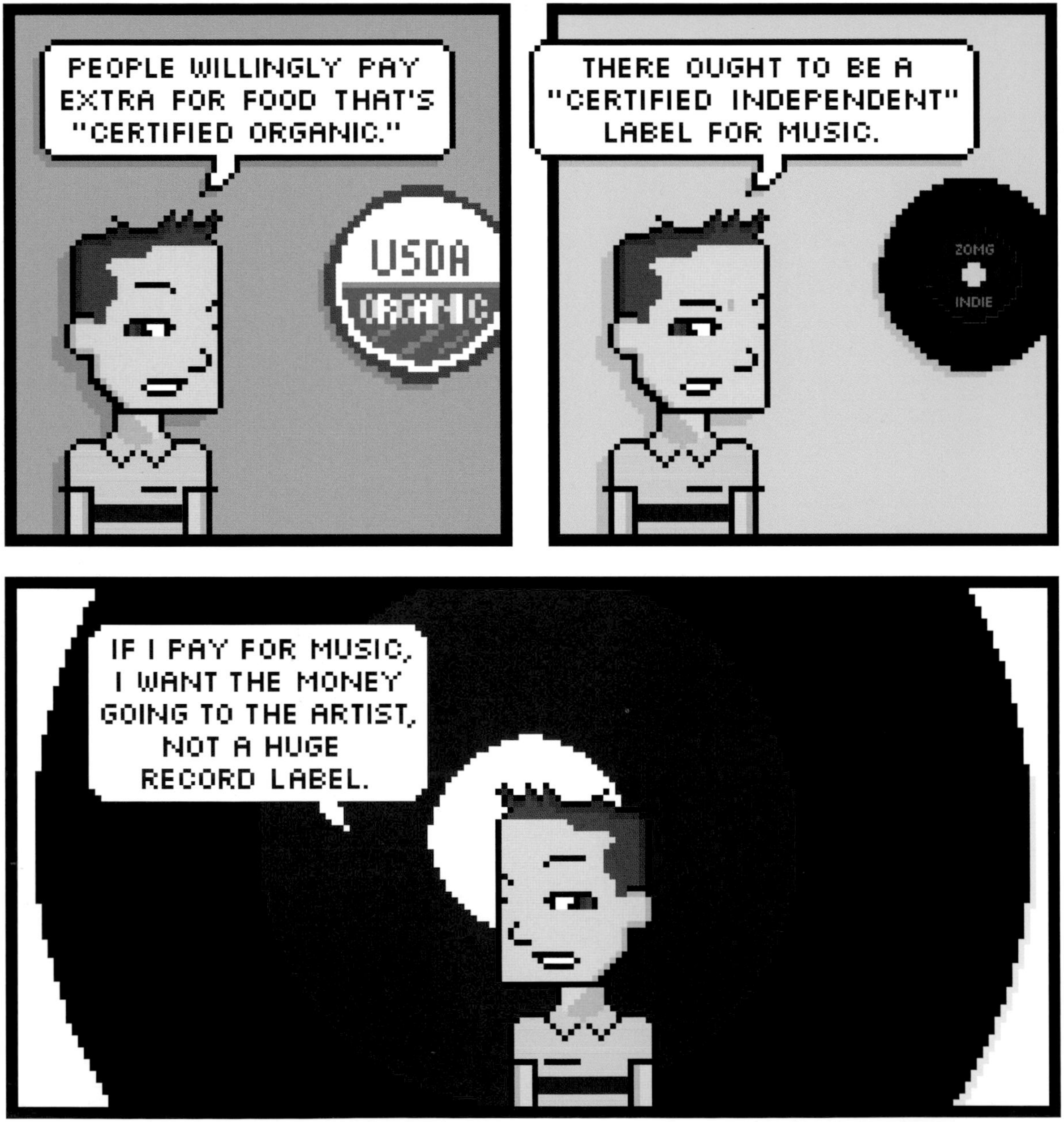
PEOPLE WILLINGLY PAY EXTRA FOR FOOD THAT'S "CERTIFIED ORGANIC."
USDA
ORGANIC
THERE OUGHT TO BE A "CERTIFIED INDEPENDENT" LABEL FOR MUSIC.
ZOMG
INDIE
IF I PAY FOR MUSIC, I WANT THE MONEY GOING TO THE ARTIST, NOT A HUGE RECORD LABEL.

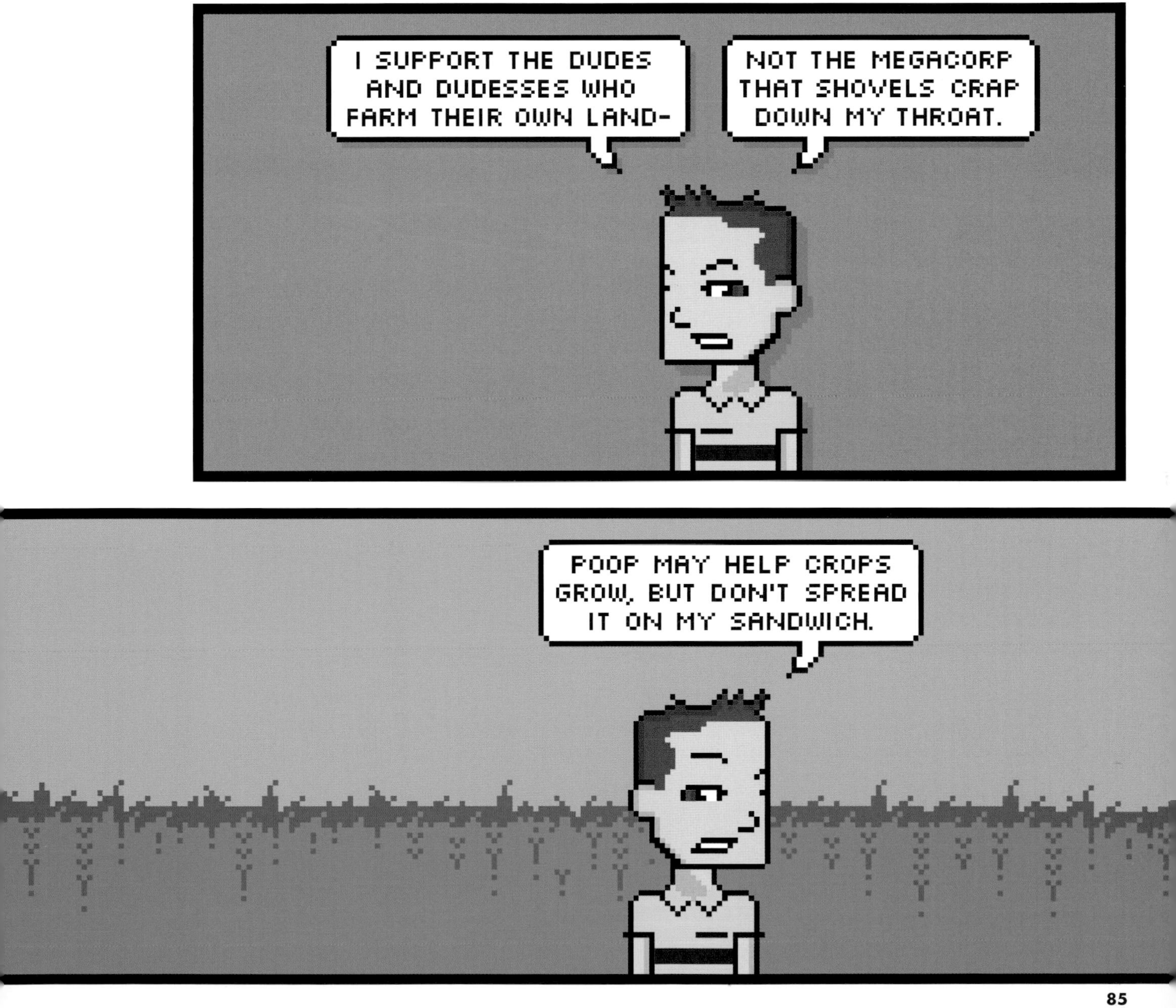
I SUPPORT THE DUDES AND DUDESSES WHO FARM THEIR OWN LAND-
NOT THE MEGACORP THAT SHOVELS CRAP DOWN MY THROAT.
POOP MAY HELP CROPS GROW, BUT DON'T SPREAD IT ON MY SANDWICH.

AMPITHEATURTLE

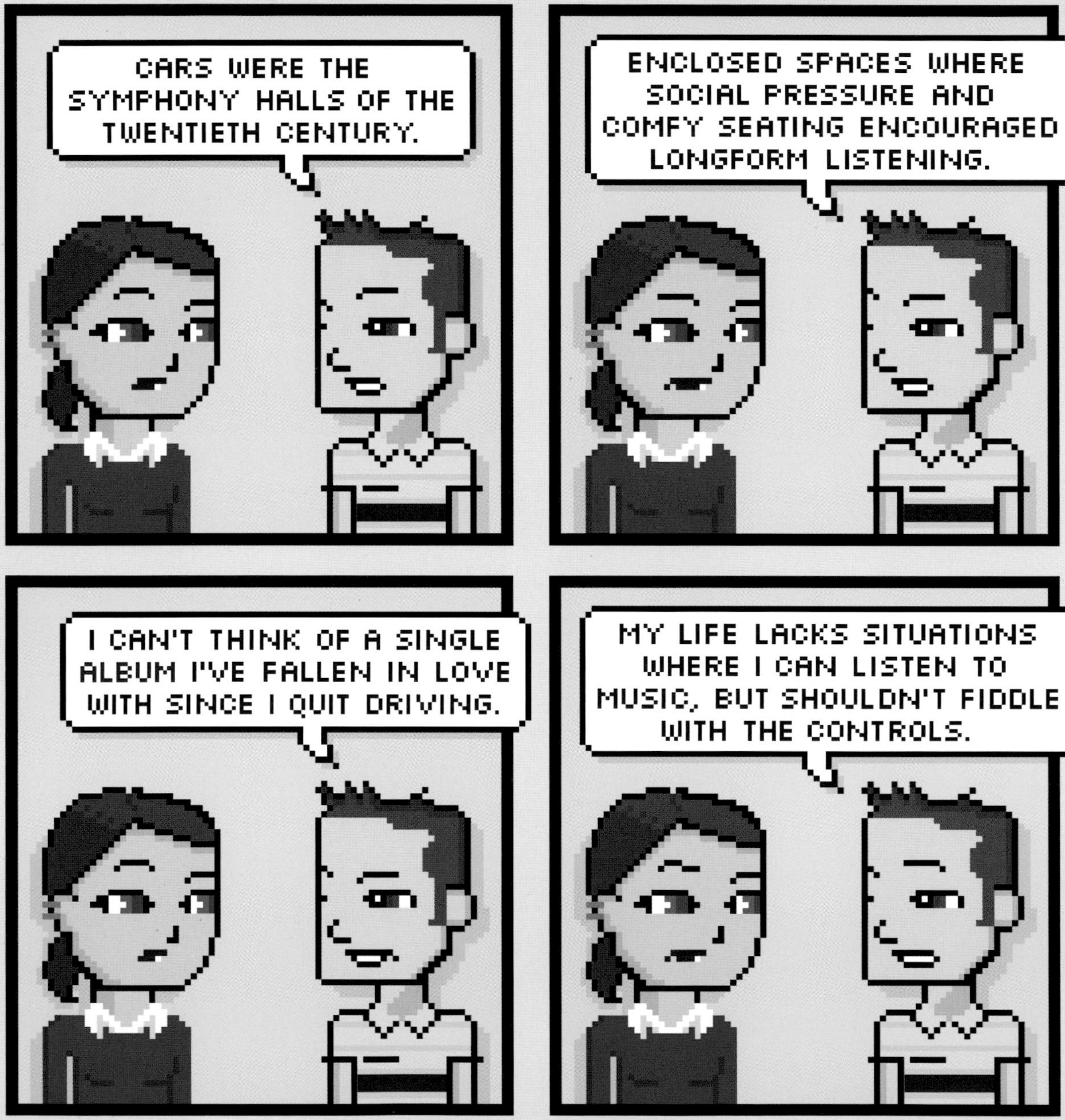
CARS WERE THE SYMPHONY HALLS OF THE TWENTIETH CENTURY.
ENCLOSED SPACES WHERE SOCIAL PRESSURE AND COMFY SEATING ENCOURAGED LONGFORM LISTENING.
I CAN'T THINK OF A SINGLE ALBUM I'VE FALLEN IN LOVE WITH SINCE I QUIT DRIVING.
MY LIFE LACKS SITUATIONS WHERE I CAN LISTEN TO MUSIC, BUT SHOULDN'T FIDDLE WITH THE CONTROLS.

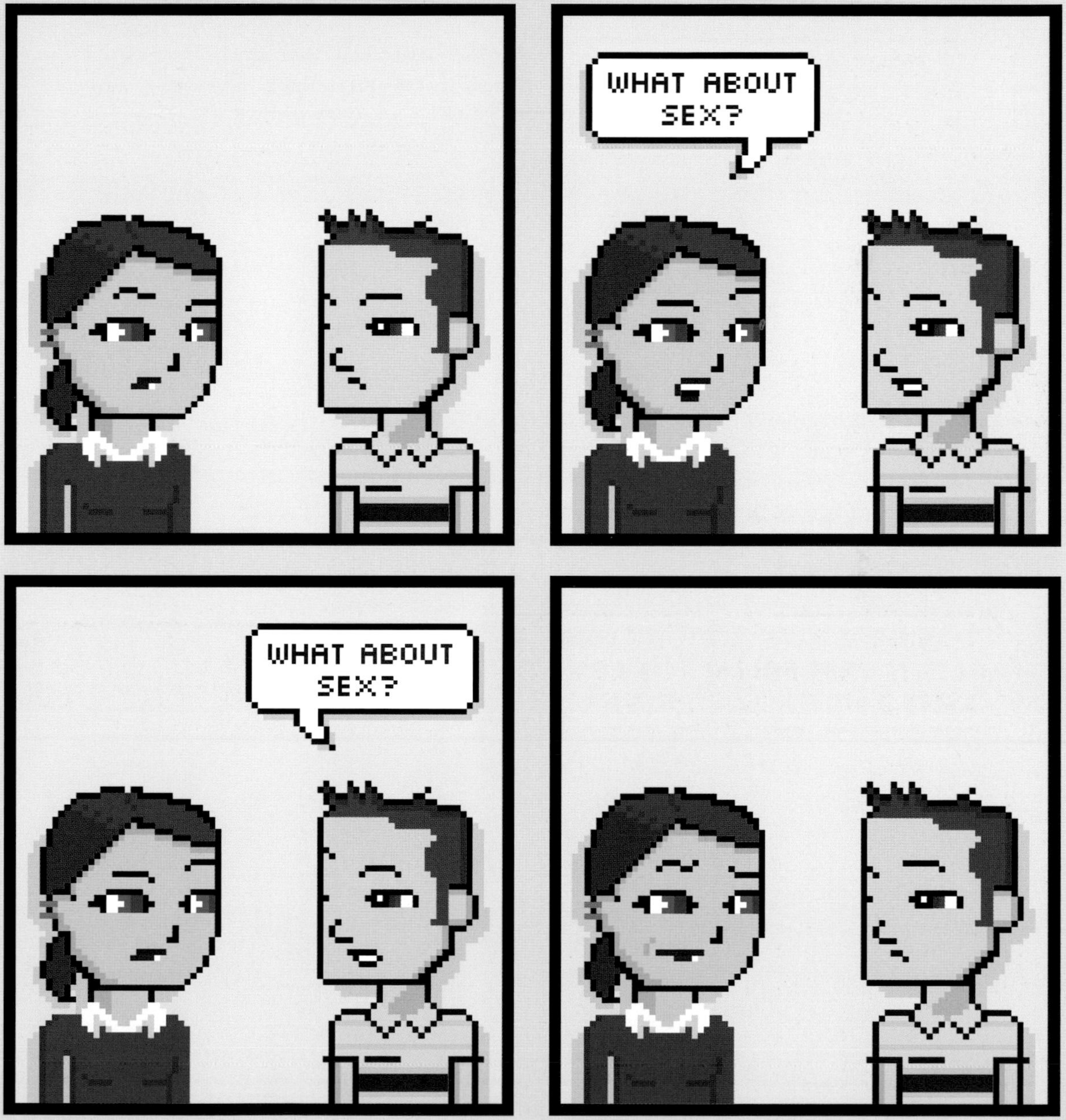
WHAT ABOUT SEX?
WHAT ABOUT SEX?

IF GWAR DRESSED LIKE LIBRARIANS

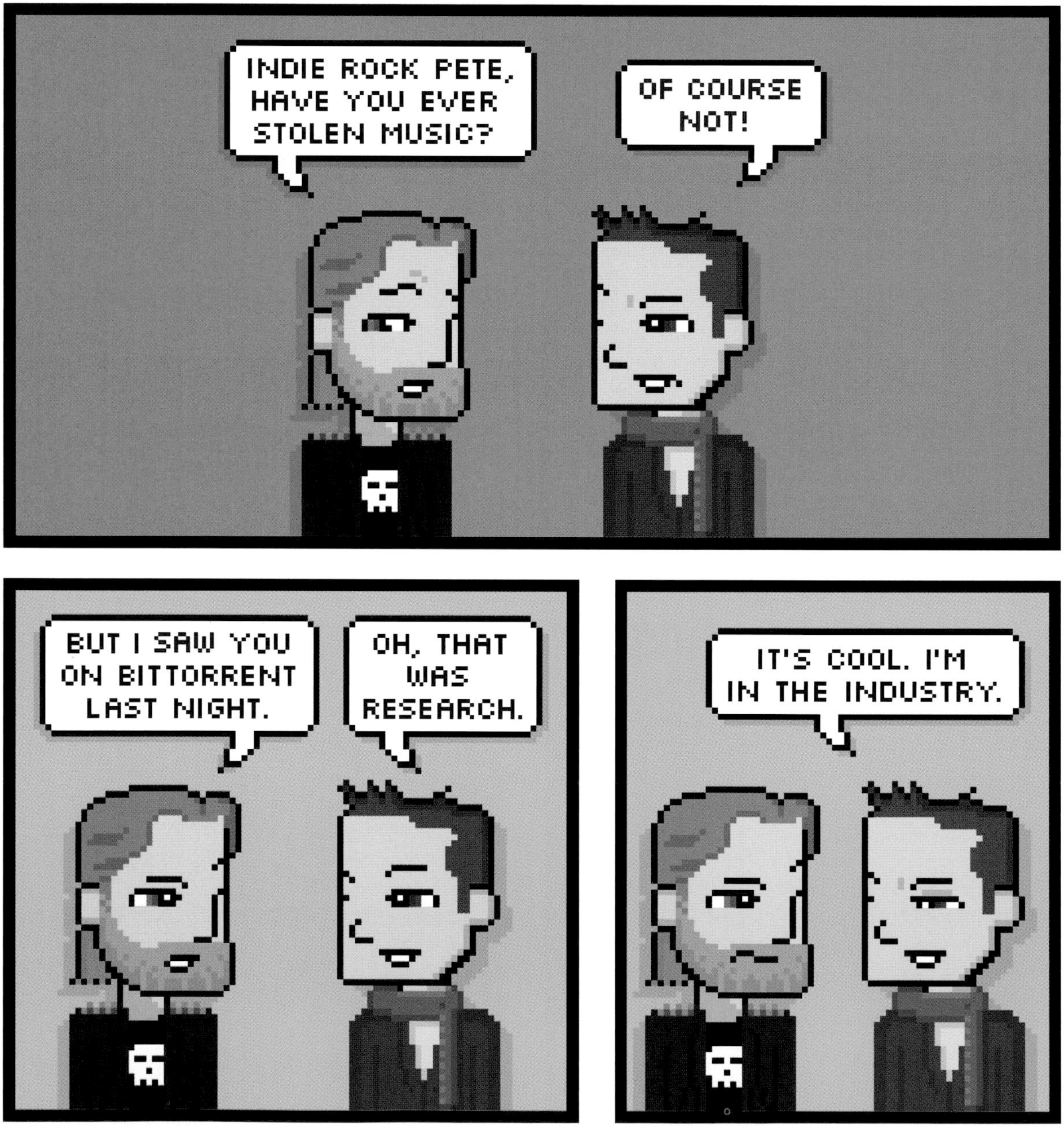
INDIE ROCK PETE, HAVE YOU EVER STOLEN MUSIC?
OF COURSE NOT!
BUT I SAW YOU ON BITTORRENT LAST NIGHT.
OH, THAT WAS RESEARCH.
IT'S COOL. I'M IN THE INDUSTRY.

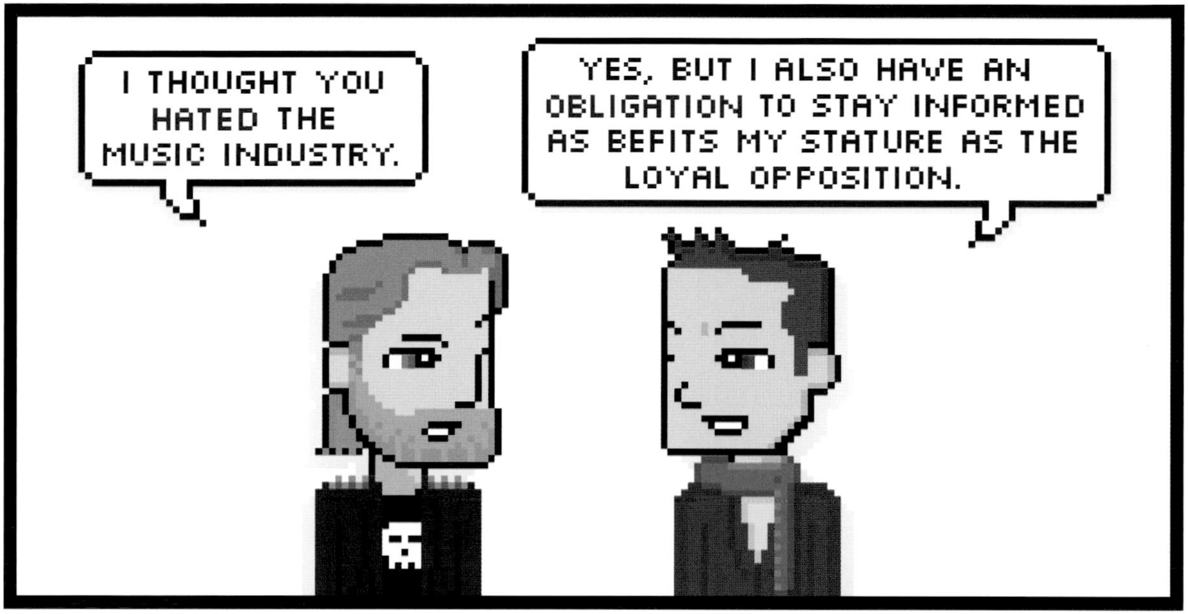
I THOUGHT YOU HATED THE MUSIC INDUSTRY.
YES, BUT I ALSO HAVE AN OBLIGATION TO STAY INFORMED AS BEFITS MY STATURE AS THE LOYAL OPPOSITION.

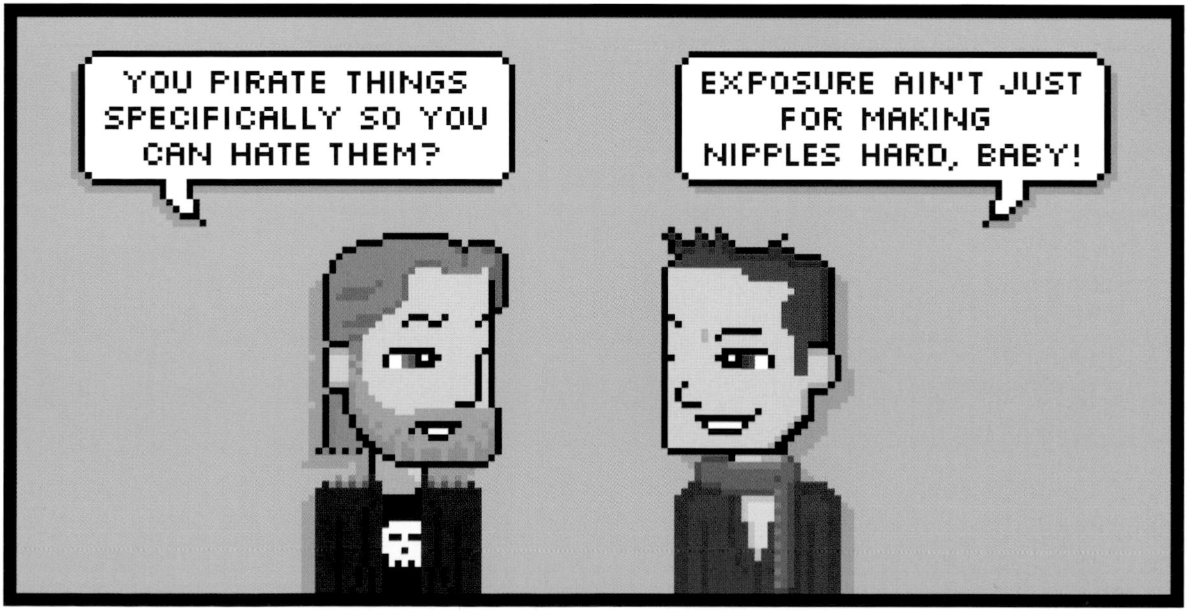
YOU PIRATE THINGS SPECIFICALLY SO YOU CAN HATE THEM?
EXPOSURE AIN'T JUST FOR MAKING NIPPLES HARD, BABY!

HONESTY IS THE BEST NOVELTY

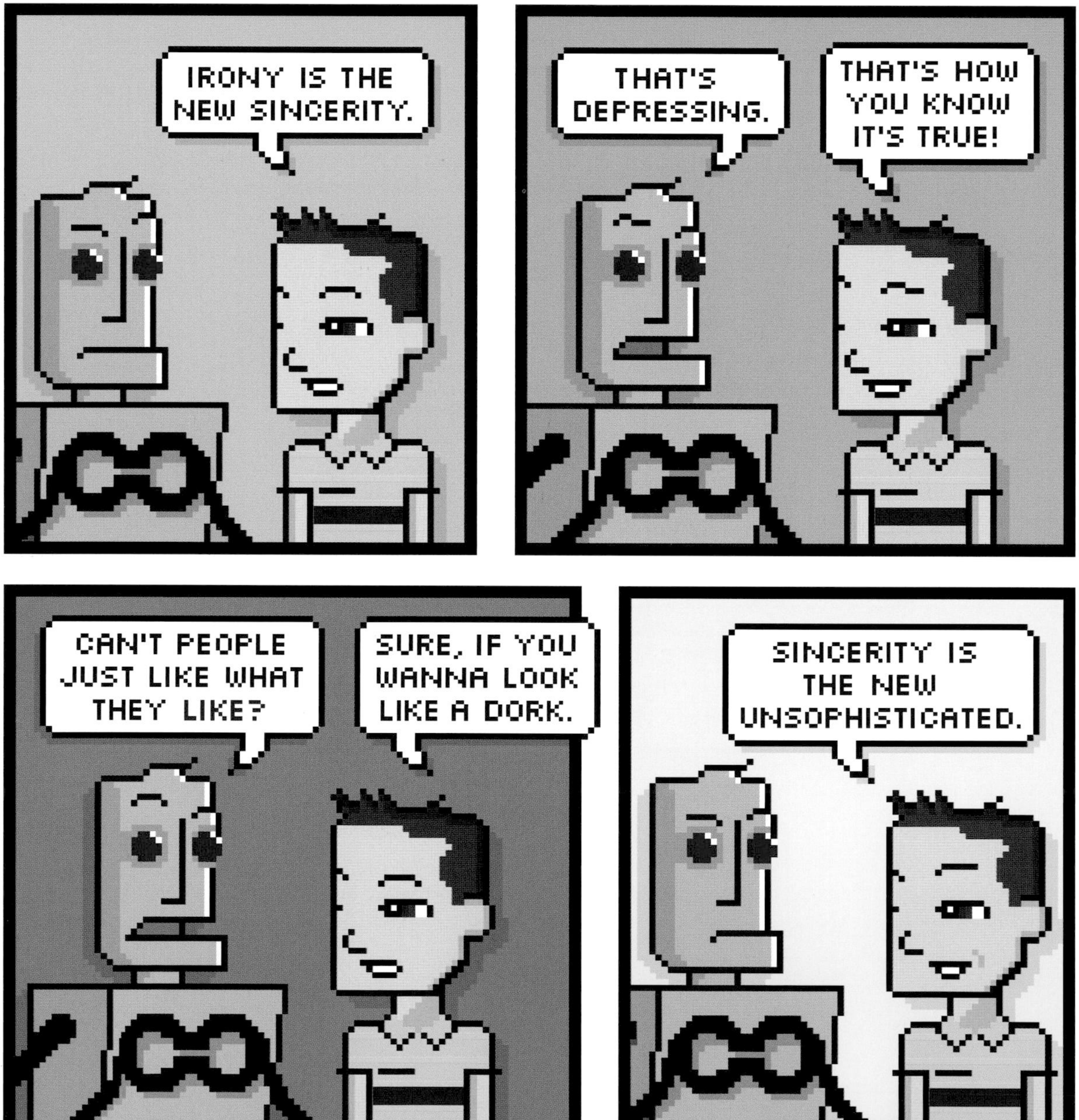
IRONY IS THE NEW SINCERITY.
THAT'S DEPRESSING.
THAT'S HOW YOU KNOW IT'S TRUE!
CAN'T PEOPLE JUST LIKE WHAT THEY LIKE?
SURE, IF YOU WANNA LOOK LIKE A DORK.
SINCERITY IS THE NEW UNSOPHISTICATED.

STRUCTURE

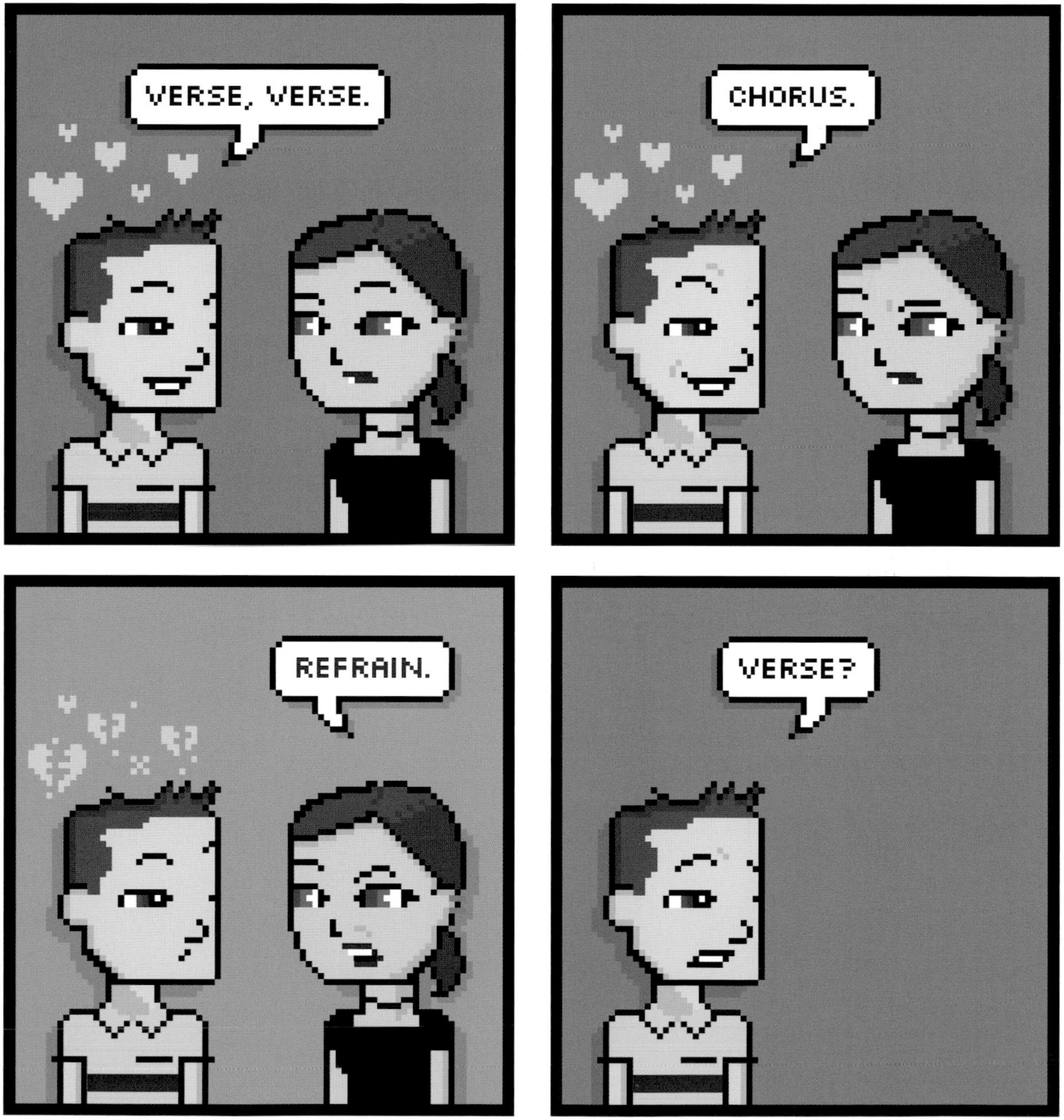
VERSE, VERSE.
CHORUS.
REFRAIN.
VERSE?

BACK UP PLANS

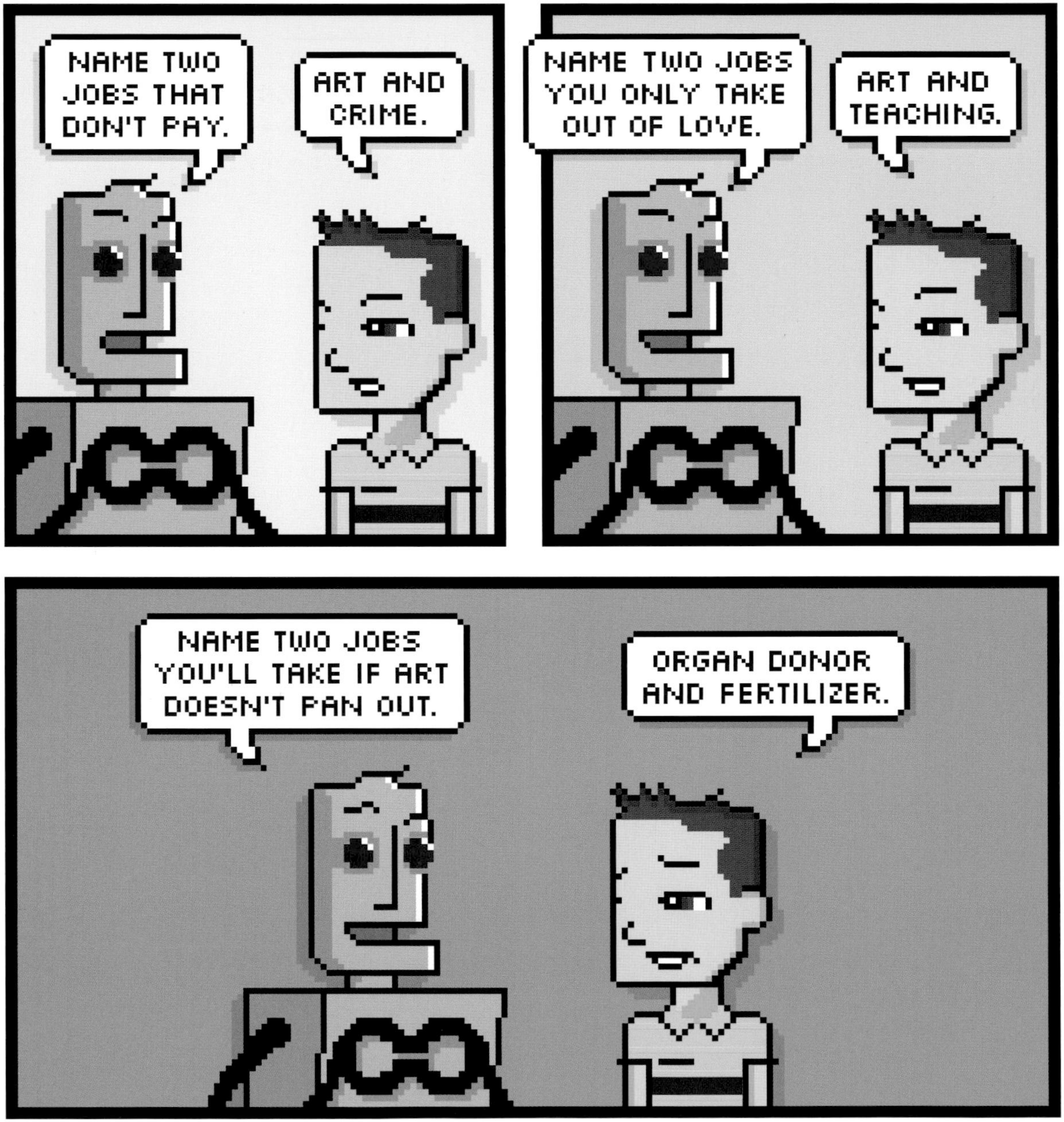
NAME TWO JOBS THAT DON'T PAY.
ART AND CRIME.
NAME TWO JOBS YOU ONLY TAKE OUT OF LOVE.
ART AND TEACHING.
NAME TWO JOBS YOU'LL TAKE IF ART DOESN'T PAN OUT.
ORGAN DONOR AND FERTILIZER.

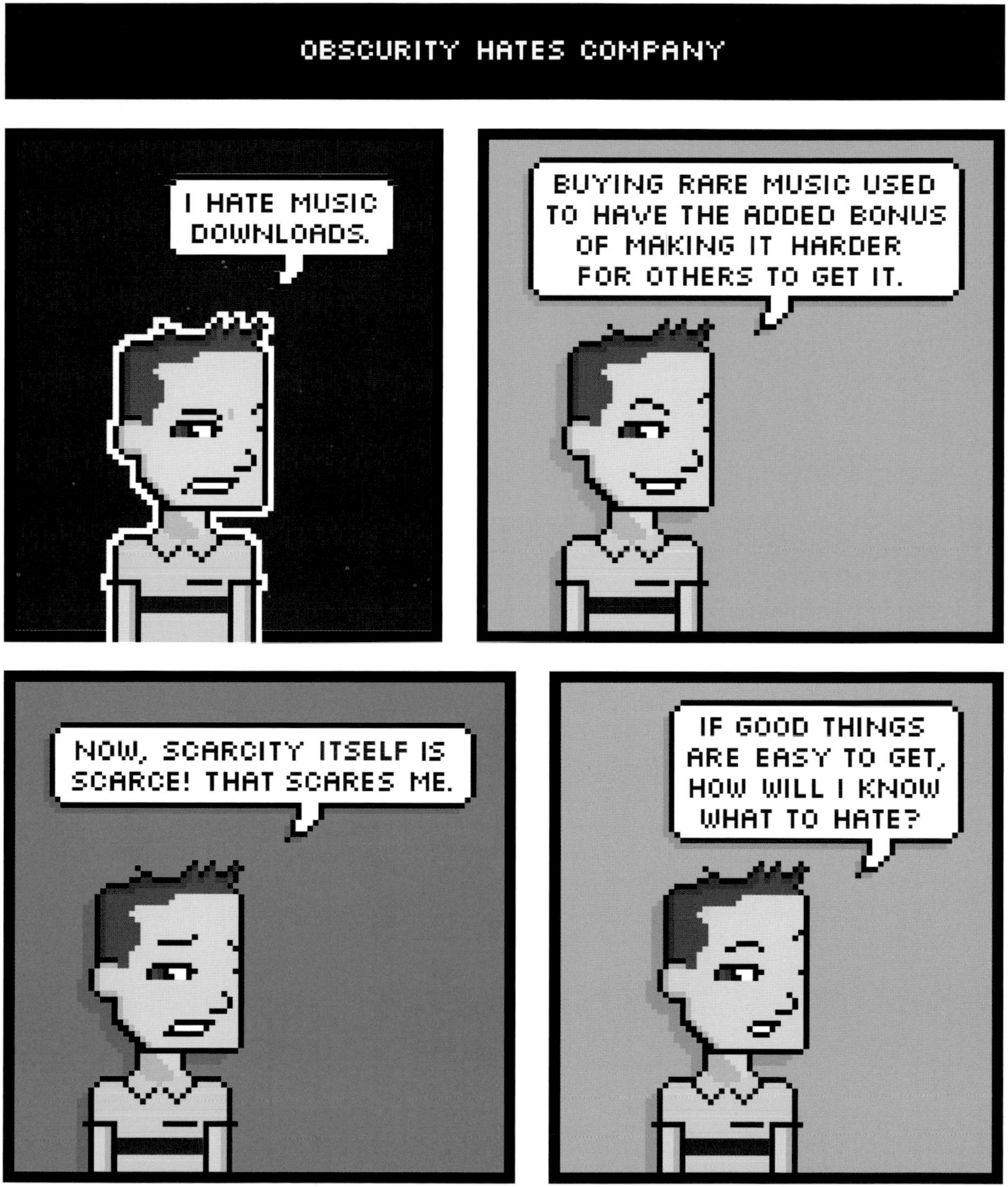
OBSCURITY HATES COMPANY
I HATE MUSIC DOWNLOADS.
BUYING RARE MUSIC USED TO HAVE THE ADDED BONUS OF MAKING IT HARDER FOR OTHERS TO GET IT.
NOW, SCARCITY ITSELF IS SCARCE! THAT SCARES ME.
IF GOOD THINGS ARE EASY TO GET, HOW WILL I KNOW WHAT TO HATE?

ELITISM = MASS MEDIA TIMES MEME SQUARED

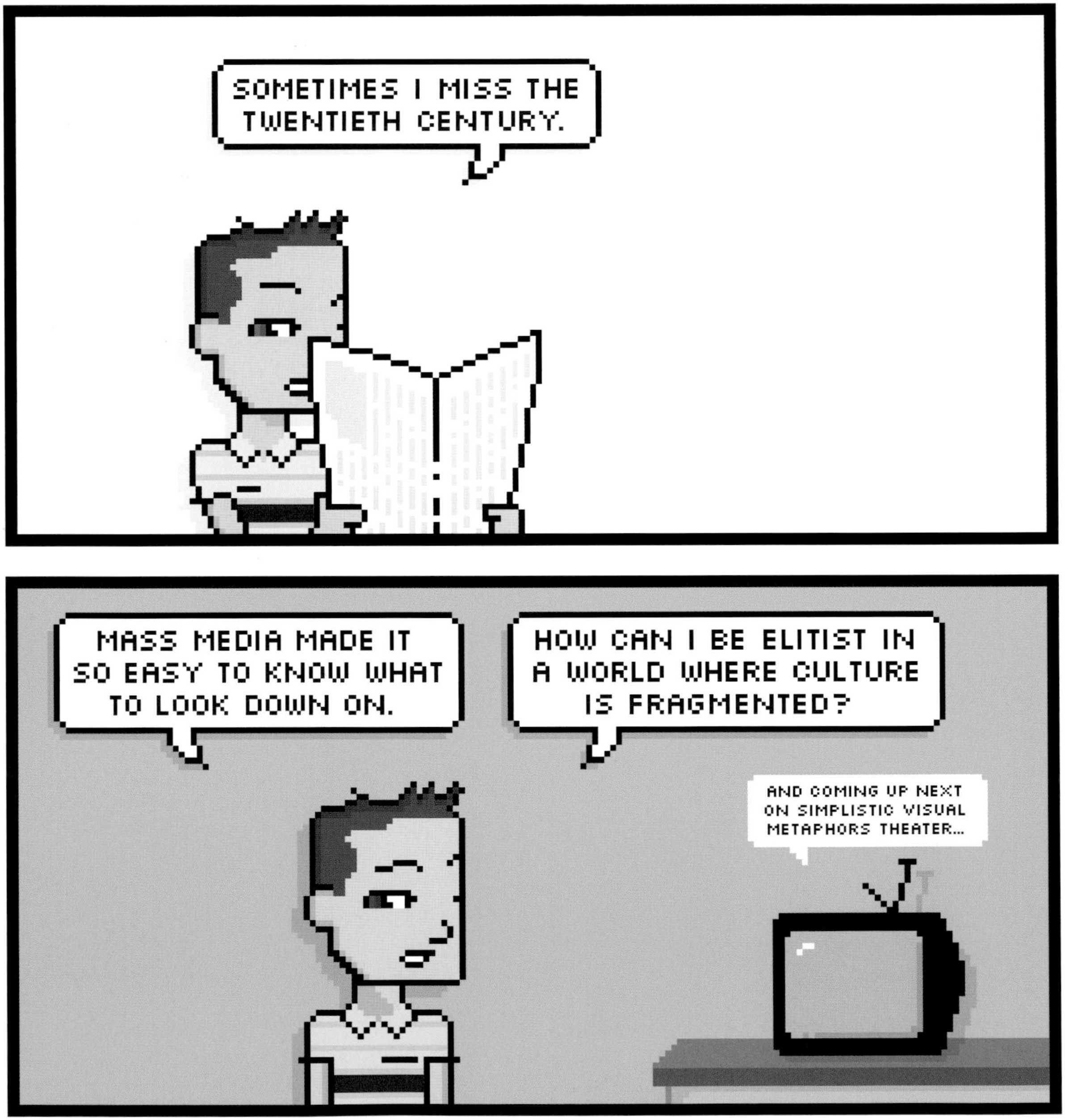
SOMETIMES I MISS THE TWENTIETH CENTURY.
MASS MEDIA MADE IT SO EASY TO KNOW WHAT TO LOOK DOWN ON.
HOW CAN I BE ELITIST IN A WORLD WHERE CULTURE IS FRAGMENTED?
AND COMING UP NEXT ON SIMPLISTIC VISUAL METAPHORS THEATER...

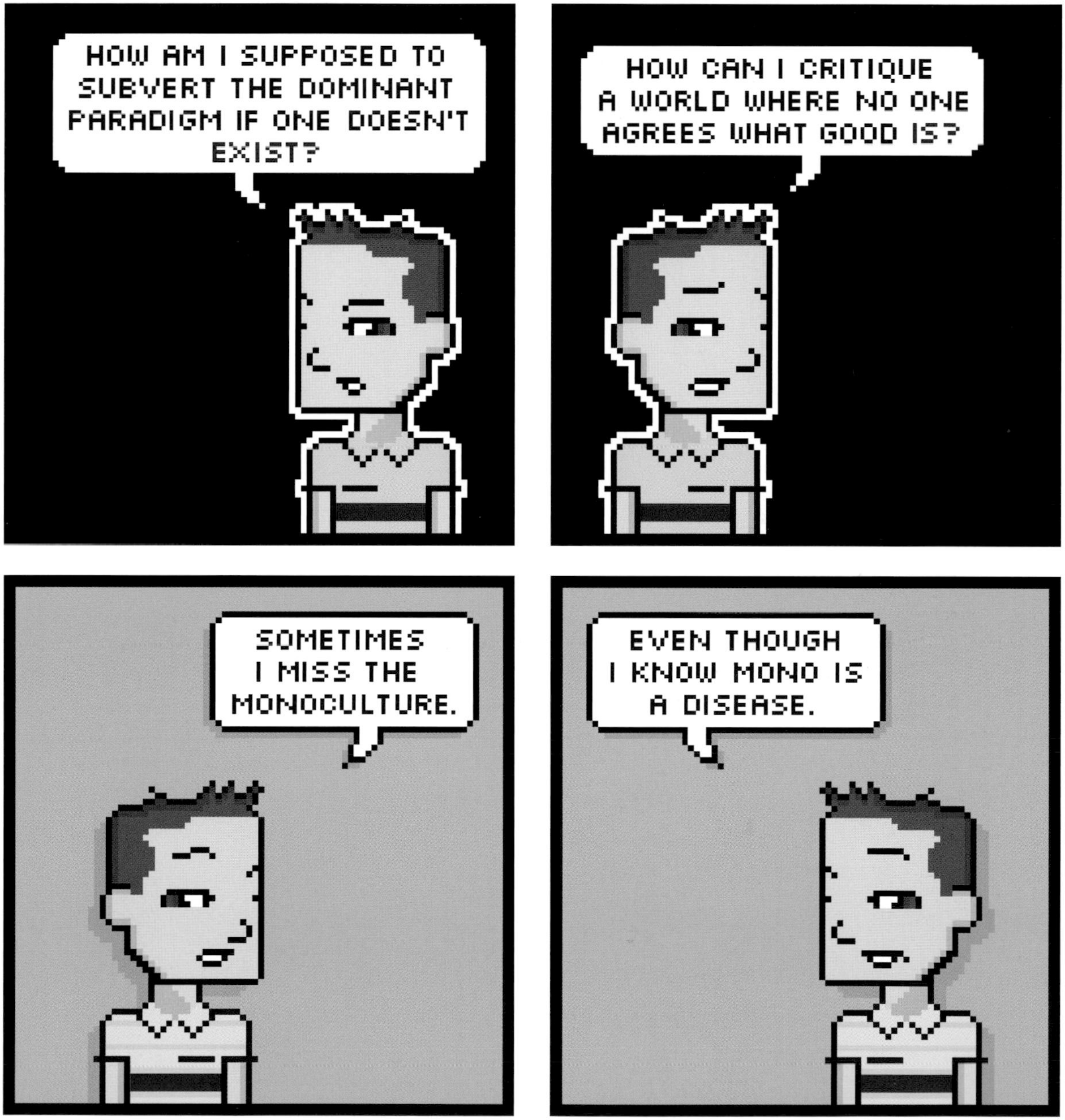
HOW AM I SUPPOSED TO SUBVERT THE DOMINANT PARADIGM IF ONE DOESN'T EXIST?
HOW CAN I CRITIQUE A WORLD WHERE NO ONE AGREES WHAT GOOD IS?
SOMETIMES I MISS THE MONOCULTURE.
EVEN THOUGH I KNOW MONO IS A DISEASE.

KING TOT

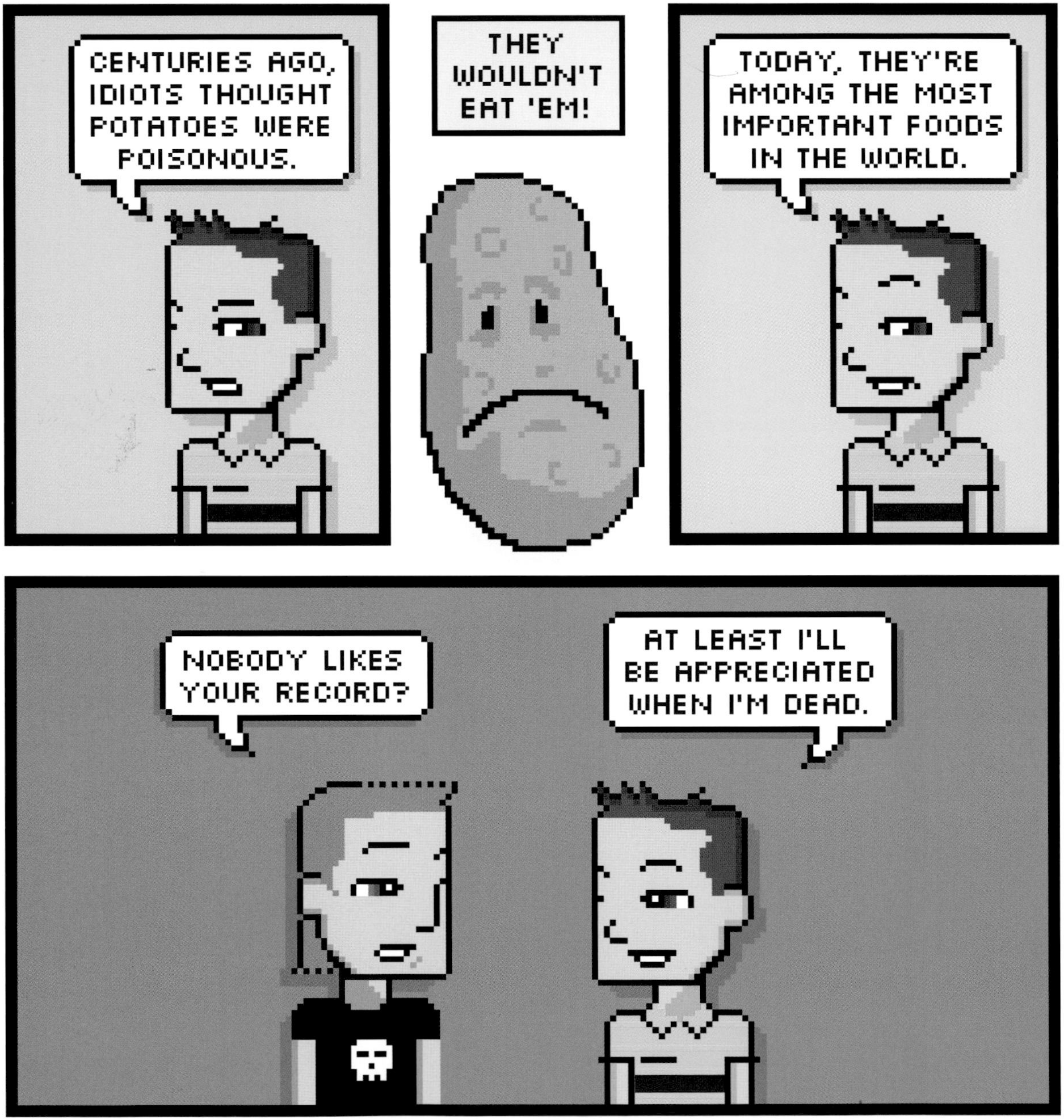

CENTURIES AGO, IDIOTS THOUGHT POTATOES WERE POISONOUS.
THEY WOULDN'T EAT 'EM!
TODAY, THEY'RE AMONG THE MOST IMPORTANT FOODS IN THE WORLD.
NOBODY LIKES YOUR RECORD?
AT LEAST I'LL BE APPRECIATED WHEN I'M DEAD.

THROUGH THE AGES

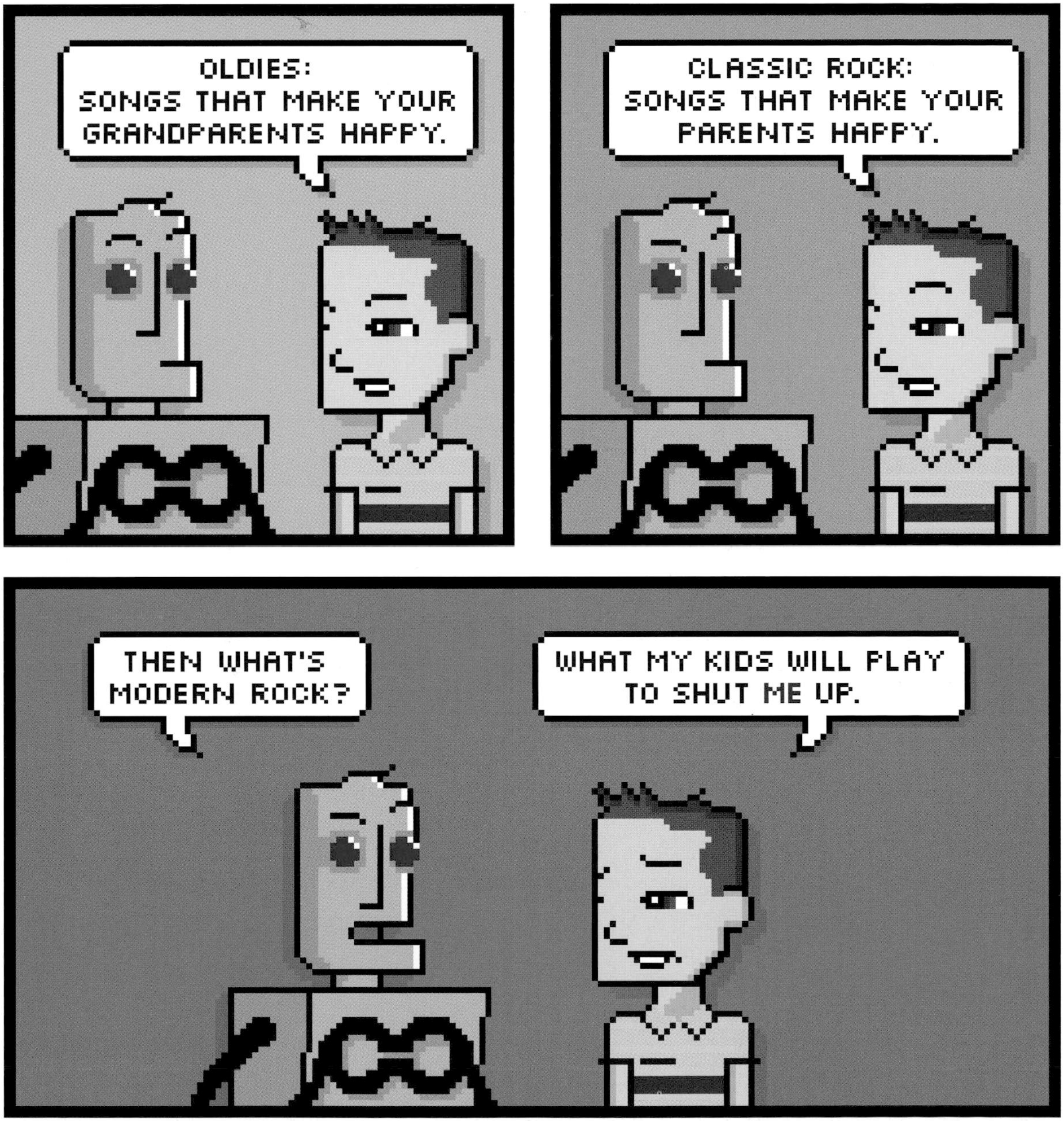

OLDIES:
SONGS THAT MAKE YOUR GRANDPARENTS HAPPY.
CLASSIC ROCK:
SONGS THAT MAKE YOUR PARENTS HAPPY.
THEN WHAT'S MODERN ROCK?
WHAT MY KIDS WILL PLAY TO SHUT ME UP.

HEIRLOOM APPLES AND ORANGES

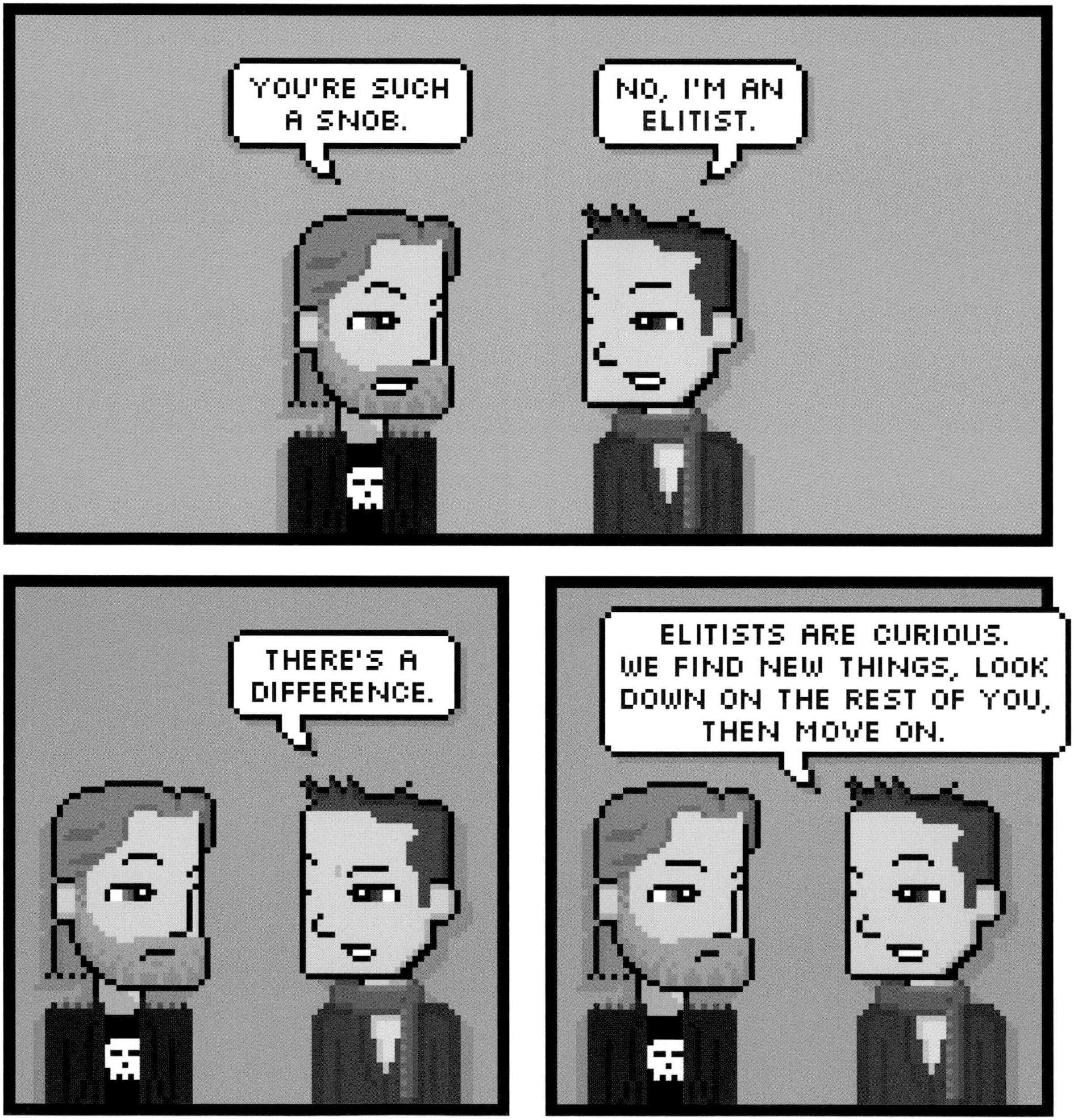
YOU'RE SUCH A SNOB.
NO, I'M AN ELITIST.
THERE'S A DIFFERENCE.
ELITISTS ARE CURIOUS. WE FIND NEW THINGS, LOOK DOWN ON THE REST OF YOU, THEN MOVE ON.

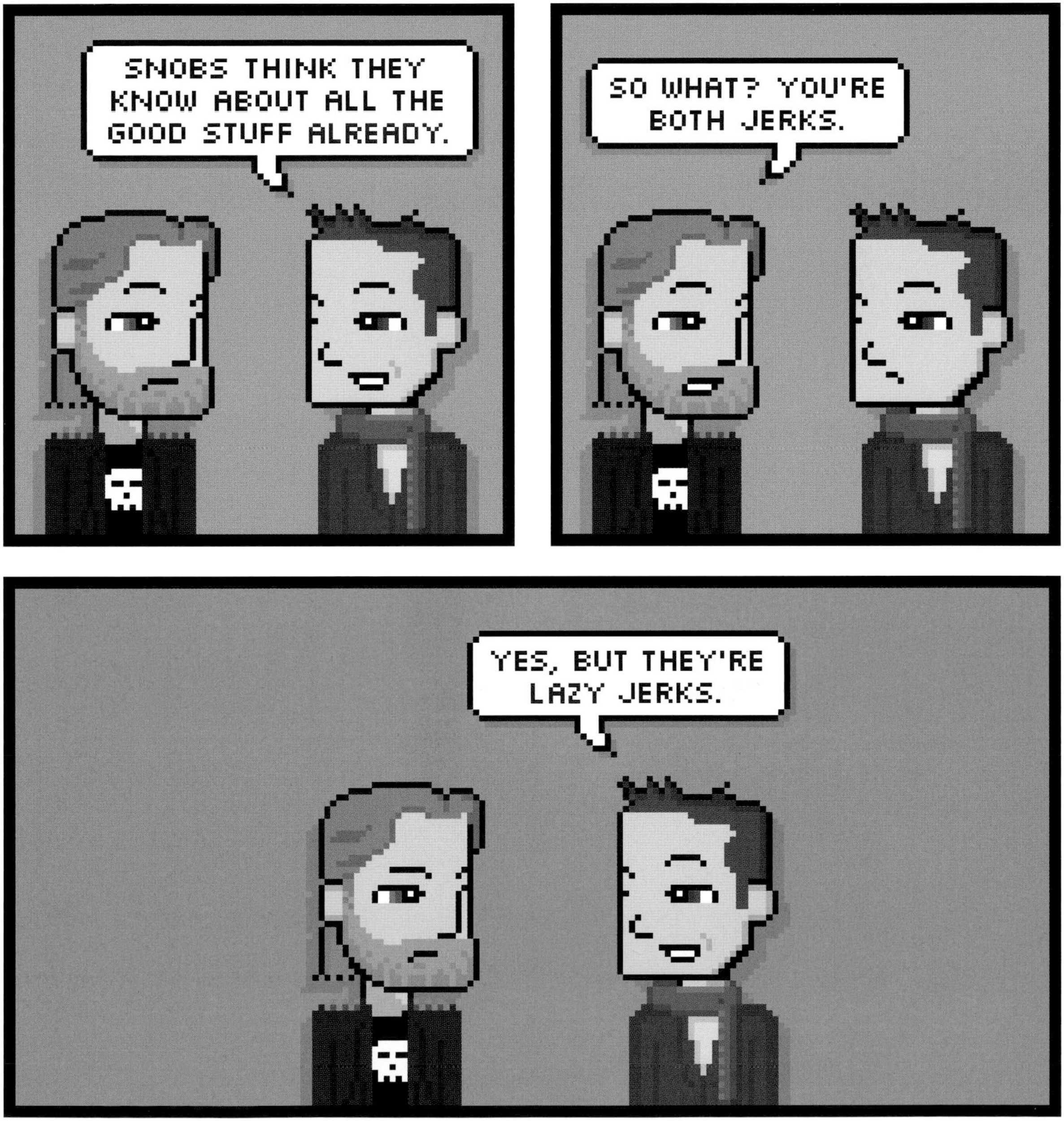
SNOBS THINK THEY KNOW ABOUT ALL THE GOOD STUFF ALREADY.
SO WHAT? YOU'RE BOTH JERKS.
YES, BUT THEY'RE LAZY JERKS.

DO ME A SOLID, LIKE A ROCK

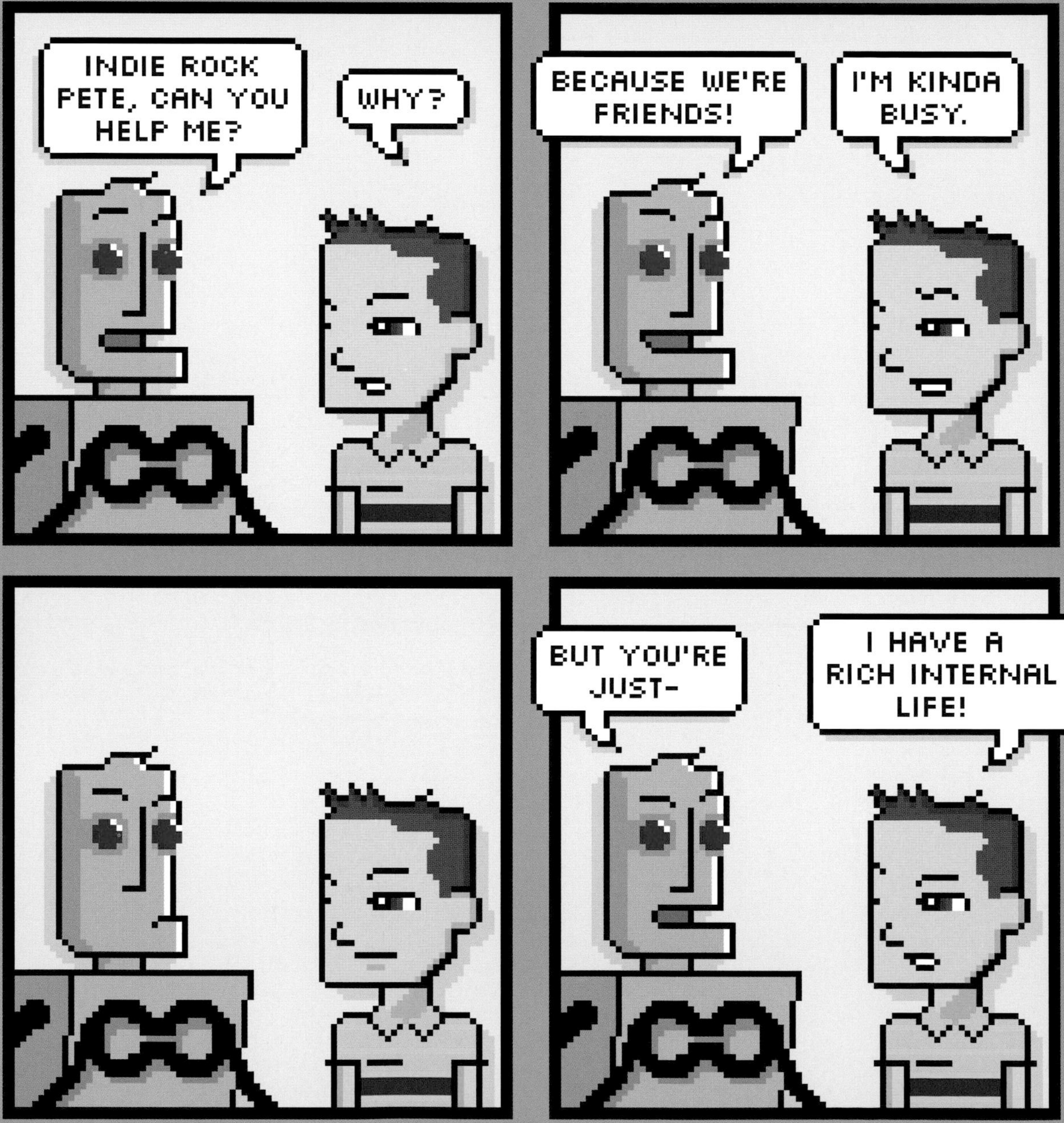
INDIE ROCK PETE, CAN YOU HELP ME?
WHY?
BECAUSE WE'RE FRIENDS!
I'M KINDA BUSY.
BUT YOU'RE JUST-
I HAVE A RICH INTERNAL LIFE!

MY GIRLFRIEND IS BEING ALL-
I DON'T HAVE TIME FOR GIRLS.
I PLAY KEYBOARDS. IN A BAND!
I'M A ROCKER. I ROCK OUT.

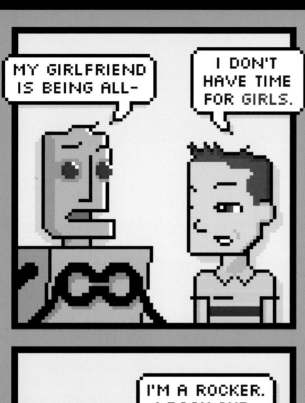

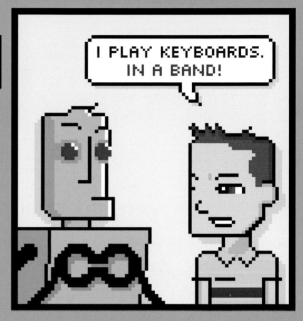

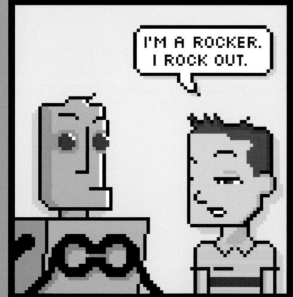

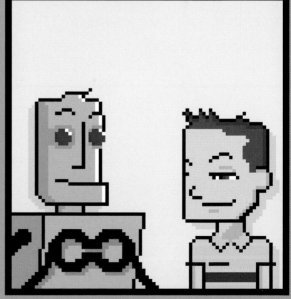

INTERSECTIONS

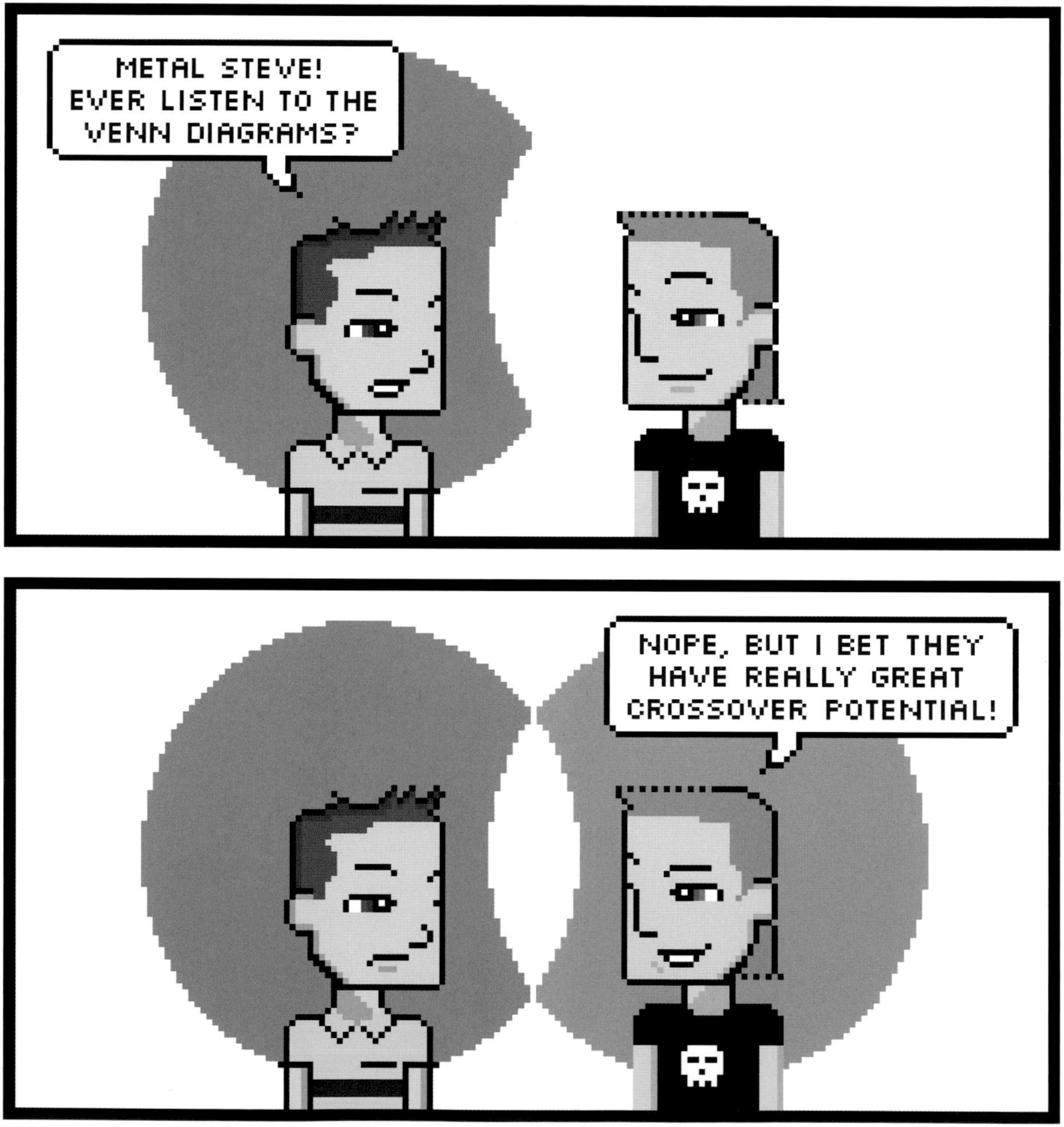
METAL STEVE! EVER LISTEN TO THE VENN DIAGRAMS?
NOPE, BUT I BET THEY HAVE REALLY GREAT CROSSOVER POTENTIAL!

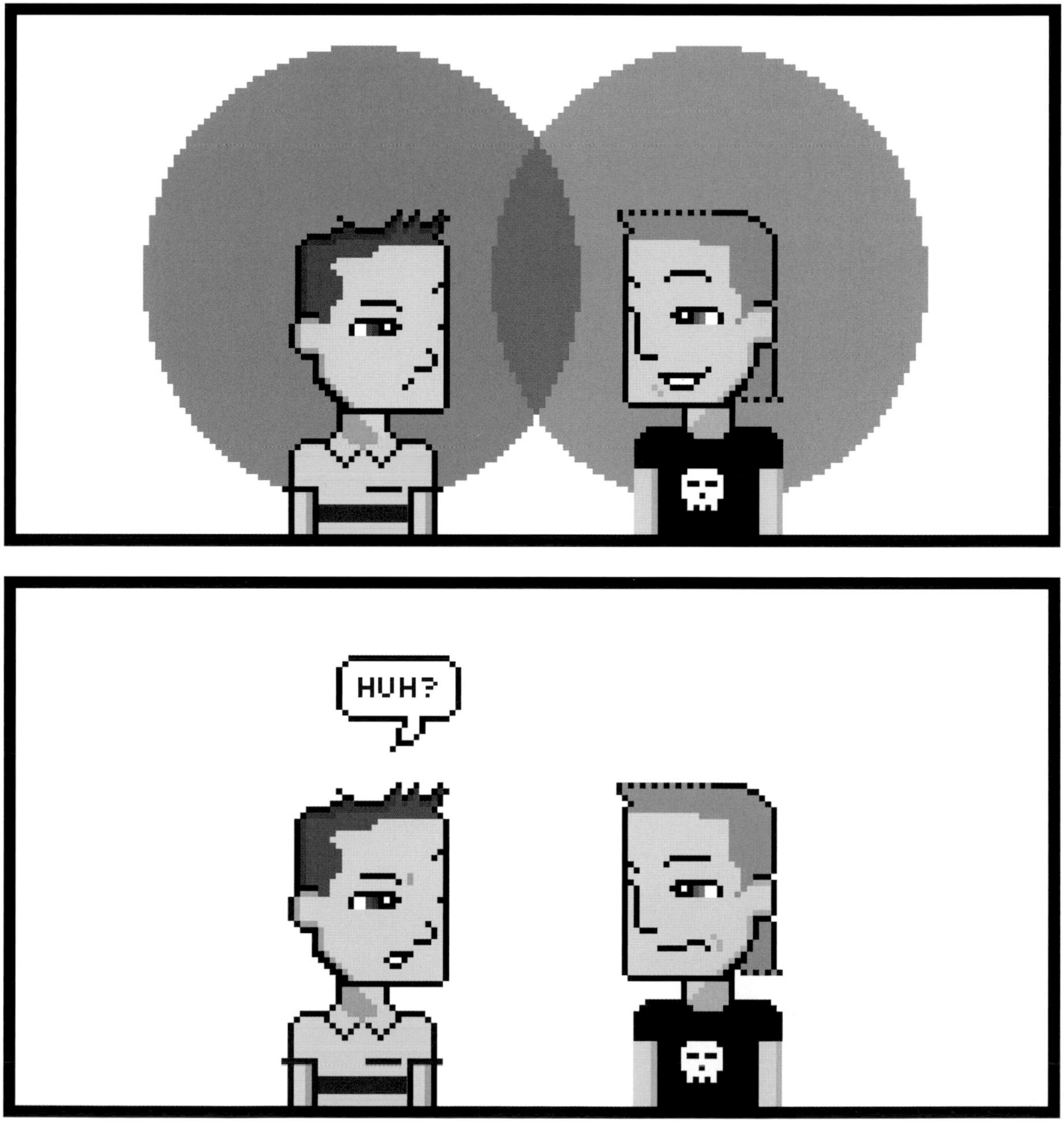
HUH?

LIVING AT FACE VALUE

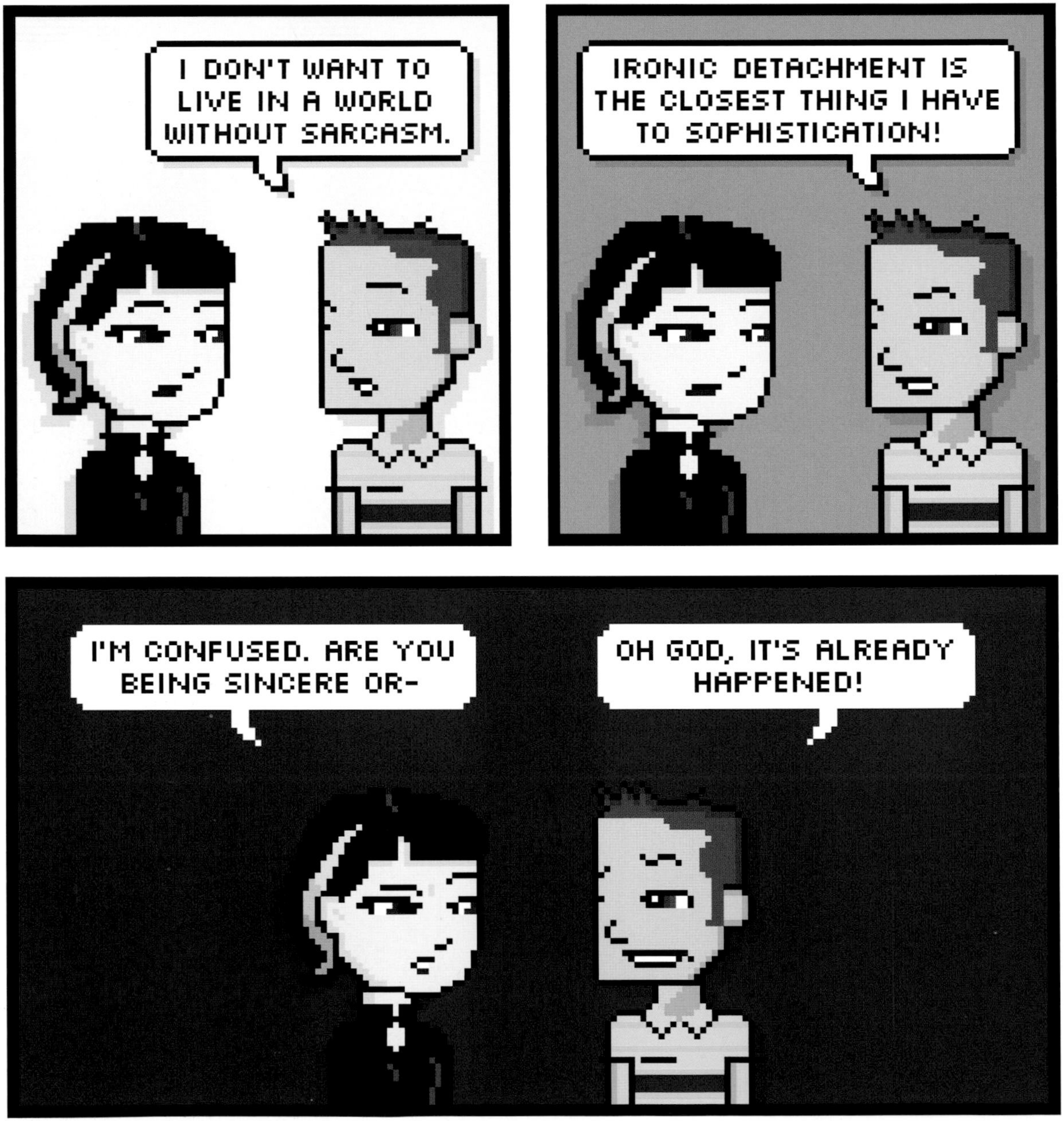
I DON'T WANT TO LIVE IN A WORLD WITHOUT SARCASM.
IRONIC DETACHMENT IS THE CLOSEST THING I HAVE TO SOPHISTICATION!
I'M CONFUSED. ARE YOU BEING SINCERE OR-
OH GOD, IT'S ALREADY HAPPENED!

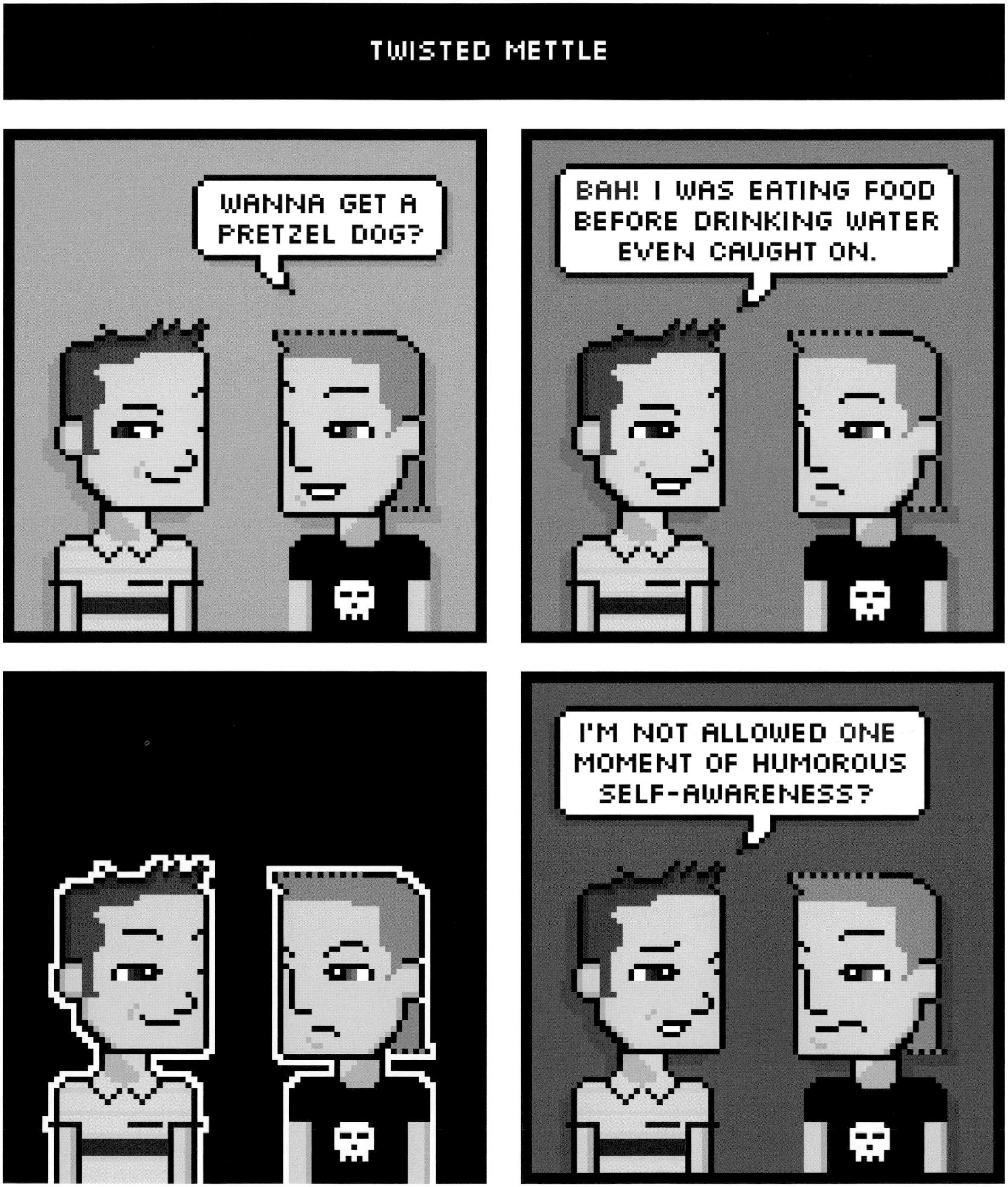

TWISTED METTLE
WANNA GET A PRETZEL DOG?
BAH! I WAS EATING FOOD BEFORE DRINKING WATER EVEN CAUGHT ON.
I'M NOT ALLOWED ONE MOMENT OF HUMOROUS SELF-AWARENESS?

WHAT'S IN A NAME?

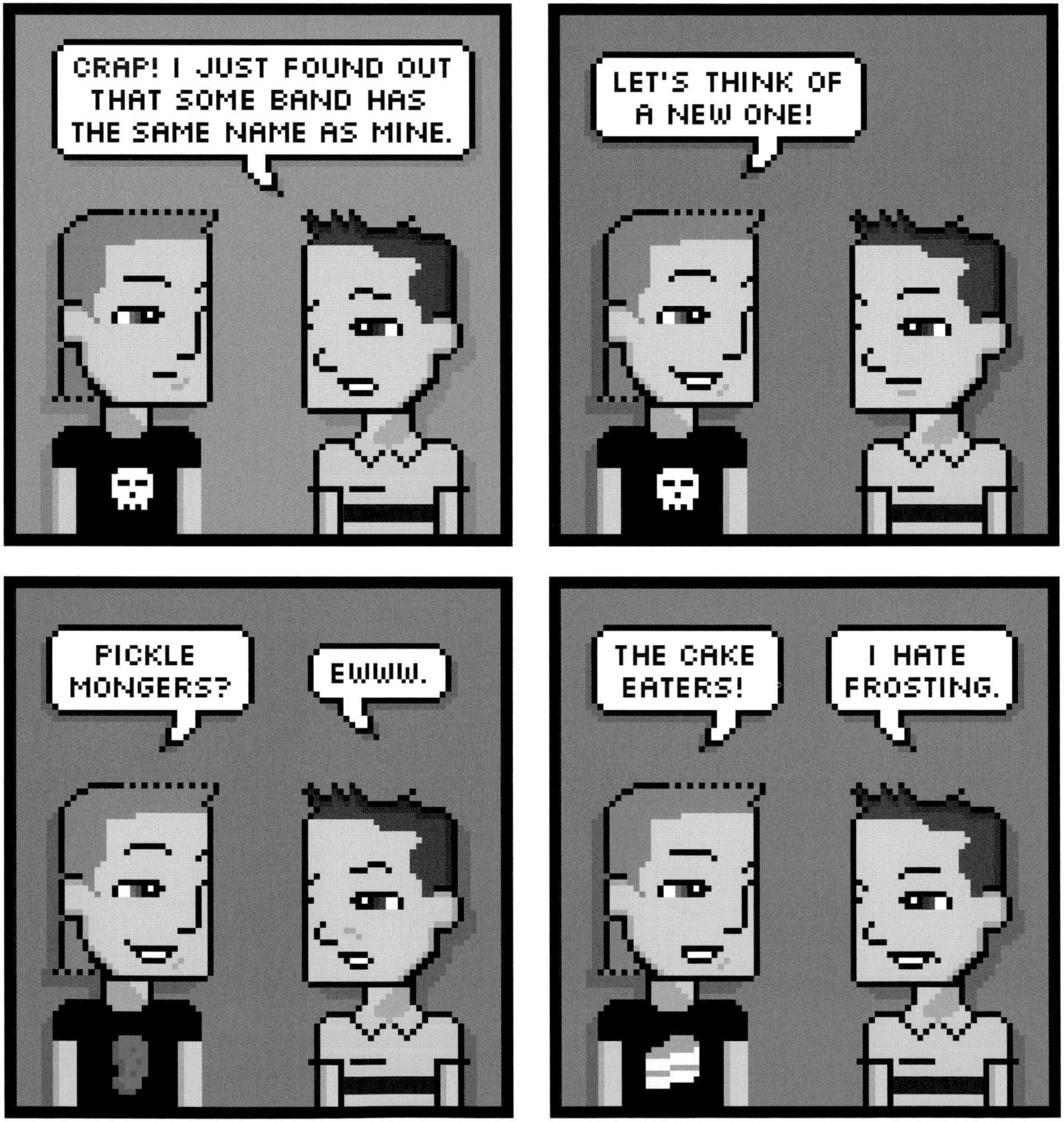
CRAP! I JUST FOUND OUT THAT SOME BAND HAS THE SAME NAME AS MINE.
LET'S THINK OF A NEW ONE!
PICKLE MONGERS?
EWWW.
THE CAKE EATERS!
I HATE FROSTING.

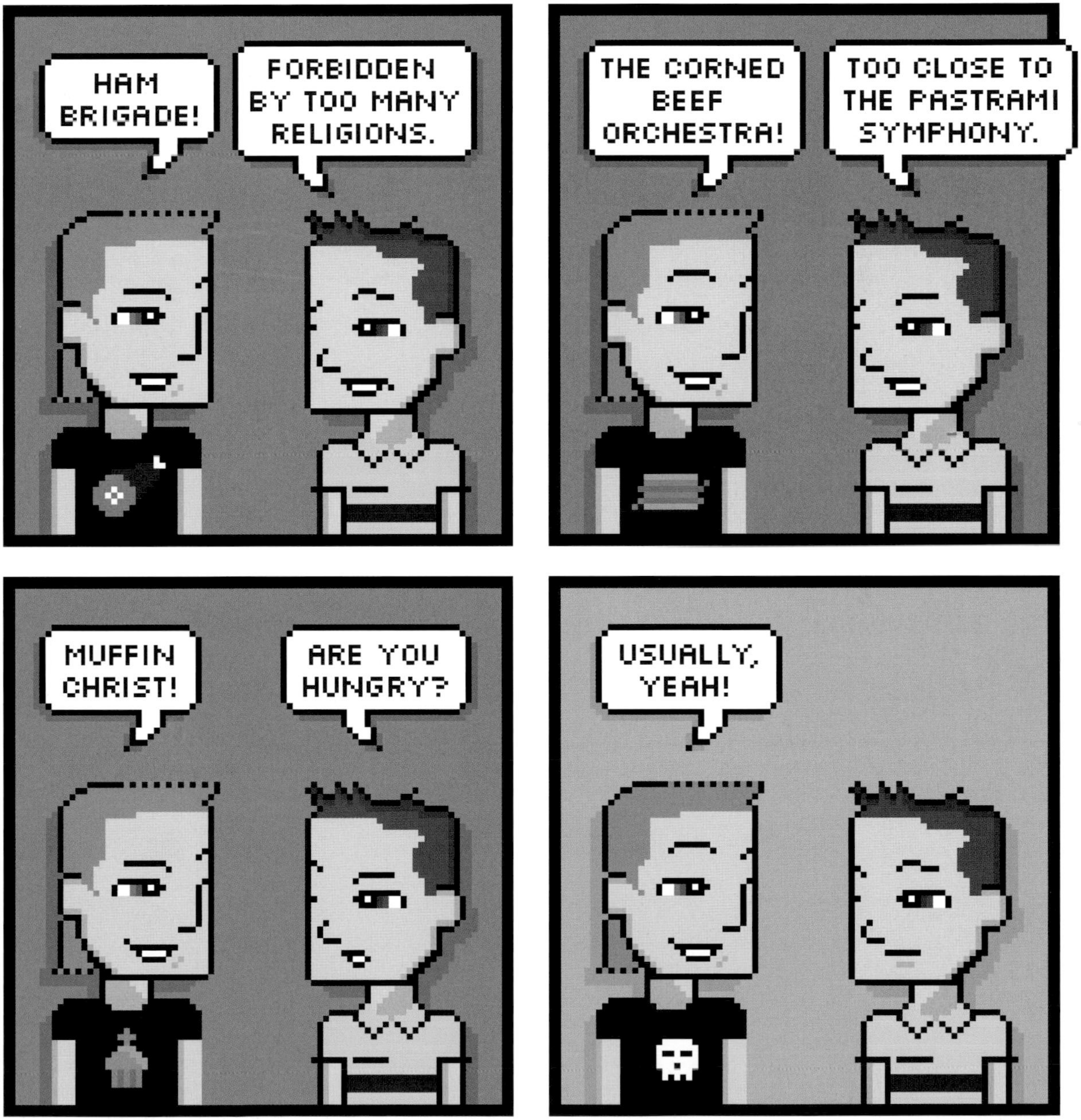
HAM BRIGADE!
FORBIDDEN BY TOO MANY RELIGIONS.
THE CORNED BEEF ORCHESTRA!
TOO CLOSE TO THE PASTRAMI SYMPHONY.
MUFFIN CHRIST!
ARE YOU HUNGRY?
USUALLY, YEAH!

PHILOSOPHOMORIC

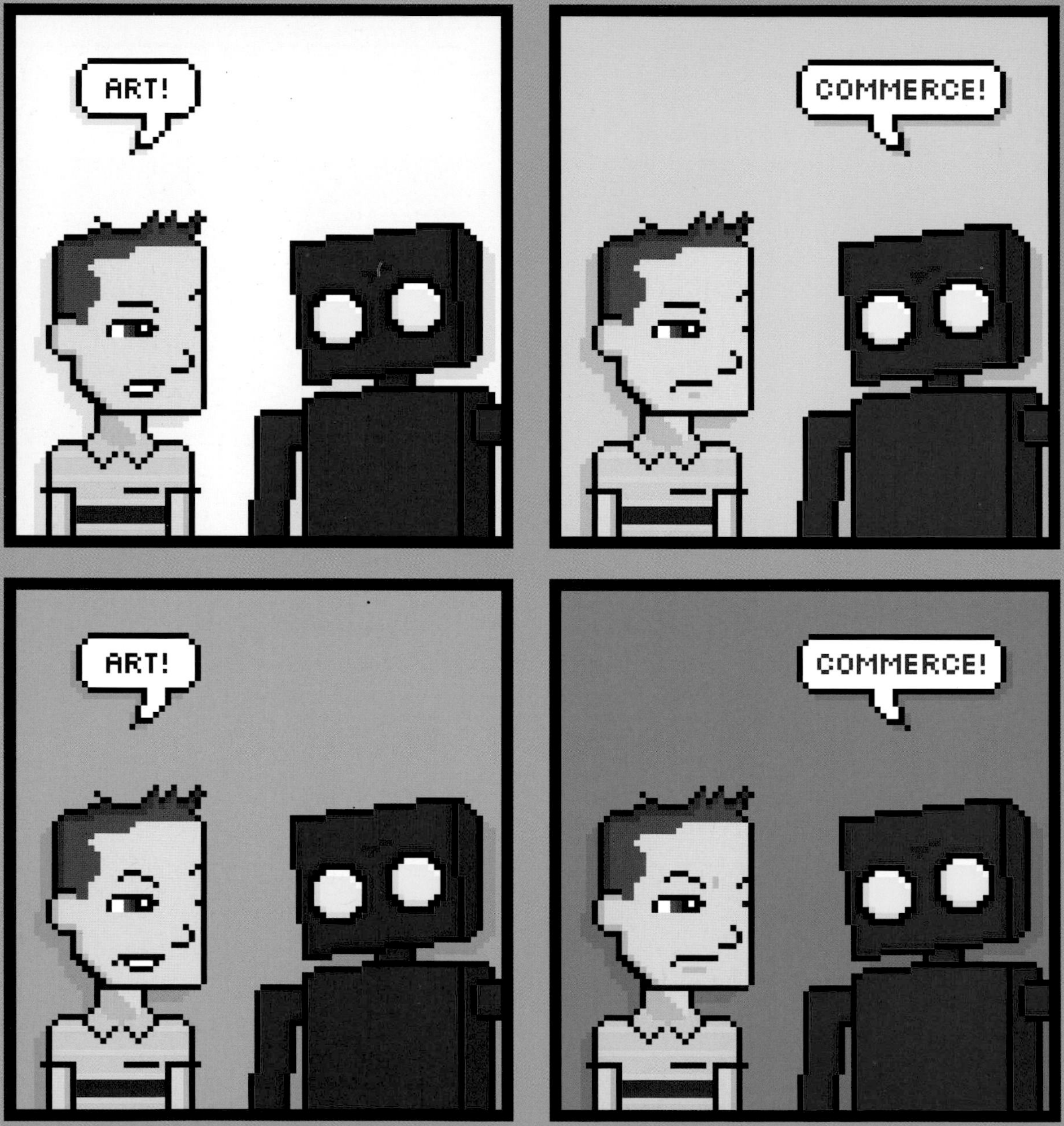

ART!
COMMERCE!
ART!
COMMERCE!

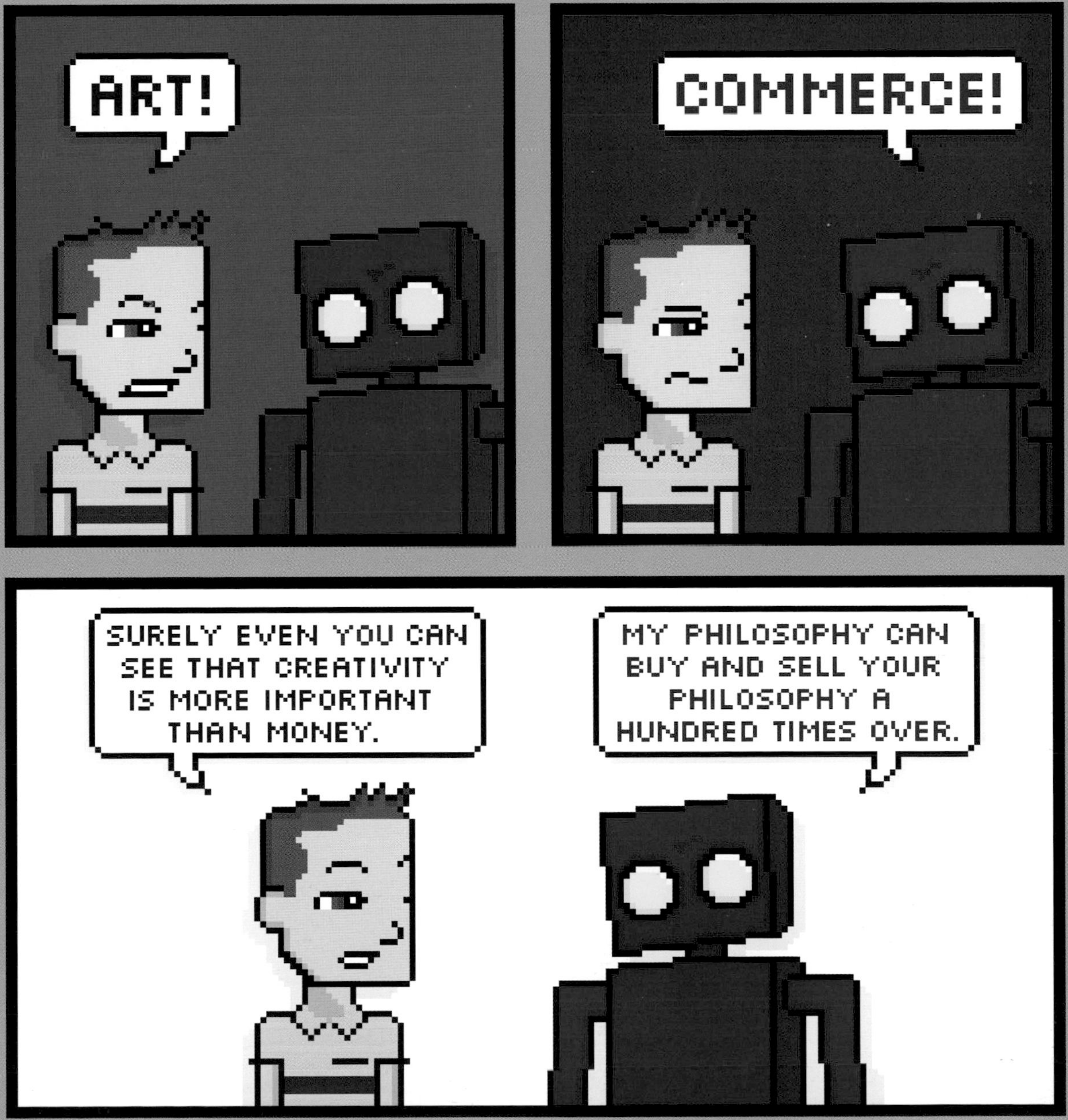
ART!
COMMERCE!
SURELY EVEN YOU CAN SEE THAT CREATIVITY IS MORE IMPORTANT THAN MONEY.
MY PHILOSOPHY CAN BUY AND SELL YOUR PHILOSOPHY A HUNDRED TIMES OVER.

THE TEMPING POINT

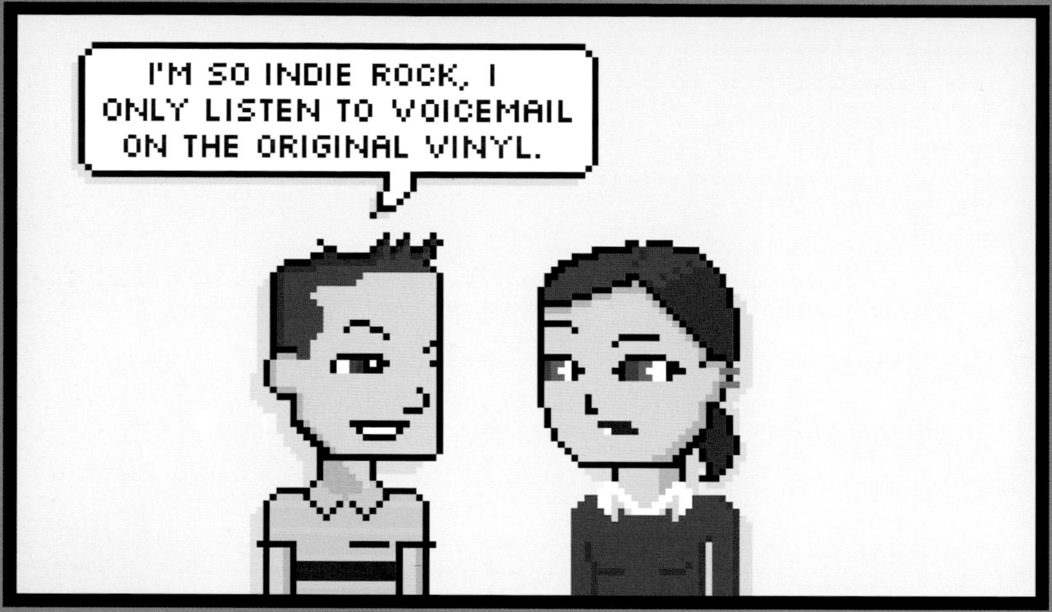
I'M SO INDIE ROCK, I ONLY LISTEN TO VOICEMAIL ON THE ORIGINAL VINYL.

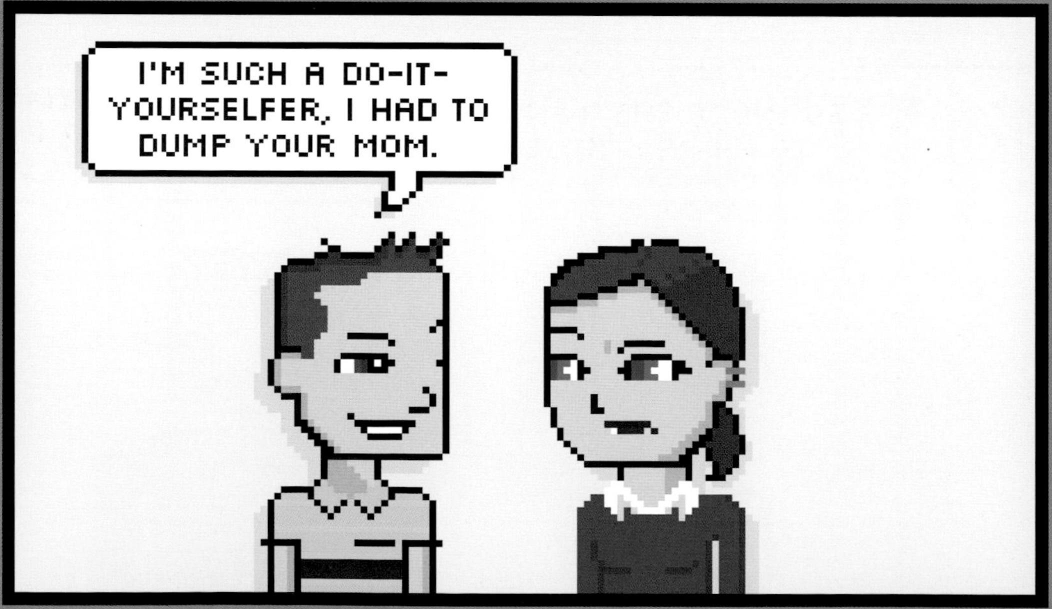
I'M SUCH A DO-IT-YOURSELFER, I HAD TO DUMP YOUR MOM.

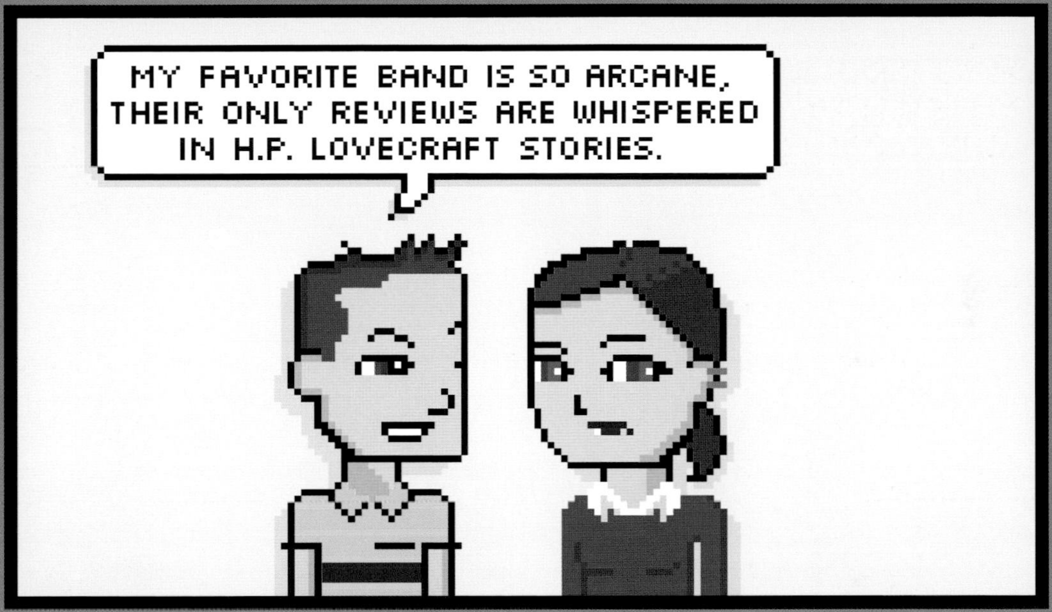
MY FAVORITE BAND IS SO ARCANE, THEIR ONLY REVIEWS ARE WHISPERED IN H.P. LOVECRAFT STORIES.

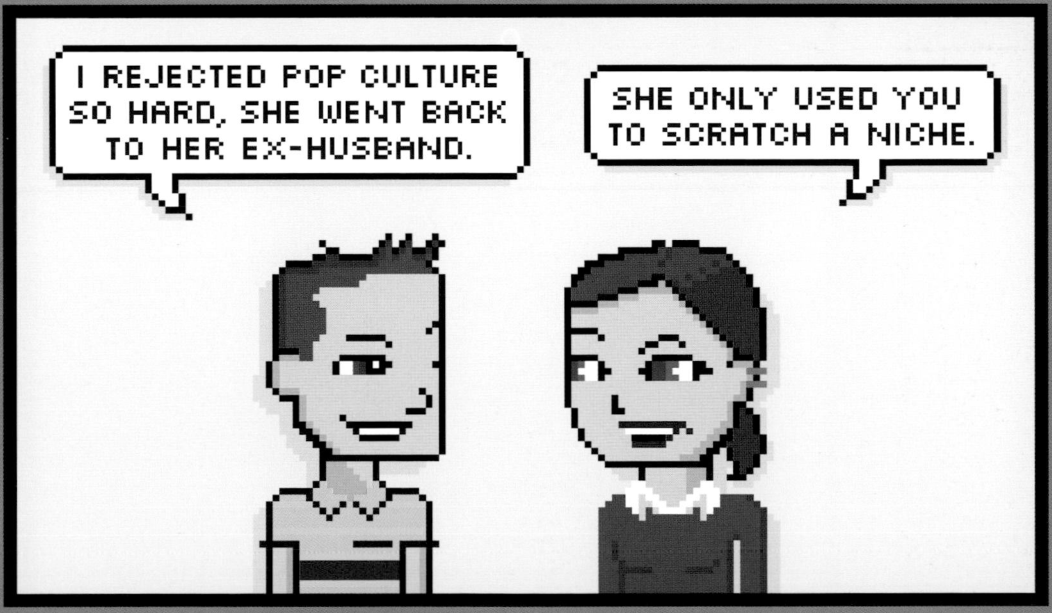
I REJECTED POP CULTURE SO HARD, SHE WENT BACK TO HER EX-HUSBAND.
SHE ONLY USED YOU TO SCRATCH A NICHE.

IN DAYS OF OLD, WHEN GENIUSES WERE SUB

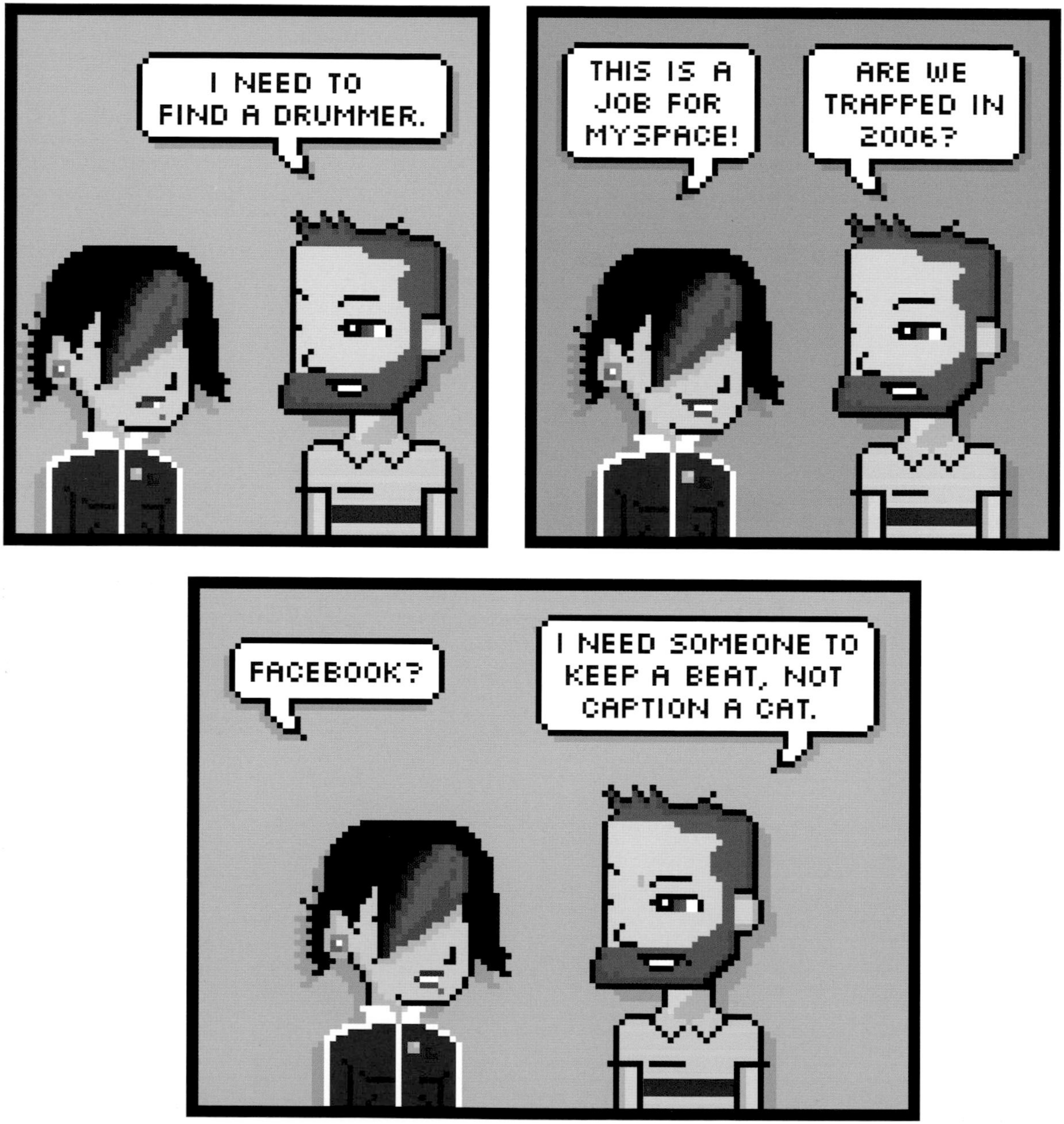
I NEED TO FIND A DRUMMER.
THIS IS A JOB FOR MYSPACE!
ARE WE TRAPPED IN 2006?
FACEBOOK?
I NEED SOMEONE TO KEEP A BEAT, NOT CAPTION A CAT.

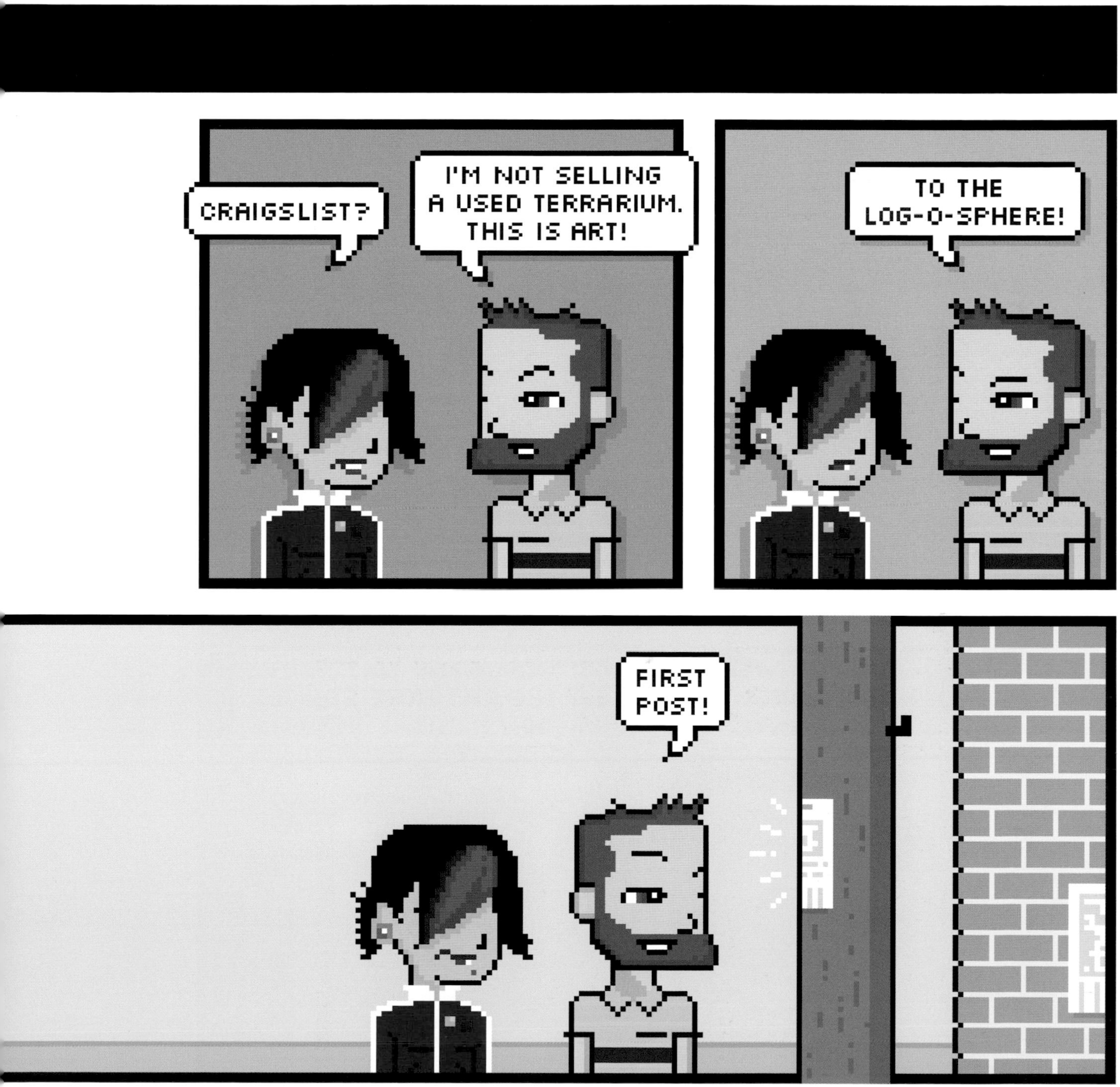
CRAIGSLIST?
I'M NOT SELLING A USED TERRARIUM. THIS IS ART!
TO THE LOG-O-SPHERE!
FIRST POST!

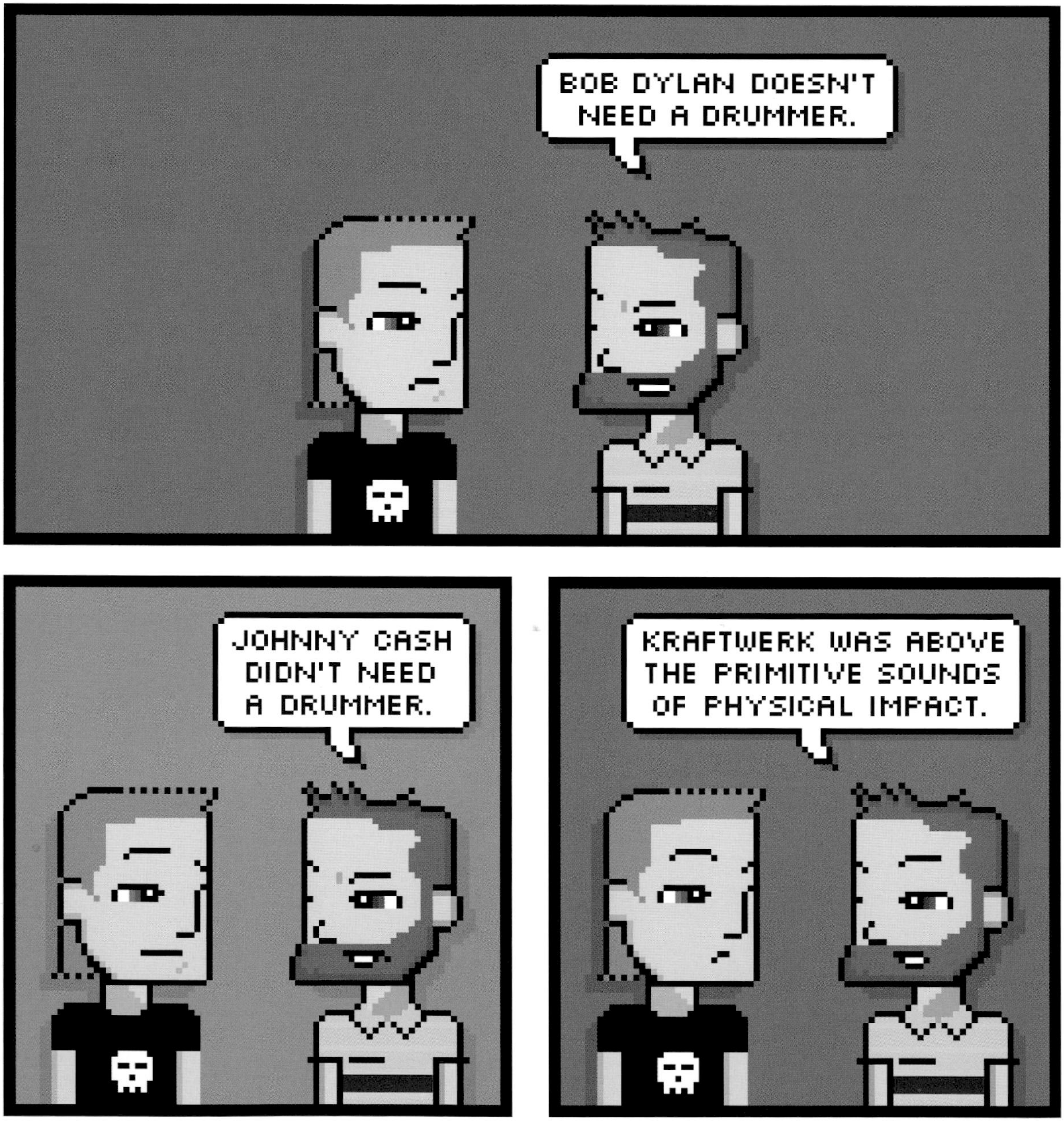
BOB DYLAN DOESN'T NEED A DRUMMER.
JOHNNY CASH DIDN'T NEED A DRUMMER.
KRAFTWERK WAS ABOVE THE PRIMITIVE SOUNDS OF PHYSICAL IMPACT.

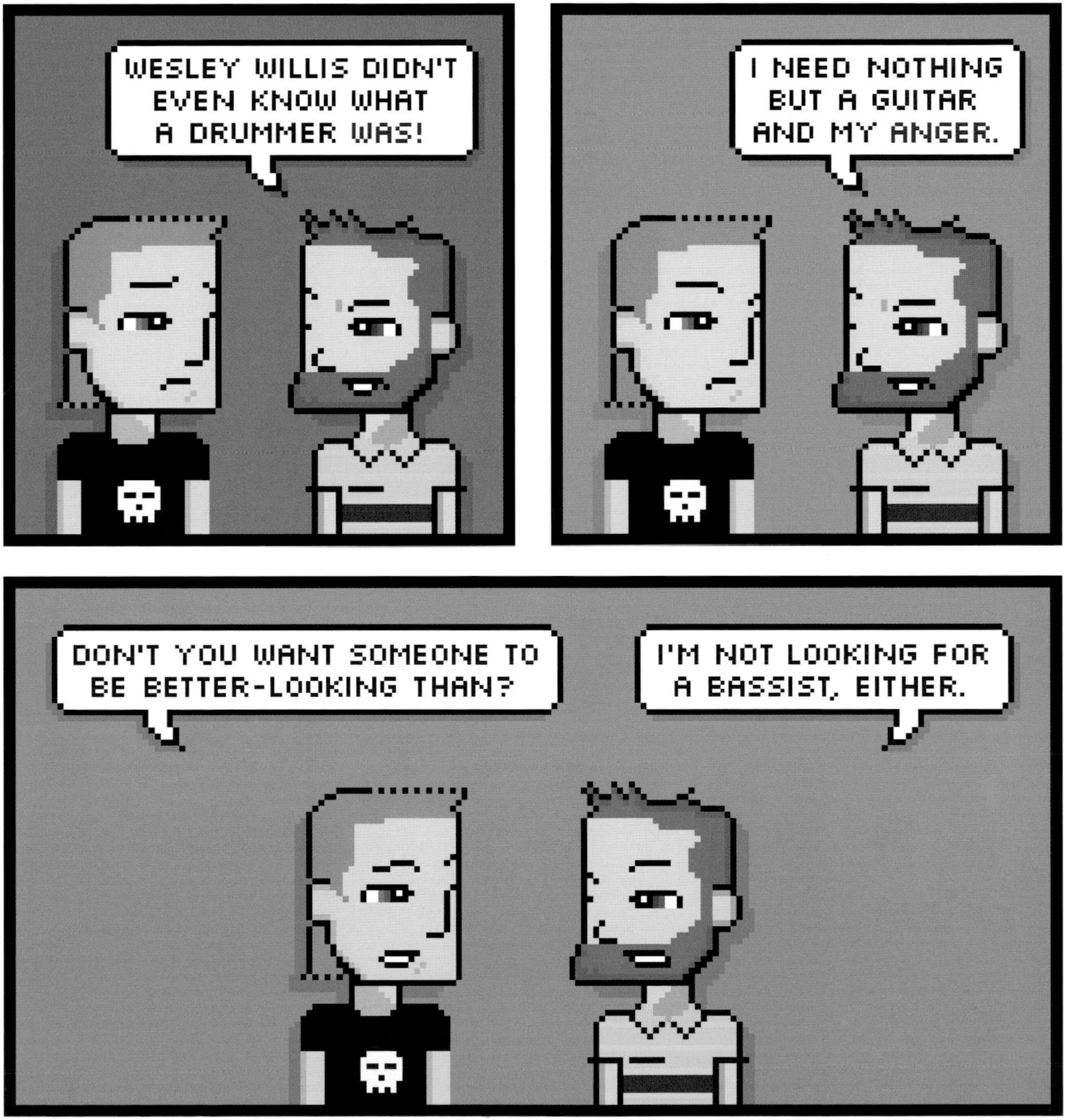
WESLEY WILLIS DIDN'T EVEN KNOW WHAT A DRUMMER WAS!
I NEED NOTHING BUT A GUITAR AND MY ANGER.
DON'T YOU WANT SOMEONE TO BE BETTER-LOOKING THAN?
I'M NOT LOOKING FOR A BASSIST, EITHER.

THOSE WHO CAN'T POO, TEACH

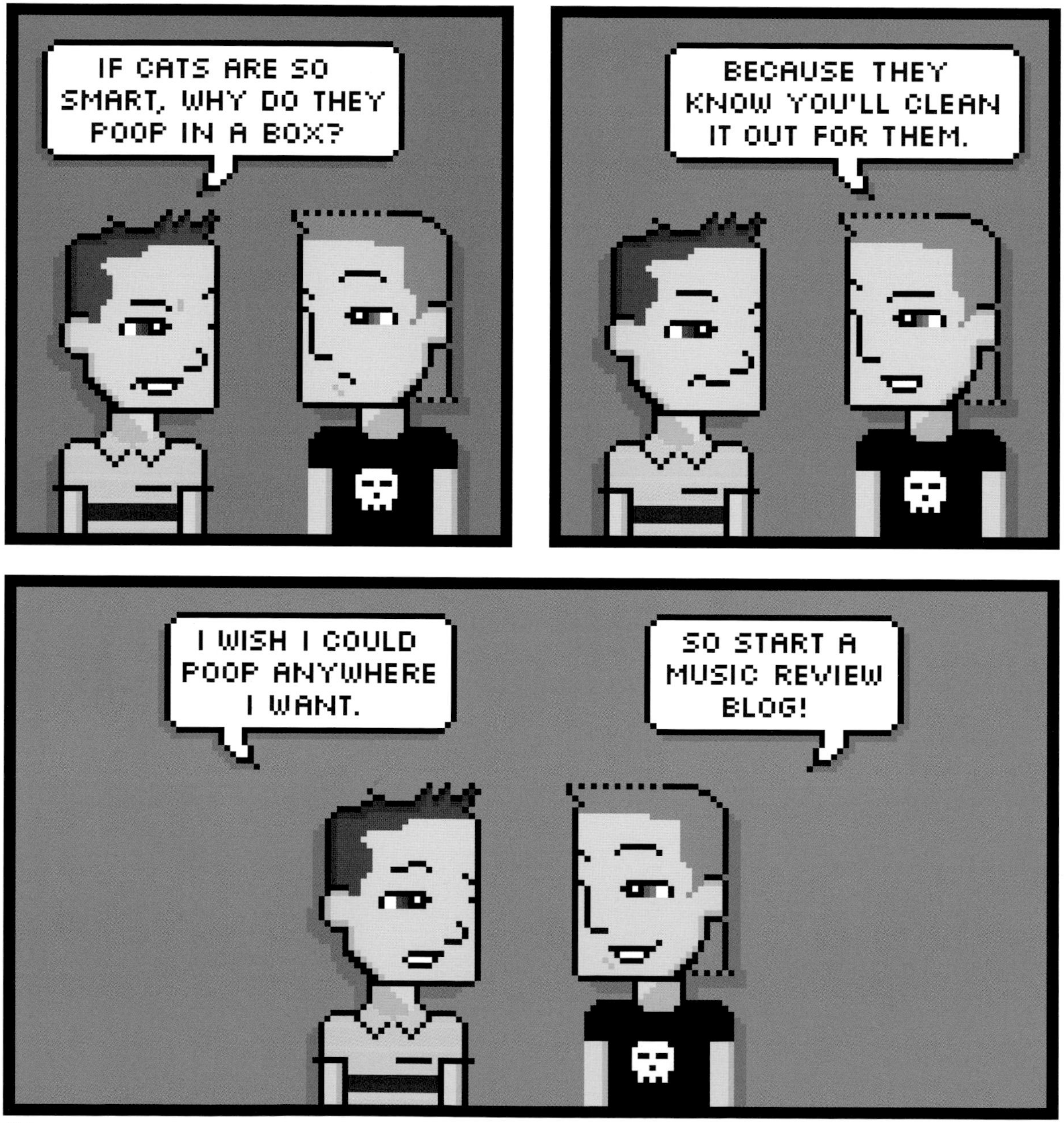
IF CATS ARE SO SMART, WHY DO THEY POOP IN A BOX?
BECAUSE THEY KNOW YOU'LL CLEAN IT OUT FOR THEM.
I WISH I COULD POOP ANYWHERE I WANT.
SO START A MUSIC REVIEW BLOG!

THE BURDEN

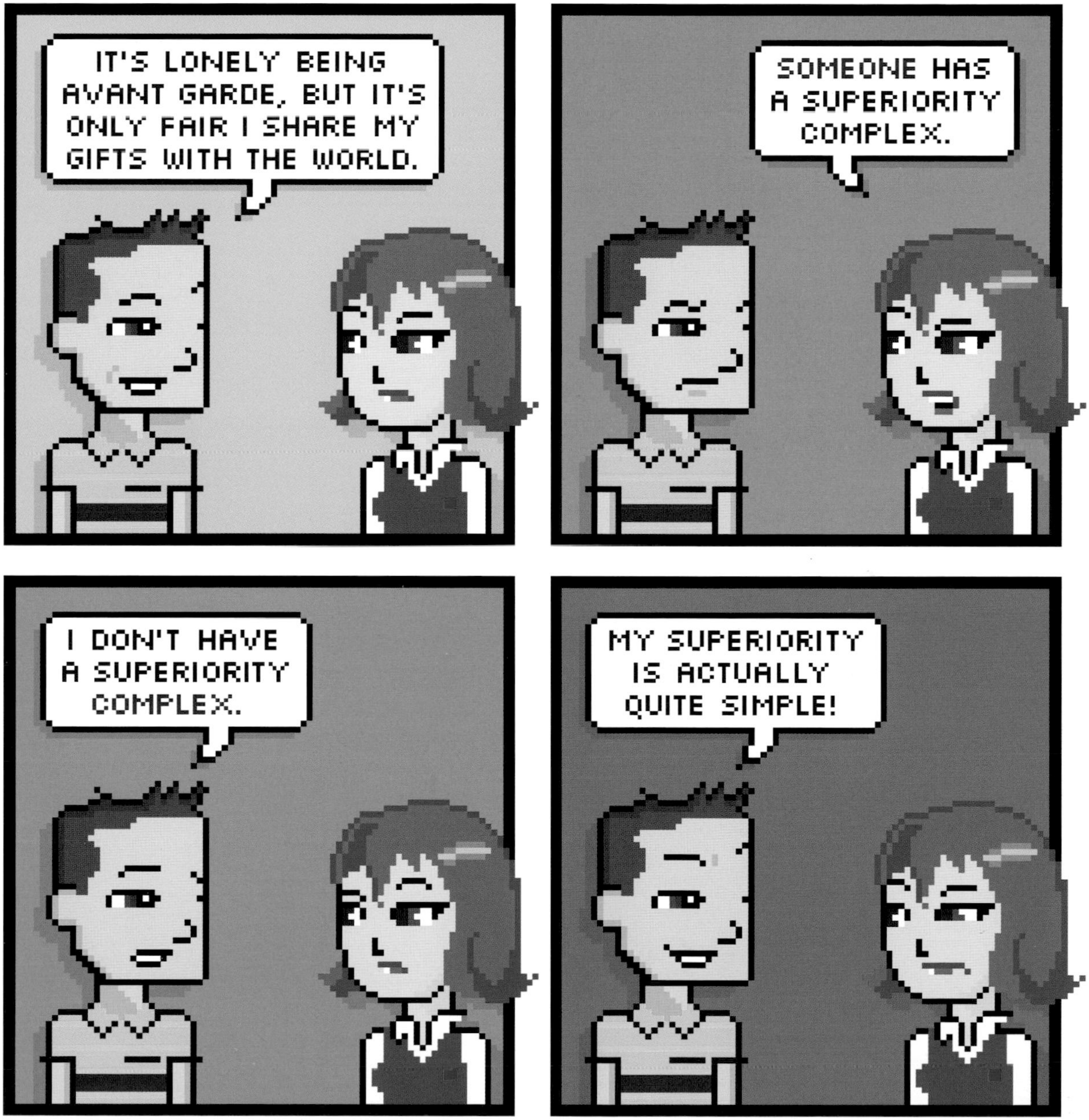

IT'S LONELY BEING AVANT GARDE, BUT IT'S ONLY FAIR I SHARE MY GIFTS WITH THE WORLD.
SOMEONE HAS A SUPERIORITY COMPLEX.
I DON'T HAVE A SUPERIORITY COMPLEX.
MY SUPERIORITY IS ACTUALLY QUITE SIMPLE!

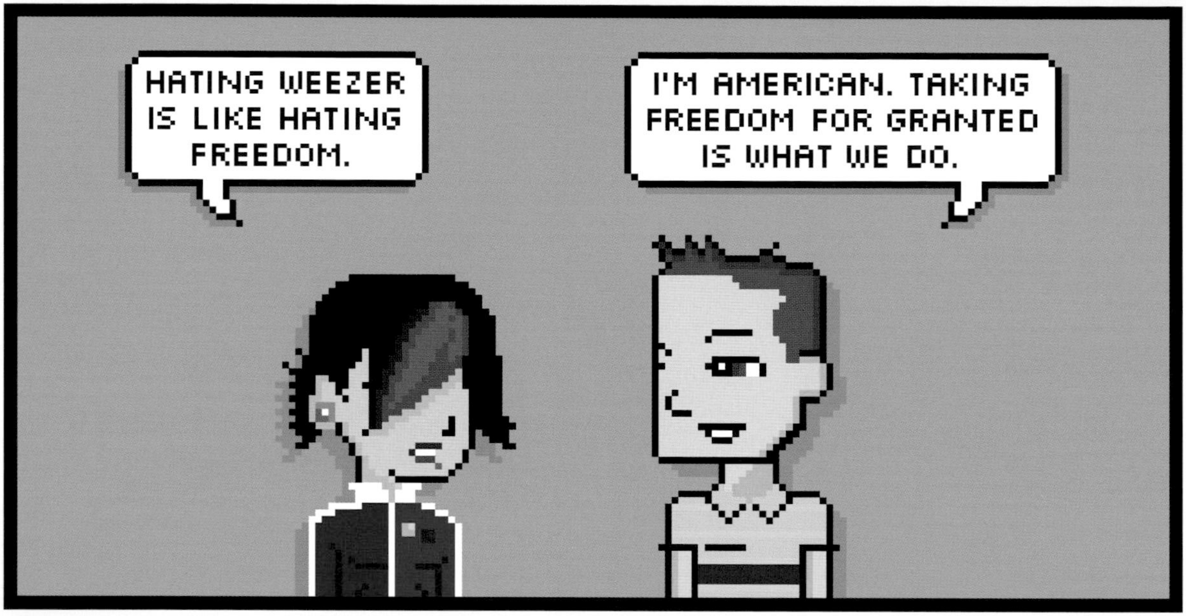
HATING WEEZER IS LIKE HATING FREEDOM.
I'M AMERICAN. TAKING FREEDOM FOR GRANTED IS WHAT WE DO.

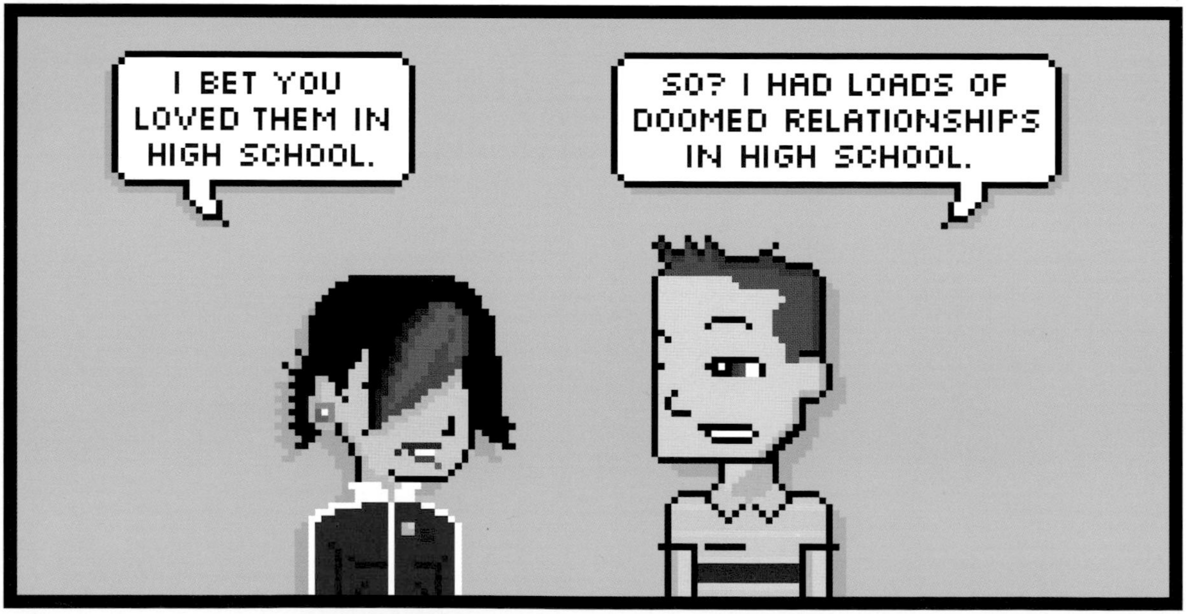
I BET YOU LOVED THEM IN HIGH SCHOOL.
SO? I HAD LOADS OF DOOMED RELATIONSHIPS IN HIGH SCHOOL.

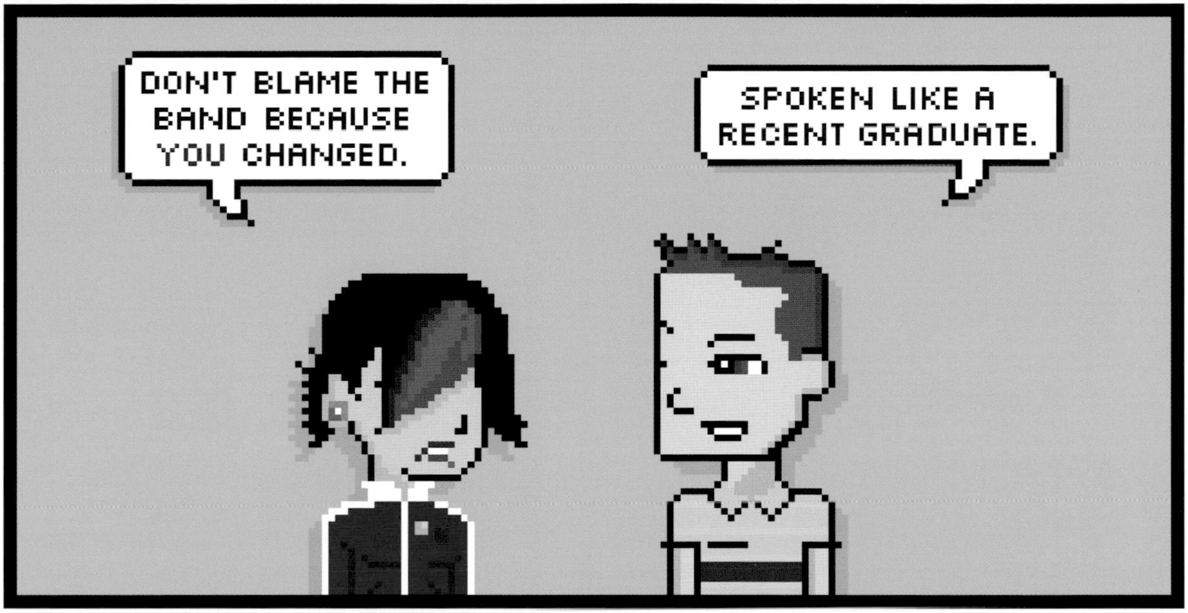
DON'T BLAME THE BAND BECAUSE YOU CHANGED.
SPOKEN LIKE A RECENT GRADUATE.

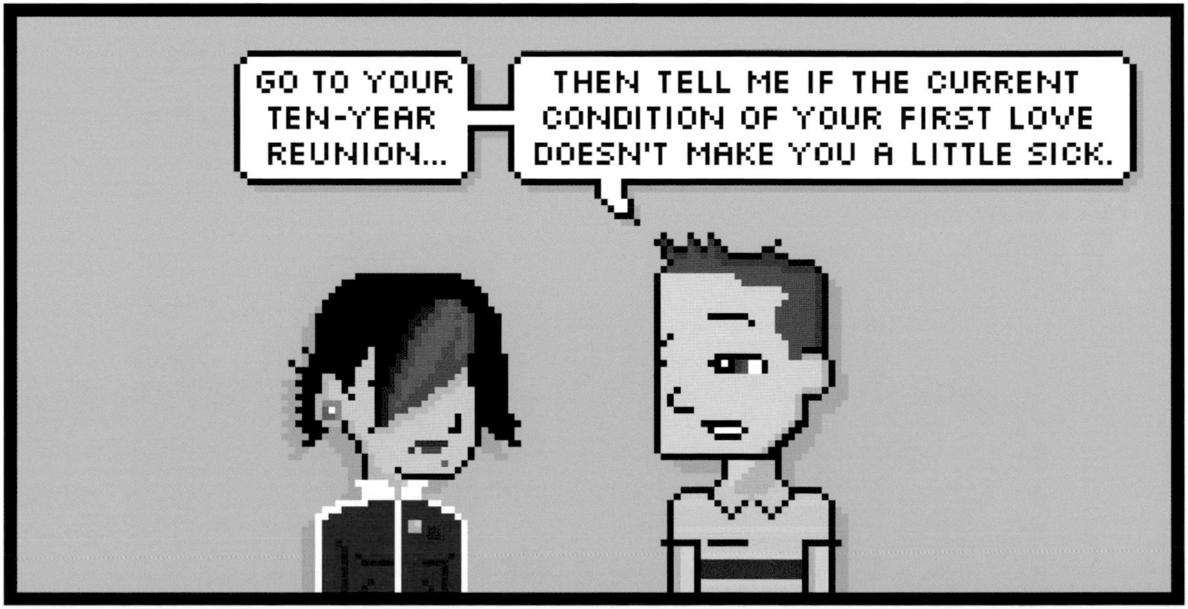
GO TO YOUR TEN-YEAR REUNION...
THEN TELL ME IF THE CURRENT CONDITION OF YOUR FIRST LOVE DOESN'T MAKE YOU A LITTLE SICK.

MY KID COULD DOO DOO THAT

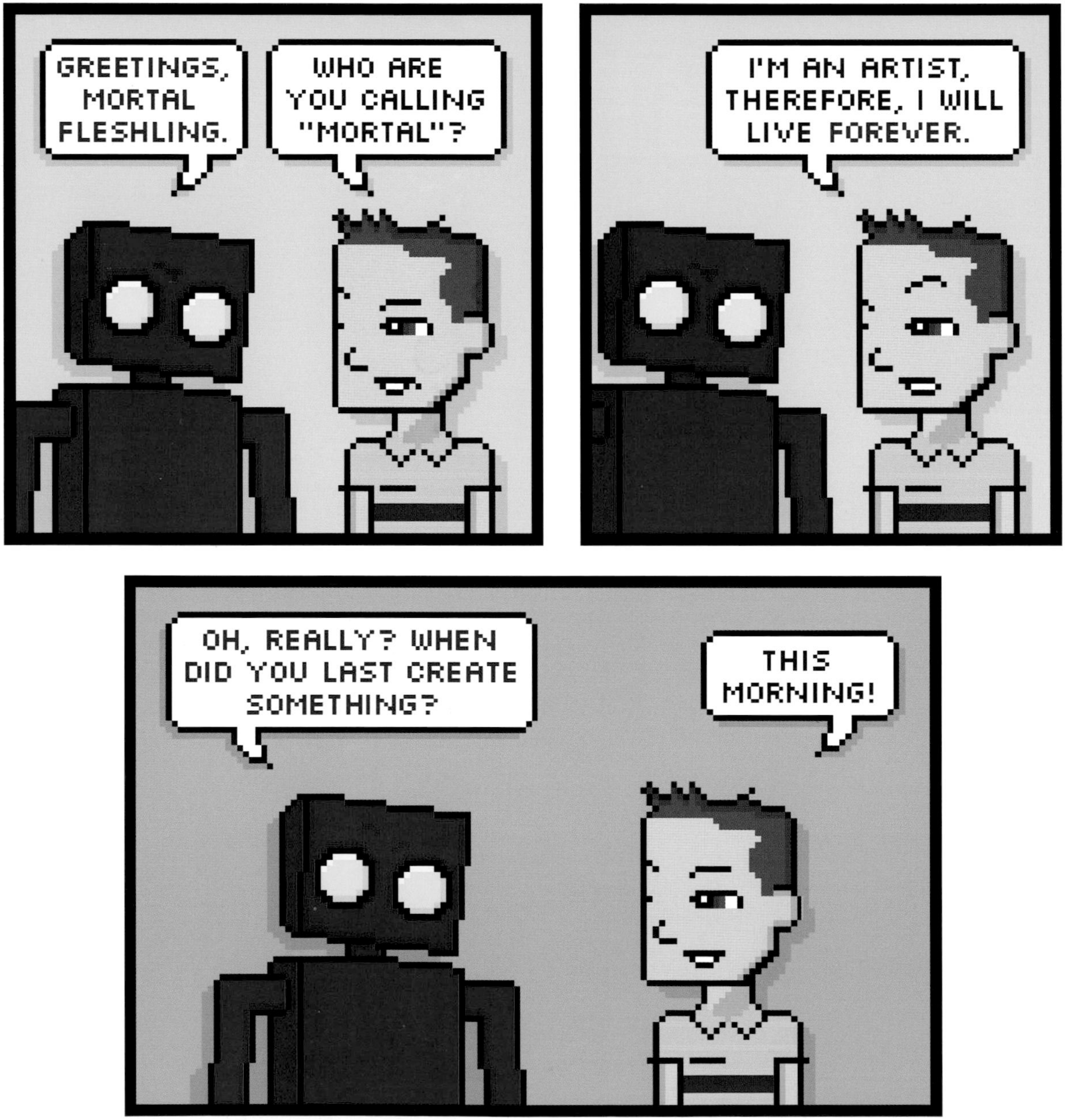
GREETINGS, MORTAL FLESHLING.
WHO ARE YOU CALLING "MORTAL"?
I'M AN ARTIST, THEREFORE, I WILL LIVE FOREVER.
OH, REALLY? WHEN DID YOU LAST CREATE SOMETHING?
THIS MORNING!

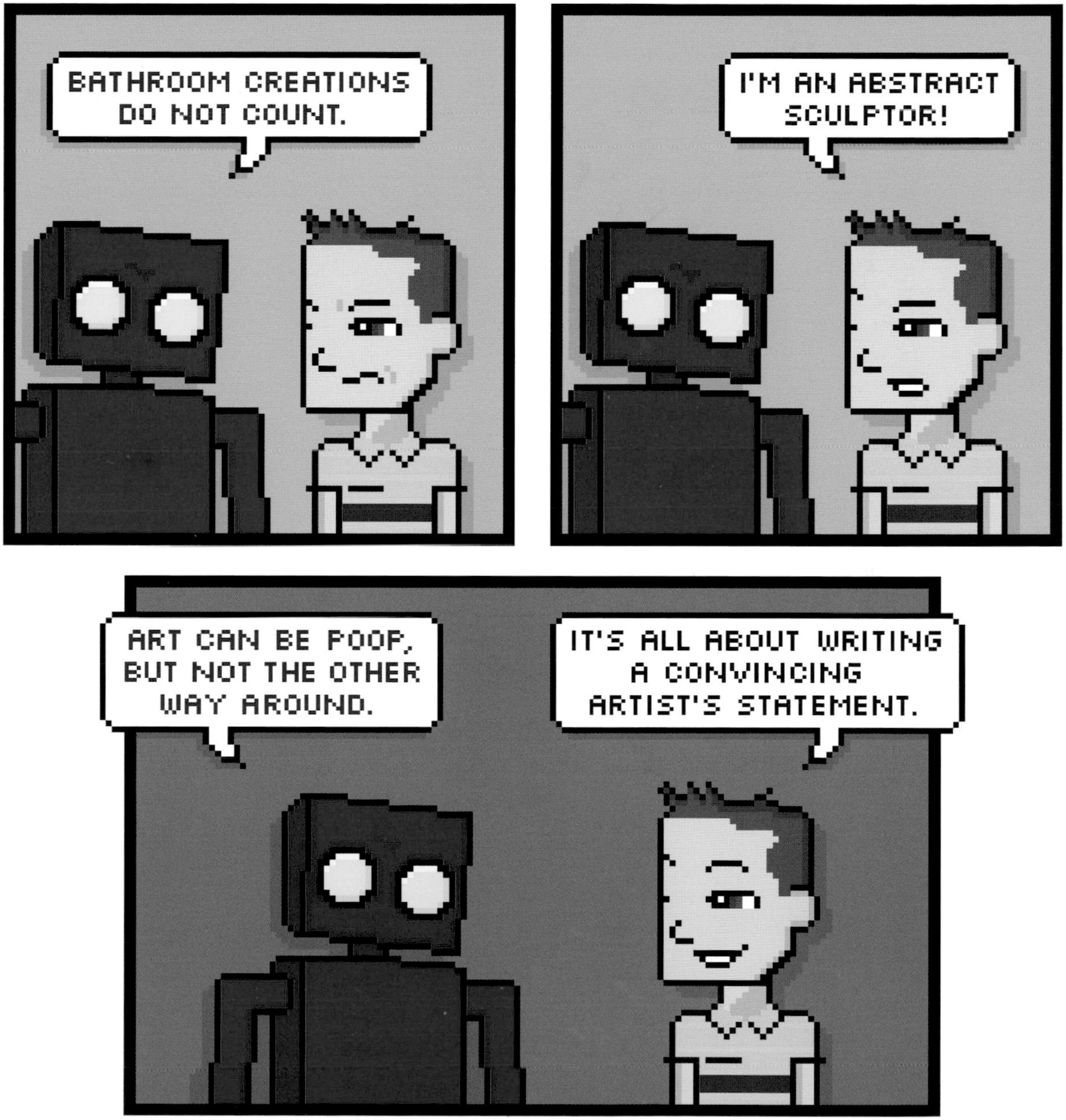
BATHROOM CREATIONS DO NOT COUNT.
I'M AN ABSTRACT SCULPTOR!
ART CAN BE POOP, BUT NOT THE OTHER WAY AROUND.
IT'S ALL ABOUT WRITING A CONVINCING ARTIST'S STATEMENT.

NO COMMENT

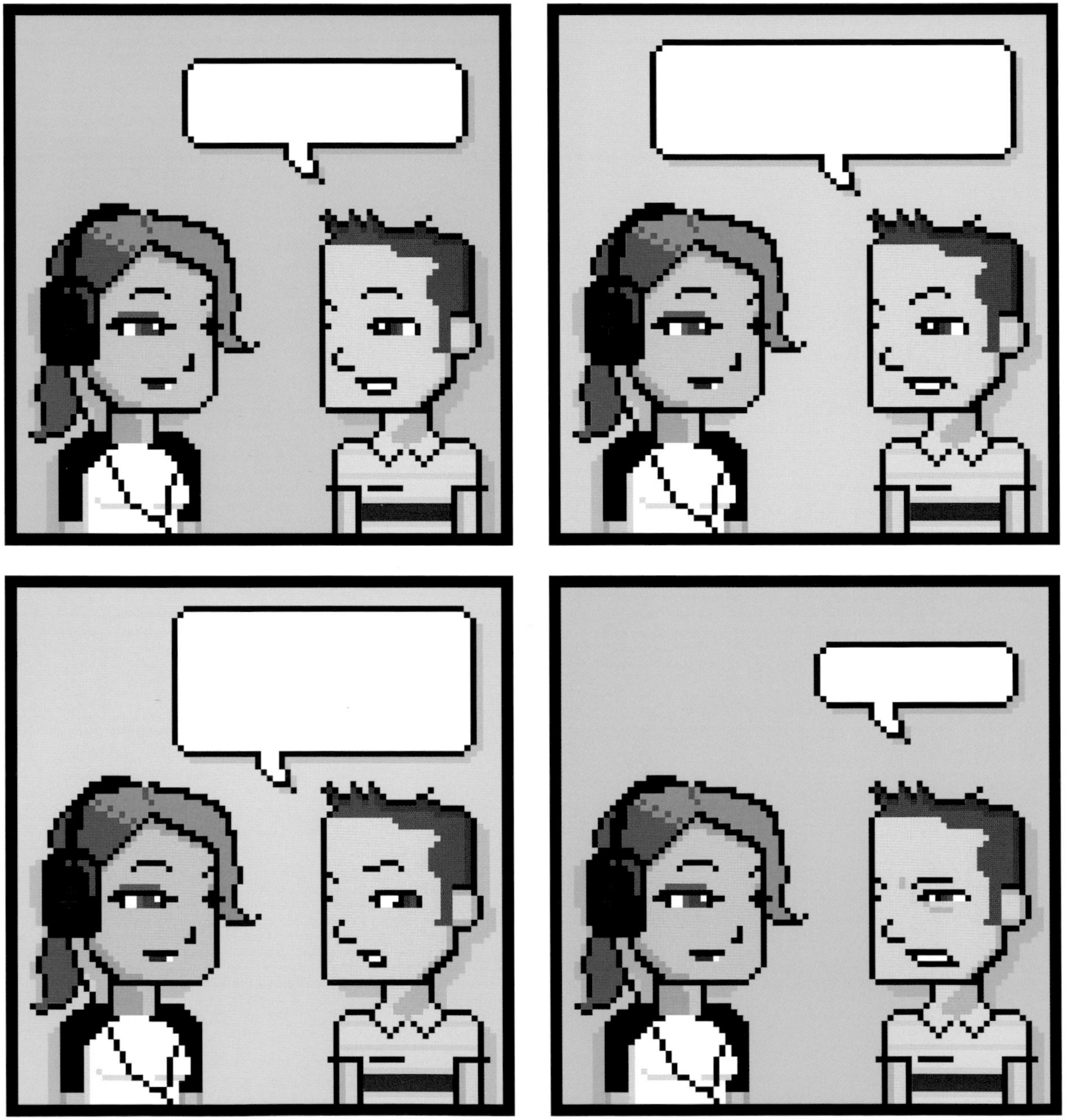

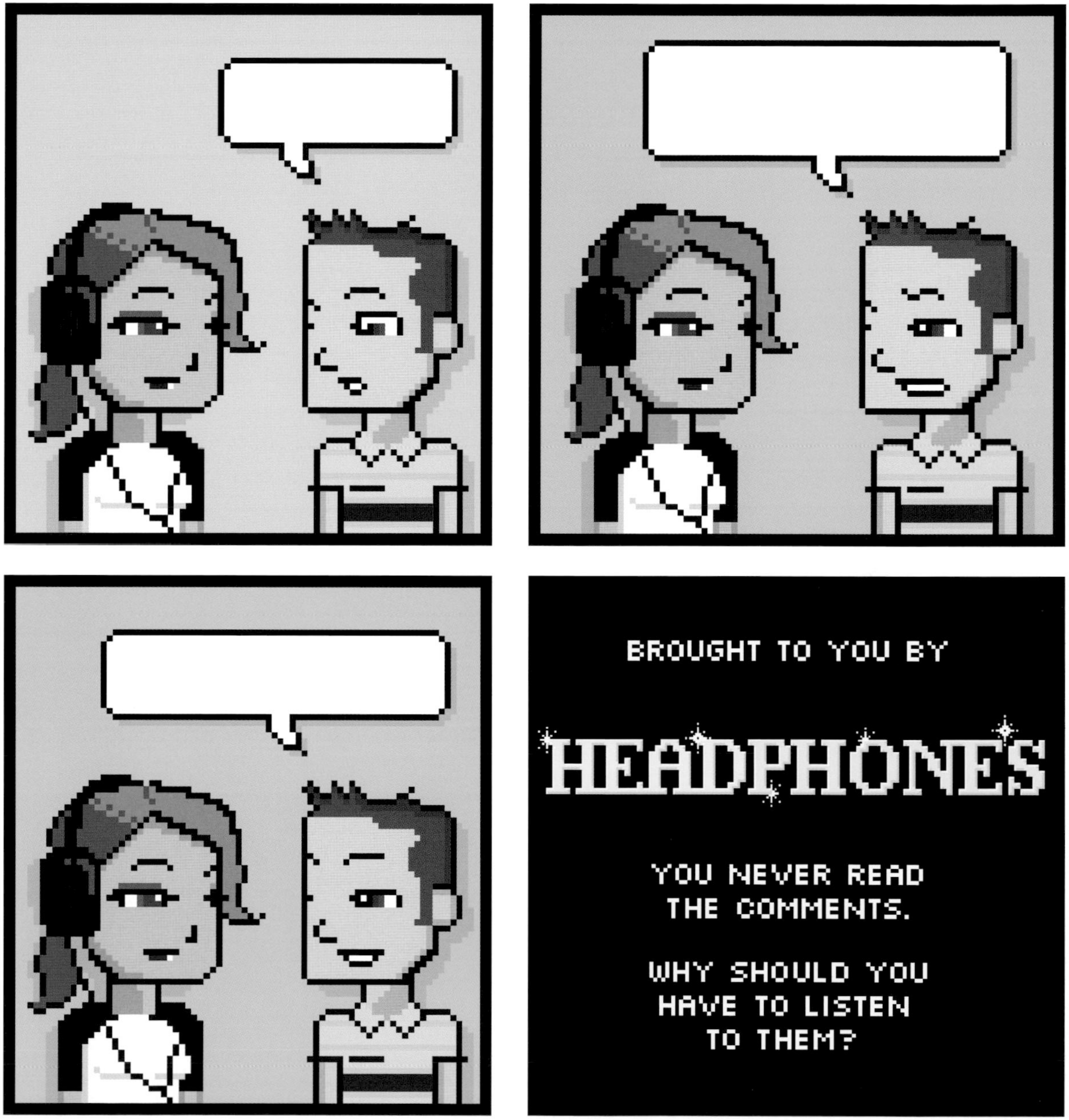
BROUGHT TO YOU BY
HEADPHONES
YOU NEVER READ THE COMMENTS.
WHY SHOULD YOU HAVE TO LISTEN TO THEM?

QUANTITY IS A QUALITY

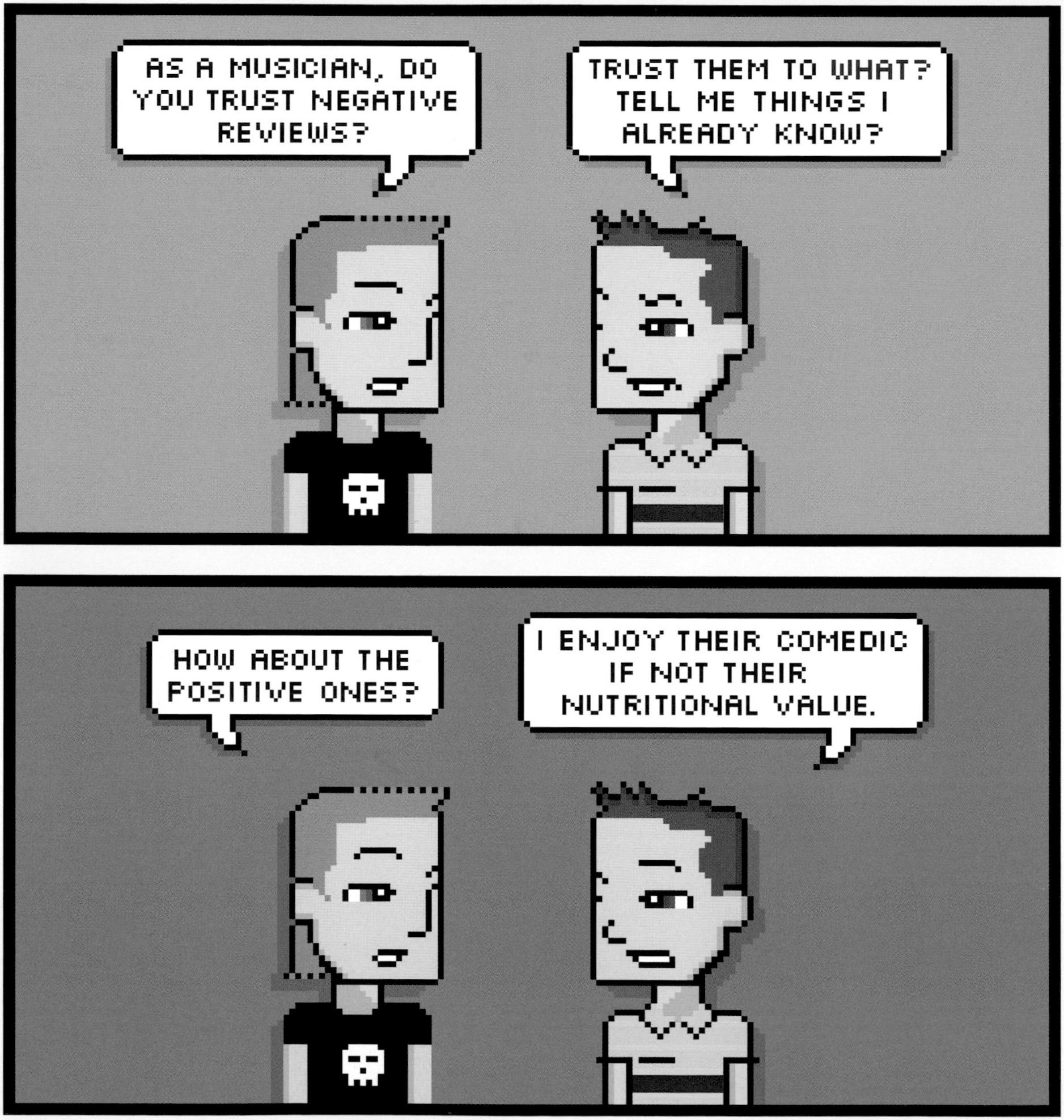
AS A MUSICIAN, DO YOU TRUST NEGATIVE REVIEWS?
TRUST THEM TO WHAT? TELL ME THINGS I ALREADY KNOW?
HOW ABOUT THE POSITIVE ONES?
I ENJOY THEIR COMEDIC IF NOT THEIR NUTRITIONAL VALUE.

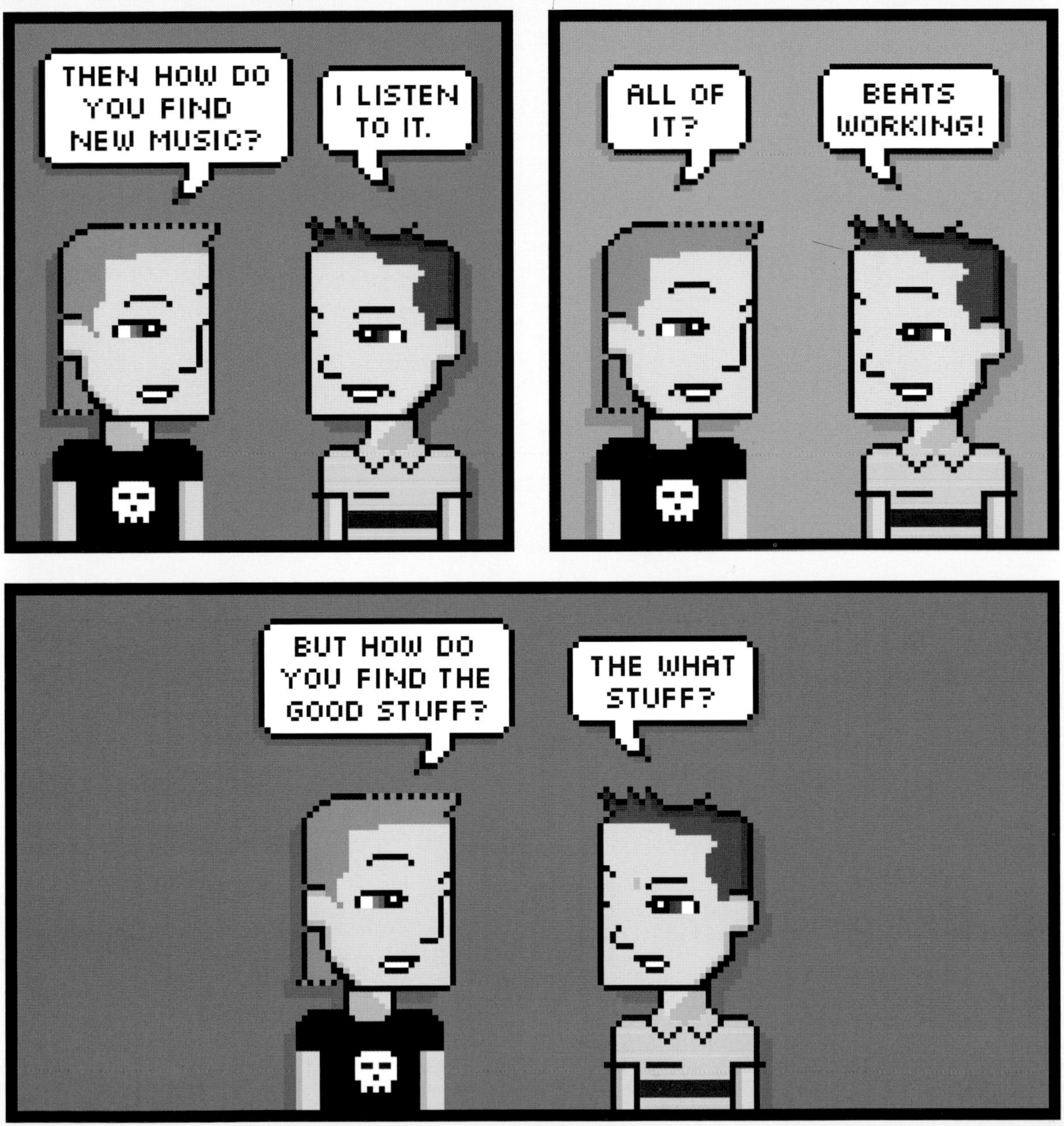
THEN HOW DO YOU FIND NEW MUSIC?
I LISTEN TO IT.
ALL OF IT?
BEATS WORKING!
BUT HOW DO YOU FIND THE GOOD STUFF?
THE WHAT STUFF?

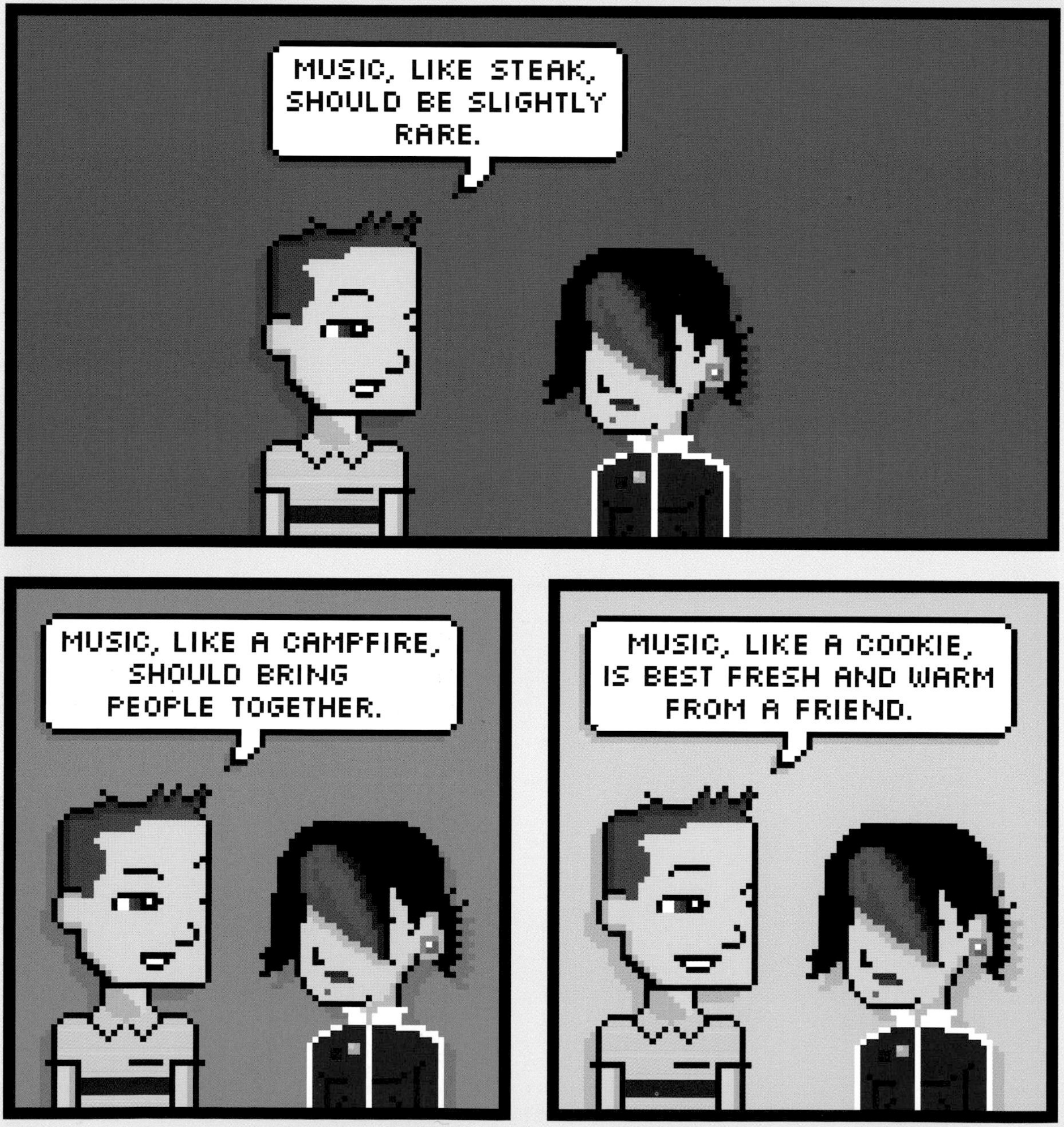
MUSIC, LIKE STEAK, SHOULD BE SLIGHTLY RARE.
MUSIC, LIKE A CAMPFIRE, SHOULD BRING PEOPLE TOGETHER.
MUSIC, LIKE A COOKIE, IS BEST FRESH AND WARM FROM A FRIEND.

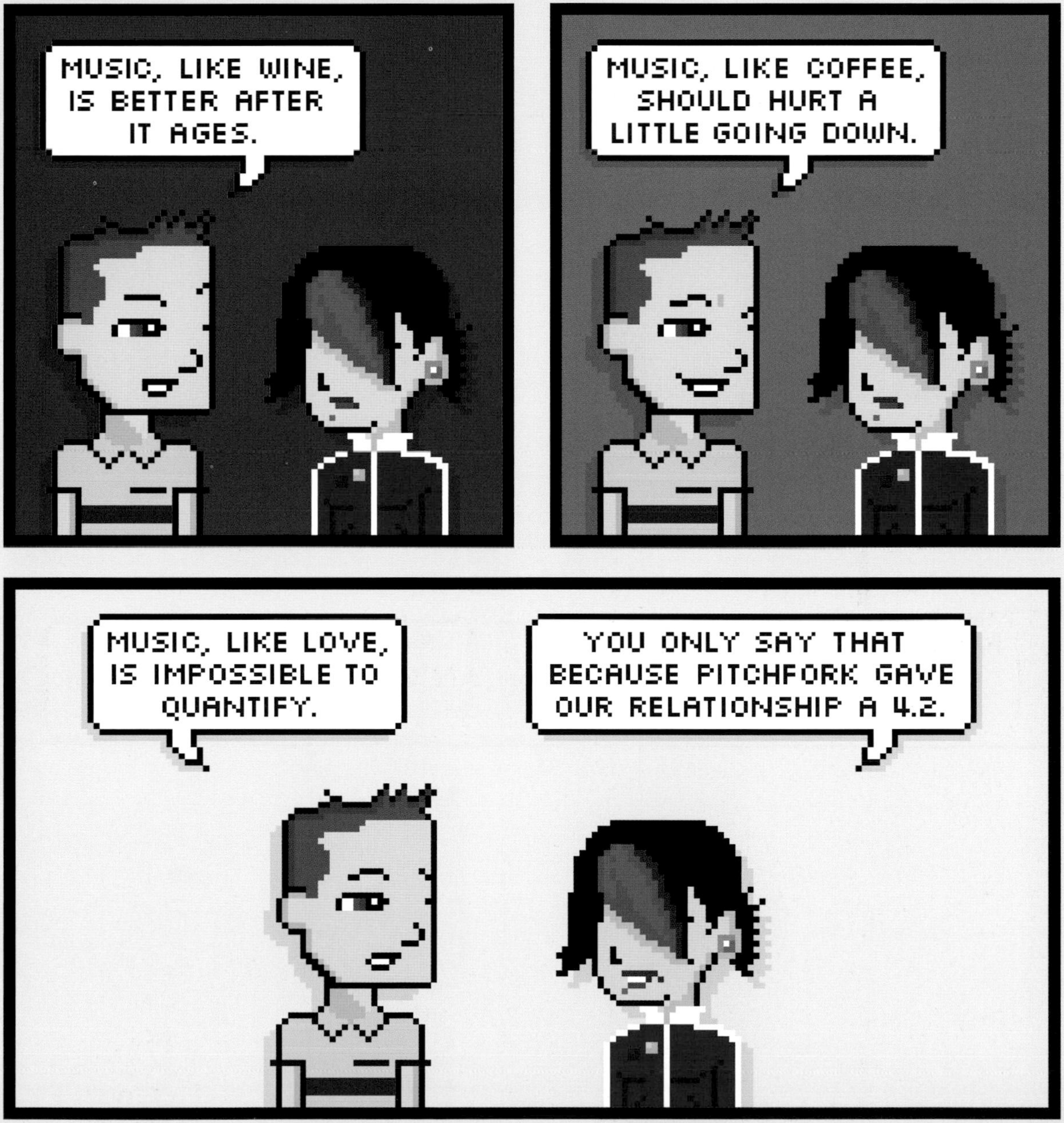
MUSIC, LIKE WINE, IS BETTER AFTER IT AGES.
MUSIC, LIKE COFFEE, SHOULD HURT A LITTLE GOING DOWN.
MUSIC, LIKE LOVE, IS IMPOSSIBLE TO QUANTIFY.
YOU ONLY SAY THAT BECAUSE PITCHFORK GAVE OUR RELATIONSHIP A 4.2.

THE HARDER YOU TRY

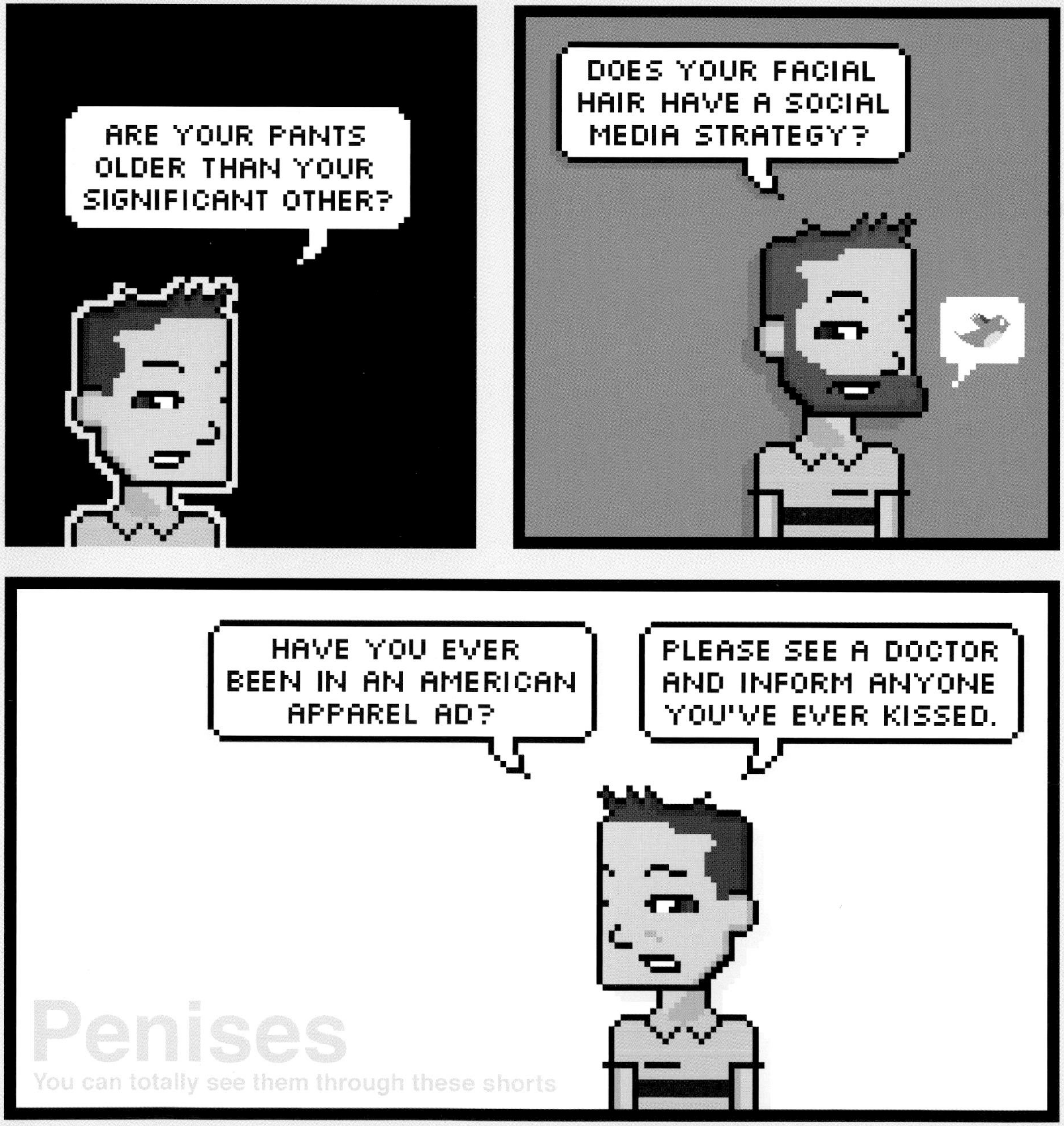

ARE YOUR PANTS OLDER THAN YOUR SIGNIFICANT OTHER?
DOES YOUR FACIAL HAIR HAVE A SOCIAL MEDIA STRATEGY?
HAVE YOU EVER BEEN IN AN AMERICAN APPAREL AD?
PLEASE SEE A DOCTOR AND INFORM ANYONE YOU'VE EVER KISSED.
Penises
You can totally see them through these shorts

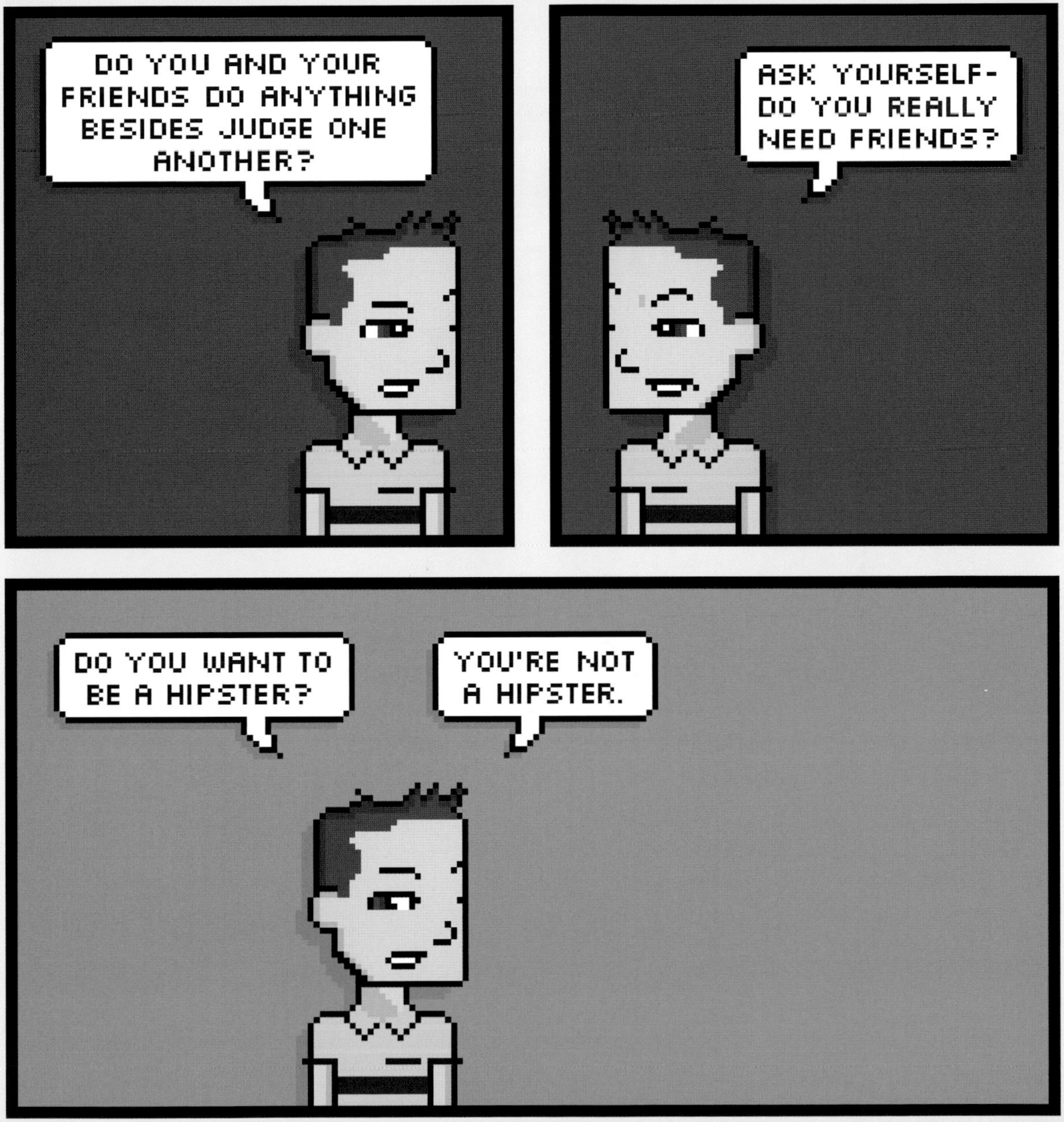
DO YOU AND YOUR FRIENDS DO ANYTHING BESIDES JUDGE ONE ANOTHER?
ASK YOURSELF- DO YOU REALLY NEED FRIENDS?
DO YOU WANT TO BE A HIPSTER?
YOU'RE NOT A HIPSTER.

GEEN SLAAP TOT BREUKELEN

AT THE SOUND OF THE TONE, IT WILL BE TIME TO GET ILL.

WANTED: DRUMMER TO HELP REDEFINE MUSIC AS WE KNOW IT.

(BUT IF YOU THOUGHT THAT BEASTIE BOYS REFERENCE WAS CLEVER, YOU JUST LOST THE JOB.)

INDIE ROCK PETE (555) YOU-SUCK

INDIE ROCK PETE (555) YOU-SUCK
INDIE ROCK PETE (555) YOU-SUCK
INDIE ROCK PETE (555) YOU-SUCK
INDIE ROCK PETE (555) YOU-SUCK
INDIE ROCK PETE (555) YOU-SUCK
INDIE ROCK PETE (555) YOU-SUCK
INDIE ROCK PETE (555) YOU-SUCK
INDIE ROCK PETE (555) YOU-SUCK
INDIE ROCK PETE (555) YOU-SUCK
INDIE ROCK PETE (555) YOU-SUCK
INDIE ROCK PETE (555) YOU-SUCK

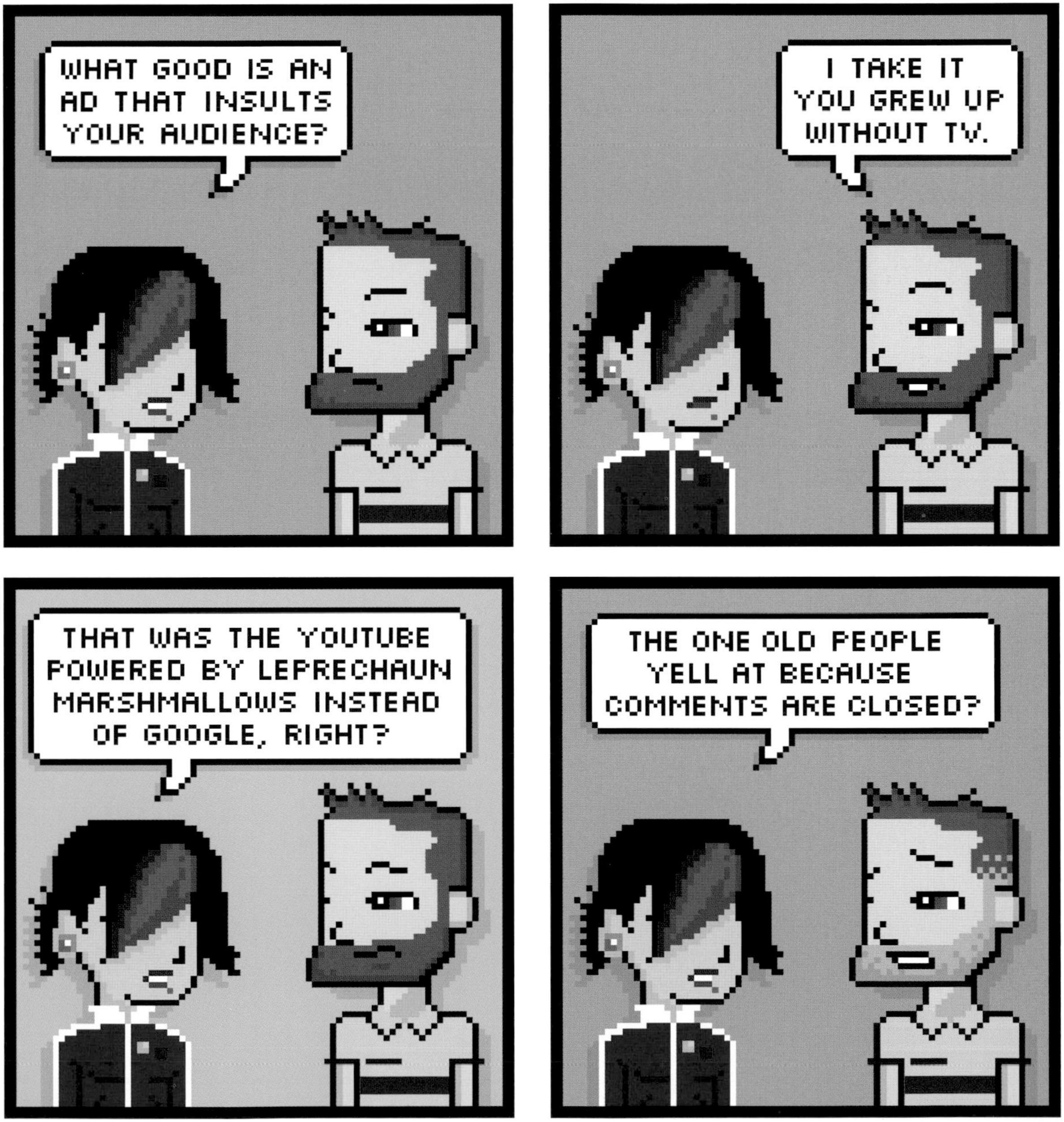
WHAT GOOD IS AN AD THAT INSULTS YOUR AUDIENCE?
I TAKE IT YOU GREW UP WITHOUT TV.
THAT WAS THE YOUTUBE POWERED BY LEPRECHAUN MARSHMALLOWS INSTEAD OF GOOGLE, RIGHT?
THE ONE OLD PEOPLE YELL AT BECAUSE COMMENTS ARE CLOSED?

COMPETITIVE ADVANTAGE

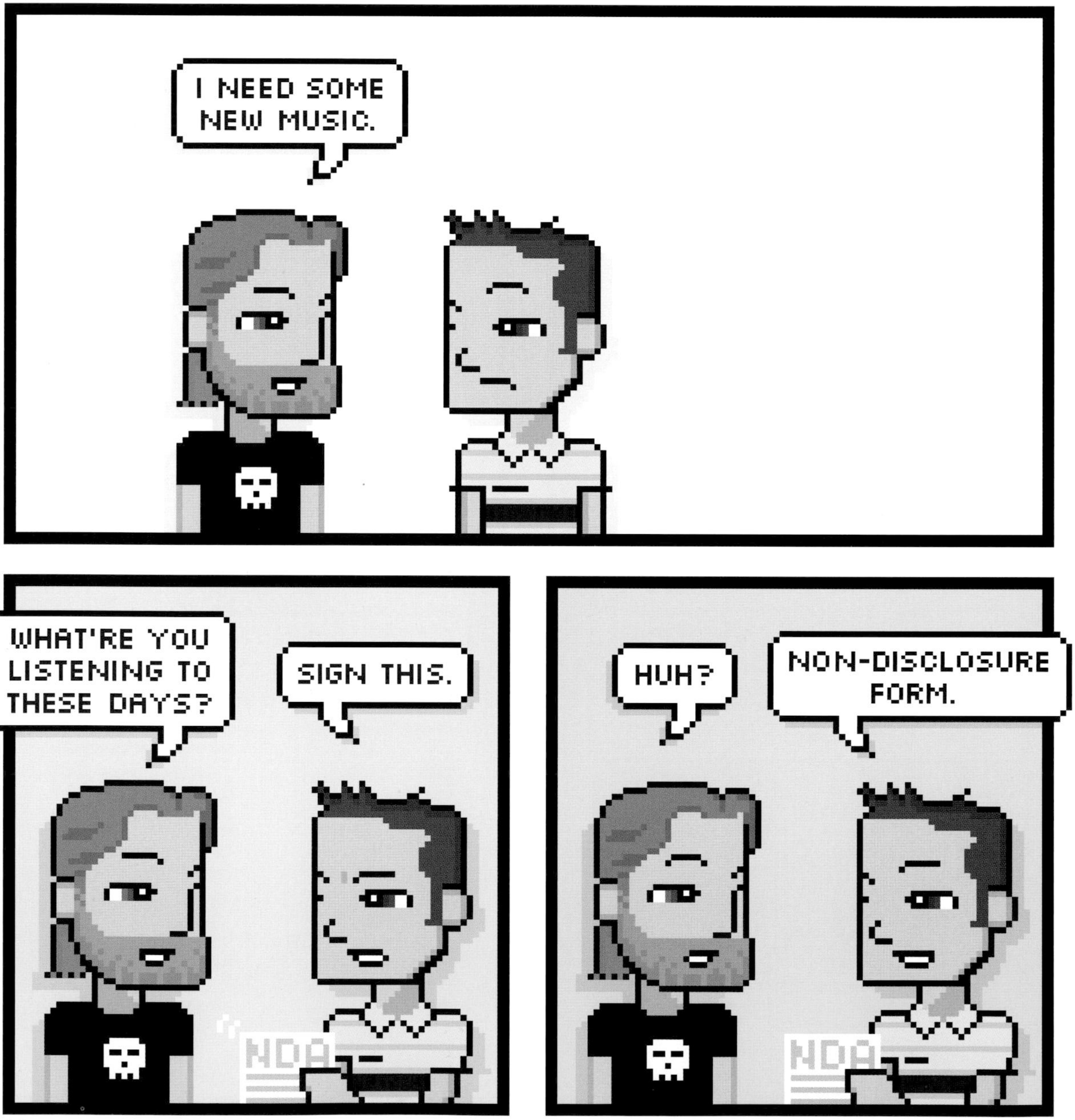
I NEED SOME NEW MUSIC.
WHAT'RE YOU LISTENING TO THESE DAYS?
SIGN THIS.
NDA
HUH?
NON-DISCLOSURE FORM.
NDA

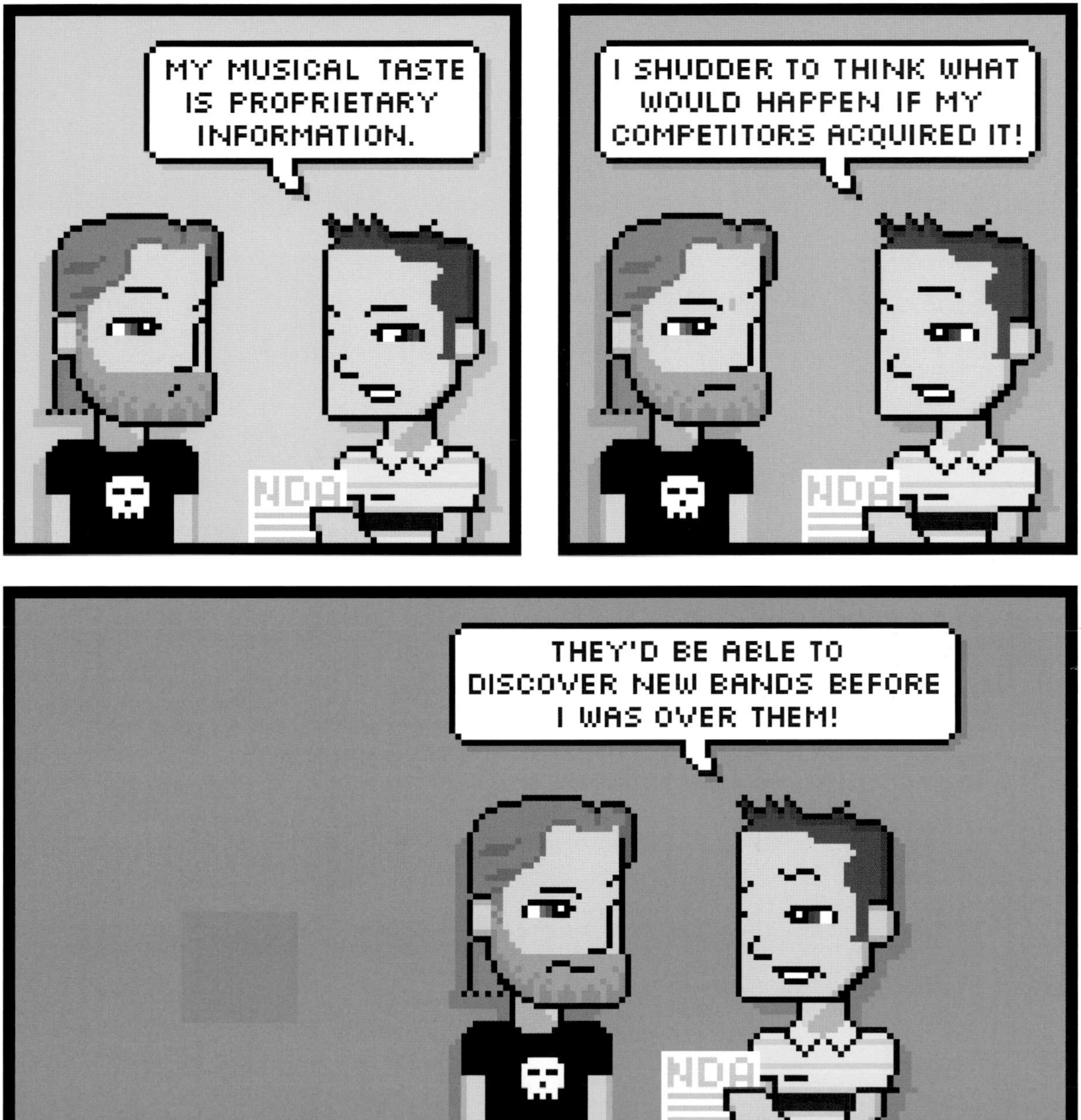
MY MUSICAL TASTE IS PROPRIETARY INFORMATION.
NDA
I SHUDDER TO THINK WHAT WOULD HAPPEN IF MY COMPETITORS ACQUIRED IT!
NDA
THEY'D BE ABLE TO DISCOVER NEW BANDS BEFORE I WAS OVER THEM!
NDA

SOPHIST'S CHOICE

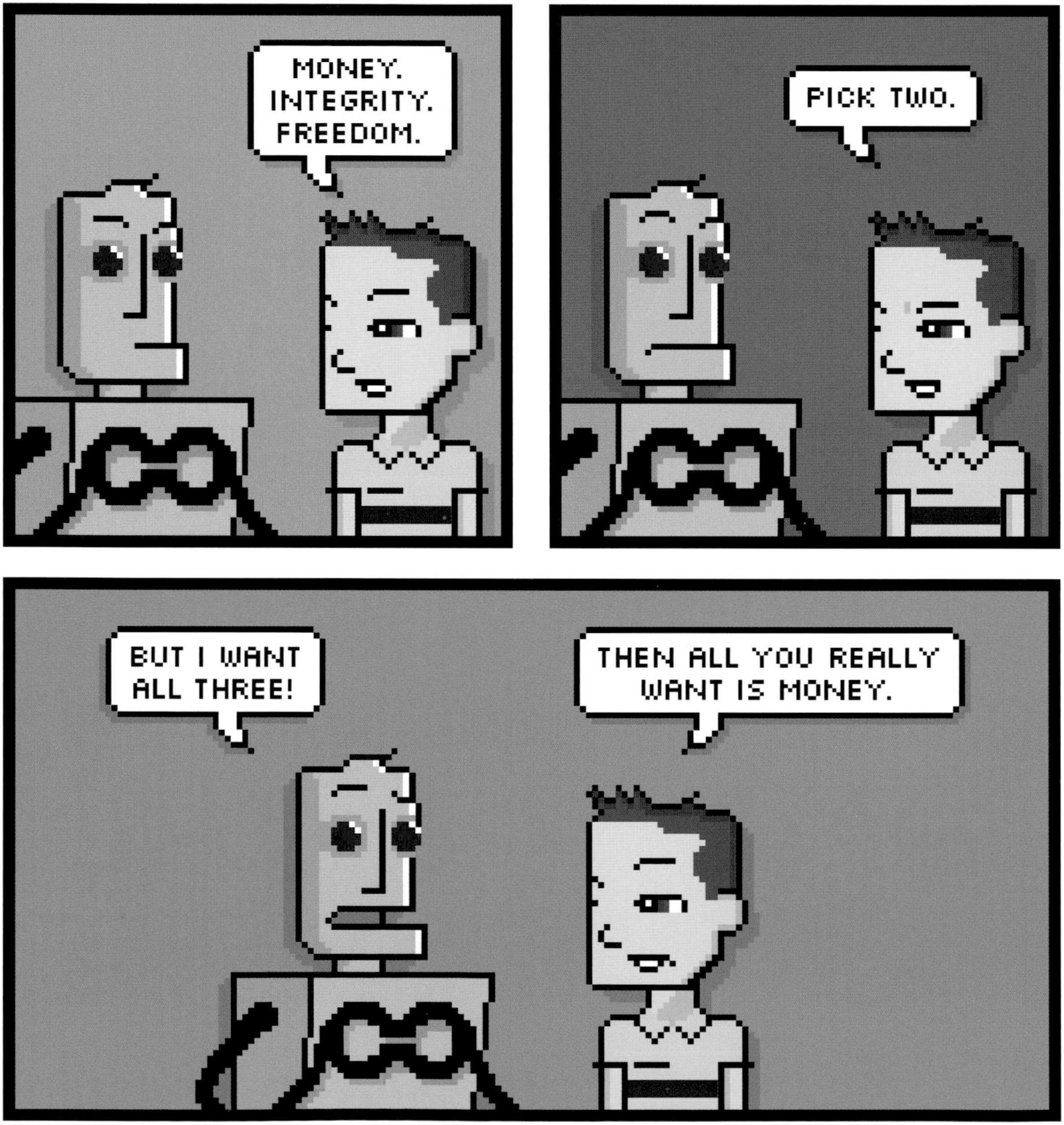
MONEY. INTEGRITY. FREEDOM.
PICK TWO.
BUT I WANT ALL THREE!
THEN ALL YOU REALLY WANT IS MONEY.

OTHER BOOKS FROM ONI PRESS...

SCOTT PILGRIM 1
SCOTT PILGRIM'S PRECIOUS LITTLE LIFE
BY BRYAN LEE O'MALLEY
COLOR EDITION

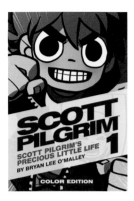

SCOTT PILGRIM: COLOR EDITION VOLUME 1
Bryan Lee O'Malley
184 Pages, 6"x9" Hardcover, Color
ISBN 978-1-62010-000-4

Courtney Volume One Crumrin
The Night Things
Ted Naifeh

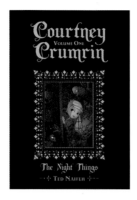

COURTNEY CRUMRIN, VOLUME 1: THE NIGHT THINGS
Ted Naifeh
136 Pages, 6"x9" Hardcover, Color
ISBN 978-1-934964-77-4

MERMIN
BOOK ONE: OUT OF WATER
By Joey Weiser

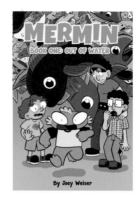

MERMIN, VOLUME 1: OUT OF WATER
Joey Weiser
152 Pages, 6"x9" Hardcover, Color
ISBN 978-1-934964-89-9

Vol. 1
DOUBLE FINE ACTION COMICS
by Scott C.

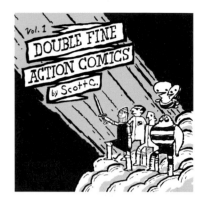

DOUBLE FINE ACTION COMICS VOLUME 1
Scott C.
128 pages, 9"x9" B&W & Color
ISBN 978-1-62010-085-1

MIKE NORTON'S
THE CURSE

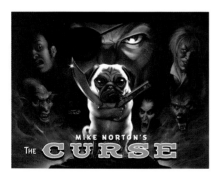

THE CURSE
Mike Norton
88 Pages, 9"x7" Paperback, B&W
ISBN 978-1-934964-88-0

Bad Machinery
THE CASE OF THE TEAM SPIRIT
By John Allison

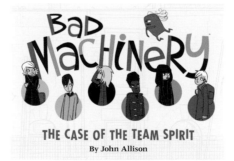

BAD MACHINERY, VOLUME 1 THE CASE OF THE TEAM SPIRIT
John Allison
136 Pages, 12"x9" Softcover, Color
ISBN 978-1-62010-084-4

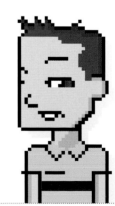

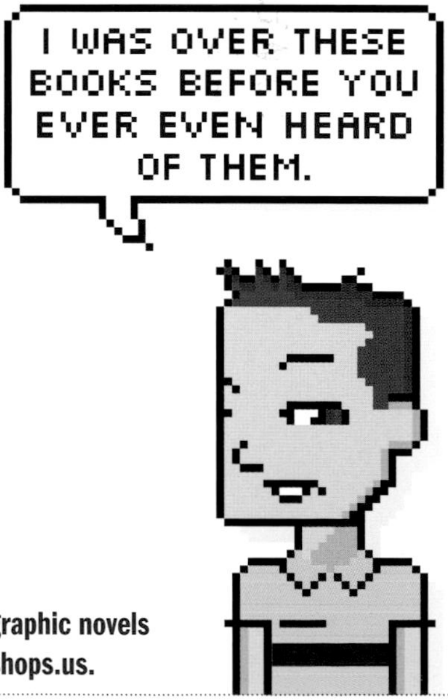

I WAS OVER THESE BOOKS BEFORE YOU EVER EVEN HEARD OF THEM.

ONI PRESS
www.onipress.com

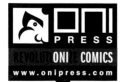

For more information on these and other fine Oni Press comic books and graphic novels visit onipress.com. To find a comic specialty store in your area visit comicshops.us.